"**What** the **devil** does the plot signify, except to bring in fine things"

George Villiers **The Rehearsal**

Books and fine things at Waterstone's

FIFTY

50

Editor: Bill Buford
Deputy Editor: Ursula Doyle
Managing Editor: Claire Wrathall
Editorial Assistant and Picture Researcher: Cressida Leyshon

Financial Controller: Geoffrey Gordon
Marketing and Advertising: Sally Lewis
Circulation Manager: Lesley Palmer
Subscriptions: Kelly Cornwall

Picture Editor: Alice Rose George
Executive Editor: Pete de Bolla
US Publisher: Anne Kinard, Granta, 250 West 57th Street, Suite 1316, New York, NY 10107.

Editorial and Subscription Correspondence: Granta, 2–3 Hanover Yard, Noel Road, London N1 8BE. Telephone: (071) 704 9776. Fax: (071) 704 0474. Subscriptions: (071) 704 0470. A one-year subscription (four issues) is £21.95 in Britain, £29.95 for the rest of Europe and £36.95 for the rest of the world.

Granta is printed in the United States of America. The paper used in this publication meets the minimum requirements of American National Standard for Information Sciences—Permanence of Paper for Printed Library Materials, ANSI Z39.48-1984 ∞

Cover design by The Senate.

Granta 50, Summer 1995
ISBN 0-14-014109-X

What happens when a leading novelist:

goes electioneering with Glenda Jackson?
spends 346 hours watching Nigel Short fail to win at chess?
shares a sandwich lunch with Mary Archer?

And just how *do* you explain Britain to the Americans?

Julian
Barnes

Letters
from
London

1990 – 1995

Fifteen already celebrated pieces from the *New Yorker* brought
together in Julian Barnes' first new book since *The Porcupine*

A Picador Paperback Original   £6.99

PICADOR

ROYAL COURT THEATRE Spring Season

MAIN HOUSE

Simpatico
by Sam Shepard

Opens 6 April
The first major new play from
Sam Shepard in nearly a decade.

THEATRE UPSTAIRS

The Steward of Christendom
by Sebastian Barry

Until 22 April
Max Stafford-Clark's production of a new
play by one of Ireland's most heralded
playwrights.

Star-Gazy Pie and Sauerkraut
by James Stock
(winner of the George Devine Award 1992)
4 - 27 May
A moving and humorous exploration of
beauty, sickness and morality.

Barclays New Stages
31 May - 17 June
Award-winning companies perform
a wide range of work from the cutting-
edge of live art.

Box Office 0171-730 1745/2554

CONTENTS

A library is thought in cold storage.

Herbert Samuel

Every week The Times Literary Supplement contains incisive reviews, not only of the latest books (over 2000 each year), but also of film, theatre, broadcasting, opera and the visual arts; debate, opinion and argument from writers of the calibre of Claire Tomalin, George Steiner, Ernest Gellner, Marina Warner, P D James and Andrew Motion.

Break the ice. Subscribe today and we'll give you your first four issues absolutely free and then 30% off the cover price for the next 6 months.

Editorial

Three months ago, I did a thing that, for a long time, I had regarded as inconceivable: I resigned from *Granta*. Even now, the logic implicit in that ordinary, adult statement—I, an employee of a publishing company, resigned from my position in it—seems to me inadmissible, if only because I find it impossible to think of *Granta* as a place of work. No one edits a literary magazine because it's a good job. And, as a rule, no one leaves. The editor stays with the ship until—well, until it goes down (which, finally, it always seems to do).

Why edit a literary magazine in the first place? The question was one of the first ones put to me by our first accountant, who—our dark balance sheet spread across the table of the pub—patiently explained why businesses exist: 'So that,' he said, 'the people who own them can make money from them. This clearly is not the reason you started *Granta*. Why, then, do you believe *Granta* is a business? Do you have any idea?'

I had none. But does any editor? The wall of my sitting-room at home is taken up almost exclusively with literary magazines. And while I have only skimmed through most, they are, all of them, a reassuring sight. My wall represents ten years in the life of John Lehmann (when he made Penguin's *New Writing*), Cyril Connolly (*Horizon*), Ted Solotaroff (*New American Review*), Charles Newmann (*Tri-Quarterly*) and Ben Sonnenberg's noble *Grand Street* (a neat decade being the conventional life, it would seem, of the successful literary magazine); as well as three years when Saul Bellow wasn't writing a novel (*The Noble Savage*), the fifteen years when T. S. Eliot wasn't writing a poem (*Criterion*), the twenty-five years when Daniel Halpern wasn't writing enough (*Antaeus*) and the eighteen months when Craig Raine was not writing anything at all (*Quarto*); and, as profound, the months of anguish suffered silently by the other editors whose labours were not allowed to endure past the first, crushing consequences of the first printer's invoice. For me, the comfort in this sight is in knowing that we all know what we've been through. Only the editors of literary magazines understand that it's a preposterous thing to edit a literary magazine. They know the labour that goes into making one—I still don't understand why it should be so much work; after all, the magazines appear only after supposedly long and restful intervals; what can be so difficult? My wall represents late nights and spilt ashtrays and bottles of drink that shouldn't have been drunk, not then and not in such quantity; and other editors know how much time is spent on everything except editing: on worrying about money, usually, and invariably on the subject of its insistent absence. And they also appreciate the exquisite, even philosophical arbitrariness with which a magazine comes into existence: the transition from nothing, that terrifying condition of no pages, to something, a physical object that exists in the world, in a bookshop, in a parcel delivered by the Royal Mail, in someone's hands on the Underground on the way to work, on a shelf in my sitting-room.

But, in anticipation of the business at hand, filling up the empty pages of this fiftieth issue of *Granta*, my last, I've also been reading through the final issues of my collection—the goodbye editorials—and find that most don't match my experience now. In a crucial respect, of course, this is simply because *Granta* is different: it has been publishing not for ten years, or three years, or eighteen months, or two weeks, but for nearly sixteen years; and, more importantly, this issue is not the last one; *Granta* will continue; and anything I write is not therefore a requiem—the gardens of the West are not closing—but a leave-taking. But I also feel that the inevitable defensiveness that characterizes most of these final editorials —chronicles of what has been achieved, or apologies, or expressions of exhaustion, or twitchy, nervous laments arising out of being unable to pay the salaries—misses something essential.

I can't think of *Granta* as employment, as a job that I'm

leaving, because *Granta* has been my life, my 'me', a thing inseparable from what I am: the normal boundaries between labour (what you do during weekdays so that something regularly enters your bank account) and self (what you are during the rest of the time) don't exist. And for some time I thought this confusion arose out of my particular circumstances. I became involved in *Granta* when I was twenty-four, a student, an American who had been in Britain all of fourteen months. I became an adult in the magazine I created, and formed the most important relationships in my life—and with my newly adopted country—through the work that I then did. It was inevitable— was it not?—that I should become confused with the magazine I made, if only because the magazine had done so much in making me. But this week I came to realize that I am not exceptional.

This week, I returned to *Granta*'s original offices. *Granta* now occupies an elegant building in north London, with space and windows and plenty of light. It has heating. But for ten years, *Granta* was published out of an attic above a Cambridge hairdresser's—the powerful smells of shampoos and peroxides and all kinds of pastel-coloured goos still permeate the original space, still empty and unrented since *Granta* moved from it five years ago. The space has no heating—it was where I learned how to type wearing gloves—and one small window that opens only by removing the frame, which became essential during English summers, however brief. There was no insulation in the roof—during windy periods dust cascaded from it, covering everything, manuscripts, your telephone, your hair, with a fine layer of dark grit—and, thus, when it was hot, it became very hot: oven hot, insufferably hot, impossible-to-work-in hot. And yet we worked there. Me alone for a time. Then me and an assistant, part-time. And then three people, five, six, eventually as many as twelve, putting in impossible hours under impossible conditions, regularly staying up until dawn to finish an issue. Why?

Because it was fun.

And it was fun because it was a privilege.

There was a time when I felt there could be nothing more alienating or dispiriting than editing a literary magazine. I was a

11

student in the United States, bewildered by the more than five hundred American literary magazines produced mainly by universities and English faculties, printed in small, heavily subsidized print-runs and read by very few people. Why put such effort into something with so few consequences? But the converse is also true: what could be more satisfying than a literary magazine that was read?

Cyril Connolly, in his last editorial, described the vocation of *Horizon* as feeling 'its way to what is, in the best sense of the word, contemporary,' and endeavouring to 'print what many years hence will be recognized as alive and original.' A modest vocation, and yet it is everything. To be in the position of making a magazine that, having felt its way to representing the contemporary, prints the most alive and original writing of the culture and finds readers for it, not just in this country but all over the world—the world's smartest and most literate strangers; to know that you are publishing what is probably the most widely read literary magazine in the world: to be in such a position is unique; it is a monumental privilege. It is not a job; it is never simply work; and it has never simply been me.

Granta exists because it has had the fortune of enjoying fifteen years of people who, like me, have been so confused that, at one time or another, they have been unable to separate themselves from the work they do: people for whom making a magazine of the best writing in the English language was an endeavour as serious as any endeavour could possibly be.

This issue is dedicated to all the people who have worked at *Granta* with me. For most, working at *Granta* was a first job, and it is gratifying to know that many have gone on to be writers or journalists or publishers: that the experience, I would like to think, has somehow never left them. Many were at *Granta* for years. I can't think of one who wasn't essential to what the magazine has become.

Bill Buford
April 1995

Philip Gourevitch
The Boat People

My grandmother lived in America for forty years before her death, yet she never stopped referring to herself as a refugee. She was a naturalized US citizen, a busy professional with native-born grandchildren and she remained a displaced person. As a child, I listened to her stories, and my imagination was filled with a succession of historical crises in Russia and Europe: revolutions, world wars, imprisonments, assassinations, executions and exterminations. What the trouble was about—the politics of it—was beyond me; I knew only that there were good guys and bad guys, and that there was always flight and more flight for the guys who survived.

Flight was *how* they survived, and for that you had to have papers. Papers, papers, papers. When my grandmother said the word, it carried a talismanic power. But I understood this notion of papers even less than I understood the politics that made them so necessary; it was too remote from my own luxurious experience of American citizenship. To elude the bad guys, you had to have certain bits of paper. You had to have papers to leave a place, and to get into a new one, and often just to go about your life where you were. The papers had to be in order, and papers that were good in the morning might not be good in the afternoon. There were never enough papers to meet the demand, and there were always people who could take your papers away. These people could also take *you* away, and you might never be seen or heard from again. You had to be very resourceful to stay on top of this business of papers, and you had to have luck.

Without papers, you were a dead letter—undeliverable and unreturnable. You had no identity; you had only your character. Years went by, and lives ran out, while refugees waited for papers. My grandmother never spoke of the suicides as insane or weak: just overburdened.

I want to say that her stories, repeated and expanded with each visit, make up my most vivid childhood memories. But I must be careful. I cannot remember another's past, only her account of it. It was my imagination my grandmother fed, not my memory.

In the spring of 1975, when I was thirteen, I watched the fall of Saigon on television, those famous scenes of aftermath—people

Photo: Ian Berry (Magnum)

15

fighting to get out of there, people carrying only a bag, people tossing their infants on to planes from which they themselves were kicked away, people hanging from helicopters, clinging to flight by their fingertips, people dropping into the South China Sea.

The moment of excitement quickly passed, and I came of age in an America in retreat from Vietnam. The war, I was taught, had been an act of national self-laceration. It was our shame and our shackle. The diagnosis of the day was Post-Traumatic Stress Disorder, and the afflicted veterans discovered that they were valued—if at all—not as men who had served when called, but as victims of crimes they were forced to commit.

I simplify, but only to describe a mood that has hung heavily over the past twenty years of American life, so heavily that, in American speech, Vietnam has become the name less of a foreign land than of a national pathology. And the Vietnamese—no longer of use as foils in our debate—have for the most part been forgotten.

Recalling the fall of Saigon, James Fenton has described how eager he was to witness the Communists' victory over 'American imperialism', and how wrong he had been to imagine that the enemy of his enemy could be his friend. But despite the horrors of Vietnam's Stalinist dictatorship, people who had opposed America's prosecution of the Vietnam war never got too worked up about the boat people. After all, they were not fleeing the war. They were fleeing the peace.

Since 1975, at least seven hundred thousand Vietnamese boat people—some say one million—crossed the South China Sea to Thailand, Malaysia, Indonesia, the Philippines and Hong Kong, where they were placed in camps to wait for refugee visas from the United States and other western 'receiver nations'. Nobody knows how many died at sea, but estimates run as high as one out of every three who set sail. Still the boat people kept coming, and in 1989, the 'international community'—led by the United States, under the auspices of the United Nations High Commissioner for Refugees—decided to stop the exodus. A new set of rules was established: escapees from Vietnam would no longer be rewarded automatically with refugee visas. They would now be known as 'asylum seekers' and subjected to a quasi-judicial screening process during which they would have to prove 'a well-founded fear of persecution.' Those who were 'screened in' would be resettled, as before. Those who were 'screened out' would be classified as 'economic migrants', a standard euphemism for illegal aliens: they would then be required to return to Vietnam under a scheme called 'Voluntary Repatriation'.

The new rules succeeded in reducing the flow of refugees to a trickle. But the screening process was characterized by sluggishness, incompetence and corruption. In November 1994, nearly twenty years after the end of the war, approximately fifty thousand boat people were still in camps, leftovers of the longest-standing refugee crisis in a world that now boasts some twenty million refugees. Most had been in detention for four or five years—they had exhausted their appeals for refugee visas, and they refused to participate in Voluntary Repatriation. The UNHCR said that the camps would close by the end of 1995. What would happen to the hold-outs?

Palawan

Approaching the Philippines First Asylum Camp in Puerto Princesa on the island of Palawan, I was surprised to see how easy it would be for detainees to escape. The camp fence was just ten feet high, a chain-link screen topped by a few wobbly strings of barbed wire. At one end, the camp had no fence—only the beach and the breakers of the Sulu Sea. I couldn't see any guards, and the fence was full of holes. As I passed by, I saw a parade of chickens wander in, and a good-sized dog wander out.

I was surprised, because Palawan was a 'closed' camp. Detainees could leave only on two-hour passes granted at the whim of camp security, and visitors were forbidden. The camp was basically a prison, and proper prison fences, in my experience, are designed to warn the escape-minded: 'Don't even think about it.' This fence did just the opposite. It said: 'Think about it.'

Think: You can go, but where? You will be without papers; your looks and your language will set you apart; you will be without protection, without rights; your children will be barred from school; you will be barred from legal employment; you won't be able to marry, or travel, or call the police if you need them.

A refugee camp is a most peculiar kind of prison, where inmates are guilty of no crime unless they try to leave without permission. Think about it, the fence said: You are your own prison.

In the midday sun, the fence was shadowless and nearly invisible. Among the palm-thatched billets, their walls painted with the flag of the former Republic of (South) Vietnam, a half-dozen barefoot Vietnamese were clustered around a communal spigot, bathing or filling buckets. A man sat in a chair, draped in a white shroud, receiving a haircut. Two little girls in straw hats trimmed with fake flowers stood hand in hand, staring out at the road.

I had been told by a State Department man that Palawan was known as the Club Med of camps. 'The people get spoiled there,' he said. 'It's the best refugee camp in the world.'

The map I had picked up at the Puerto Princesa airport listed the camp as one of eight 'Major Places of Interest' for tourists. It said: 'Food trips are the craze of visitors to this area, where they can sample a variety of noodle flavors, porridge, mouth-watering kebabs, French bread, and other Vietnamese cuisine at very low prices. Silver jewelry may also be ordered from enterprising Vietnamese whose shops are found near the main gate.'

The map was out of date.

'Restaurant finished,' a security officer told me when I presented myself at the main gate. Over the past year, the camp administration—officers of the Armed Forces of the Philippines and of the UNHCR—had severely curtailed camp activity. Business was banned; schools, vocational and language training and the social and cultural programmes provided by relief agencies were shut down; many camp facilities, including several housing zones, were destroyed. The cuts were imposed to pressure detainees to return to Vietnam. Even medical services were reduced, and those who sought care were advised that they should first sign up for repatriation. But in the six months before my visit, the rate of applications for Voluntary Repatriation had tapered off sharply. As a Vietnamese woman I met at the gate explained, the two thousand four hundred remaining boat people refused to be bullied. There had been demonstrations, troops had been called in; nobody was budging, and conditions were getting bleaker.

'They cut and cut,' the woman said. 'Soon, there will be nothing left to cut but the people.' She gestured at a wide, gravelly area that stretched from the gate to the sea. 'That used to be streets and houses, Zone One and Zone Two. People lived there. Now it's all flat. Everything is done little by little to make a smooth surface, but underneath it is like a volcano and you don't know where will it explode.'

The guard would not permit me to enter the camp, but he made no effort to stop me from talking to this woman. When I told her I was a journalist, she said: 'The people can't do anything. Some run away and don't come back. Some commit suicide. I'm glad you are here to rise up your voice for them.'

I told her that I was staying nearby at the Badjao Inn, and she said she would pass the word along to the boat people.

For the next six days, I hardly left my hotel. It was a strange time. A clerk would knock at my door and say, 'More Vietnamese to see you, sir.' I received thirty-three visits. I spent hours with people—some very poised, some in an evident state of breakdown, some swinging back and forth—who were frightened and helpless: they said they had left their homes to save their lives, and now their lives were being lost. They believed that the only way to reverse that loss was to wait for an external force they called 'the world' to recognize that it was treating them unfairly and rectify its mistake. To the boat people, I was both a representative of that world, and their representative to that world, and so they were not just telling me their stories but pleading their cases.

The stories—by no means equal in their coherence or their appeal to conscience—often had a strange, posthumous quality, as though the tellers were reciting their own obituaries. The boat people had been told they were not the politically violated people they said they were, but their invalidated stories were all they had. They felt buried alive, and they offered their stories to me as evidence of the dirt thrown over them and as the trowel with which they hoped to be excavated.

Ninety per cent of the boat people I met at Palawan had arrived in 1989. Many had set sail between late March and mid-June, when the risk of storms is low, and the prevailing winds drive east to the Philippines. They could not have known about the new rules because they were not in effect until 14 June, and they certainly had no idea that the cut-off date for refugees had been set retroactively for 22 March.

It was rare to escape Vietnam on the first try. 'We attempted seven times,' said Trinh Tanh Hung, my first visitor. 'At the end, my father decided we should get our own boat and the whole family should go together. But my uncle was thirteen years in re-education camp, so we had to wait until 1988, then buy the boat and prepare.'

Twenty-eight members of Hung's extended family sailed together. They made the trip at night, because they knew that fishermen would chase them for the reward, and that they could only escape when the fishing boats were loaded down with catch. After eight days at sea, on 1 May 1989, they reached Palawan. Nearly eighteen months later, Hung's parents and younger sister were accepted as refugees. They now live in Oregon, but Hung and his two brothers were rejected because they were over eighteen and considered independent of their parents.

'When we learned our screening decision,' Hung told me, 'my father said the UNHCR is worse even than the Communists. Even the Communists did not destroy the family.' In fact, UNHCR regulations state that the immediate family of anyone determined to be a refugee should also be considered refugees, and Hung had seen people over eighteen get accepted with their families. 'It's very stupid,' he said. 'They say I'm too old to depend on my parents, but they are now old, and they need to depend on me.'

Hung had come to me in shorts, a T-shirt and sneakers, breathing hard and pouring sweat. He had run the two miles from the camp in the heavy evening heat and he apologized for being so informally dressed. 'It's how I got out,' he said. 'I'm a runner and I told them I wanted to go for a run.' Later, when I asked if he shouldn't get back before his pass expired, he said it wasn't important; he would slip through the fence. 'It's good to talk,' he said. 'It's good to remember what I am—my life. I am waiting to live, and I forget sometimes that this is my life.'

Hung learned his English at Palawan, and became the principal of the camp secondary school. In June, when the school building was destroyed, he started teaching children in secret, because, he said, 'If children don't study, I'm afraid they will fool around, and it's important for me, too, to have something to do.'

Nearly a fifth of the camp population was under the age of ten, and most of these children were born in the camp. 'It's not good,' Hung said. 'They don't have to do a thing. They just receive. When I was a child, I knew how to plant crops, or fix a bicycle, but they don't even know about traffic. They just hear about red light, green light. The world for them is a world in theory only.'

Their parents, generally, were not much better grounded. Many had endured forced labour in Vietnam, and here they found themselves in a forced idleness camp. 'When it was allowed, I used to work,' one woman told me. 'Now I have only free time. I take care of some flowers. I think too much. I get hurt in my head.'

Money was a constant worry; when business was banned, a limit of fifty dollars per family per month had been imposed on the funds detainees could receive from overseas. The weekly food ration was just enough for one meal a day, and it included no spices, no oil, only staples—rice, fish (often claimed to be inedible), pork, vegetables and either one egg or one tin of sardines.

Accommodation was equally spartan, generally ten people to each twenty-metre-square billet. When Zones 1 and 2 were demolished, their residents, including Hung and his brothers, had to split up and live with others. Electricity had been cut back, and every other night half the camp went without. Nobody I spoke with liked the living conditions, but I rarely heard complaints. It was their lives that oppressed the boat people, the emptiness of the present, and the hopelessness of the future.

Depression was endemic, and the less there was to do, the more people drank. Hung recalled five or six suicides during his time in the camp. 'Just last month,' he said, 'one man got drunk and went to the sea and he drowned. But that's not a real suicide. If you do a suicide, that's political. You plan it and write a letter and tell everyone.'

Hung was silent for a moment, then he said, 'Sometimes it's

hard to know what's politics and what's depression.'

The best one might hope for in these circumstances was to resist being crushed by them. In this, Hung had succeeded. He saw the camp as a dangerous place; he understood that when you're wasting time you have to be very careful not to let time waste you. He was traumatized in ways he seemed to know he could not yet reckon with, but he had made something of himself and he worried about others. He was an impressive young man.

So was Che Nhat Giao, a twenty-nine-year-old who had led demonstrations in the camp against medical service cuts and unfair screening practices. His father had been a first lieutenant in the South Vietnamese army, and later an English teacher. In 1975, when Giao was ten, and the Communists took Nha Trang, his family was placed under strict surveillance. Their house was occupied by the People's Committee, and the family was sent to work in a New Economic Zone, as rural labour camps were called. Giao had tried to flee by boat many times, and two of his brothers, who made it in 1988, now live in Washington State.

'I didn't escape from the country but from the tyranny of the regime,' Giao told me. 'My first dream is to return to some kind of democratic Vietnam. If I'd stayed, I'd probably be a dissident now, but as a returnee I'd be under surveillance or in jail. It is very insulting to be called an economic migrant. We stay here now because we want to show how much we crave something higher.'

I was struck by Giao's switch from 'I' to 'we'. To him, history was not something external. He was a part of it. He was reading *Beyond Peace* by Richard Nixon and *Diplomacy* by Henry Kissinger, and he admired both men, but with reservations. 'When the Americans left South Vietnam,' he said, 'we felt abandoned, and it was all about China. I was very young at the time, but I still remember the feeling that it was very outrageous. The Americans were playing God with us.'

Later, Giao used the words, 'playing God' again to describe the high-handed, careless way in which asylum screening was conducted. It was a common refrain at Palawan—'They play God with us'—and the phrase made me think of the scene in Genesis, when Abraham, realizing that God intends to wipe out Sodom, asks the Lord: 'Wilt thou indeed destroy the righteous with the

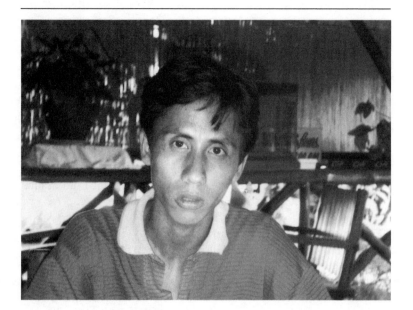

wicked . . . Far be that from thee! Shall not the Judge of all the earth do right?' God replies that if fifty righteous men can be found, the city will be spared. Abraham asks: What if there are only forty-five? No destruction, says the Lord. Abraham presses on: What if there are only thirty, or twenty, or ten? God says that even for the sake of ten righteous men, he will not destroy the city. And, with that, 'the Lord went his way . . . and Abraham returned to his place.'

They never discuss the bottom line: what if only one righteous man can be found in Sodom? But the question is answered with the ensuing fire and brimstone: one righteous man is not enough. The one righteous man who was found, Lot, became a hapless refugee. If there were others—there could have been as many as eight more by the formula—they were slaughtered with the city.

G iao told me this story:
    Two sisters left Vietnam together with the boyfriend of the older one. During the screening interview, the Filipino

Above: Che Nhat Giao.

23

immigration officer asked for sex. The older sister felt that she couldn't have sex with him because she was in the company of her boyfriend; on the other hand, the boyfriend could do nothing to help her through the screening. Eventually, the sisters gave in, and had sex with the interviewer and his friend. Shortly afterwards, they and the boyfriend were granted visas and resettled in the Netherlands. The boyfriend couldn't stop thinking about what had happened, and especially about his inability to prevent it. The couple split up. The younger sister, who was just sixteen, is now in a mental hospital. She wrote to a friend in the camp, saying: 'I am in a free country, but my heart cannot be free of what I did in life.'

Giao said: 'It's a sad story.'

Three women from the camp arrived at my door, claiming that their husbands had all been resettled—in America, Australia and France—but that they had been left behind. Was this true? Not entirely, I found out. None of the women had actually been married at the time of their screening interviews. One had a two-year-old son with a man in the camp; the son went with the father. Another had married the previous year, after her screening, to a man who had resettled in America in 1977: although the marriage may have been legitimate, it fitted the classic profile of an immigration scam and did not constitute a claim for political asylum. The third woman was merely engaged to be married; she had met the man in the camp and they had fallen in love just before he resettled. She had a sworn affidavit, notarized in Ontario, that stated that her fiancé would marry her immediately upon her arrival in Canada. It was a meaningless document, but it was her only hope.

Everyone had documents; they brought me these bundles of papers to prove their claims were real: birth certificates, property confiscation certificates, re-education camp release certificates; photographs of themselves or their menfolk in uniform, posing with American GIs; wedding photographs; summonses from the People's Committee in their village; notices of 'employment termination' in 1974 from US firms or the US military. There were letters written to the White House, pleading in mangled English for special consideration, as well as the replies saying that the President could not answer all his mail personally and that the matter would be referred to the appropriate government agency.

Several hundred people had documents approving them for a family reunification immigration visa to the United States or Canada, but to collect the visas they would have to return to Vietnam and wait—possibly for several years. Hung had such a document. 'It's not right,' he said. 'My family is my home, and if we didn't care what is right and what is wrong, we could have stayed in Vietnam all along. Until they let me emigrate directly from the Philippines, this paper is just paper.'

Papers, papers, papers.

A woman showed me a document carefully wrapped in plastic. Her photo floated above seven big rubber stamps with flamboyant signatures underneath. 'Proof of my husband in America,' she said. It was only an expired travel permit, allowing her to meet him at Manila airport, but she held it out as if it ought to be immediately convertible into a passport and plane ticket. She seemed to have no clue which paper was which, so she offered her prize document, the one that had brought her the most satisfaction. She was doughy-faced and depressed, a bit hard to look at directly—so much anguish—but she had this husband, and the husband loved her, and she loved the husband, and her heart was breaking in the camp. A broken heart, however, does not constitute 'a well-founded fear of persecution'. I asked her about her life in Vietnam. She said she taught at a high school in Saigon. Why did she leave? Why had she decided in 1989 that she had to risk her life at sea to get out? She seemed unable to remember that other life, just as others were unable to stop remembering it. She could only say, 'My husband sponsored me in 1993,' and 'You will help me? You will reconsider my case?'

I greeted my next visitor, Tran Thi Kim Truong, with the words: 'Let me guess. You've got a husband in America.'

'No,' she said. 'My husband recently died here. He was thirty-three and he had a very slight fever, and they took him to the hospital. The doctor said it was a very normal sickness. They gave him IV fluid and medicine. Then the IV ran out, and the nurse didn't notice. He went into the hospital on the third of January and he died on the seventh of January.'

Truong was left with three daughters, aged ten, six and one. After the rest of her family escaped from Vietnam in 1988, she said, the authorities made it very hard for her and her husband. Her relatives now live in Texas. She showed me a sharp letter from the Secretary of Justice for the Philippines, telling her to stop wasting her time and money sending pleas for reconsideration. She said, 'I am glad you have come to my aid.'

'What can I do?' I asked.

She looked hurt. She said: 'I don't know. Help me.'

It was easy to get impatient. Within hours of my arrival, the rumour had spread that I was a lawyer, and even as I explained over and over that I was not, that I could only listen to the boat people's stories and perhaps recount a few of them, I became invested with ever greater powers. 'Is it true,' an earnest young woman asked me, 'that in the United States you are a member of Congress?' And a sixty-three-year-old veteran came to find me with a two-page typed letter 'respectfully requesting' that I reconsider his case, because, he wrote: 'Having perceived your humanity and kindness by nature, I was almost fainted when I received the Decision denying my refugee status.'

I went out for a walk one afternoon, and when I returned, the desk clerk said a Vietnamese man had come by who wanted to talk to me for one and a half hours. The man reappeared a few minutes later, and talked to me for three and a half hours. He was in his sixties, with eyes that appeared slightly filmed with cataracts, and a vaguely conspiratorial air. He started by explaining that I must not publish his name because a leader should not appear to be promoting himself when he is representing his people. 'You can help me,' he said. 'But you must not dishonour me.'

I asked what he was the leader of, and he showed me his membership card from the Veterans of the Vietnam War, Inc., in Wilkes Barre, Pennsylvania.

'I am secretary-general of the Palawan post,' the Vet said. 'I was an engineering captain in the South Vietnamese army from 1961 to the end. I was in re-education for twenty-one days, then I bribed the local authority so they didn't call me any more. But I couldn't work legally. I went to the square to repair keys, and they confiscated my tools. So I decided to escape, and someone betrayed me. At ten-thirty in the night the police came to my house. They beat me and tied me to a chair like that.'

The Vet twisted his right hand behind his head and midway down his back, and reached his left hand from around his waist to meet it—an awkward position to achieve, much less maintain. The Vet said that after being tied this way and beaten for five hours, he underwent three months of acupuncture before he could use his arms again. He showed me the scar where his left ear had been torn in half by a policeman beating him with a ruler. 'I try and try and try,' he said, 'but I cannot live in Vietnam.'

Each incident he described was accompanied by a deft pantomime—the process of making keys; his beatings; the way he had to scrunch himself up when, at last, he got on to a fishing boat about twenty metres long and three metres wide with 246 other people; the way their bodies swayed against each other when the boat was struck by a typhoon. Suddenly, he clutched his forehead with his hands, shut his eyes, shook his head and declared: 'But I did not come to talk of myself. I planned to talk of my people.' He let go of his head and scolded himself: 'Be a leader. Be a leader.'

He told me that the Vietnam Veterans of the War post at Palawan represented 224 people—members and their families. He didn't say much about them. He seemed to think that their situation spoke for itself: they had fought alongside the Americans, they had been abused for this by the Communists, the UNHCR said veterans should get asylum, and the Americans ought to come to their rescue.

The Vet was adamant that all of his members had legitimate cases, but he was a practical man. Citing his own case, 'for example', he said that he had missed his opportunity to facilitate justice with 'a little gift'. After his screening interview, the interviewer said she also needed a document about the background of his father. The Vet was annoyed at this irregularity, but he returned with the document. The interviewer glanced at it and asked if he had brought anything more. The Vet didn't understand. What else did she want?

'Then,' he said, 'I got my decision, and I thought, I'm very stupid. If I said I have a little envelope, or I would like to see you outside, I would be a refugee. She wanted money. She needs to repair her home, to buy a new air-conditioner, a fan. I need a visa. She is a woman. I am a man. Humans are weak, and we can co-operate together. But I'm not mad at this woman. What makes me very, very mad is the UNHCR which made this bribery necessary.'

In fact, the Vet said, Americans should withhold that portion of their taxes which goes to supporting the UNHCR. He found it astonishing that the plight of the boat people had not sparked a widespread tax revolt. 'The American people,' he said, 'look at the Vietnam veterans, with the long hair and the beard and the problems, and they think they are just hooligans. We fought for freedom. When they understand, it will be too late.'

A woman named Thu came by to drop off some documents while I was talking to the Vet. She said she needed just a minute of my time, and the Vet said, 'Go ahead,' but he seemed annoyed. Once we were alone, Thu said, 'Vietnamese are very jealous. Everyone's afraid you have a better story.' As soon as she left, the Vet said to me, 'Everyone wants to make their personal appeal, eh? Everyone wants to push forward his own case.'

Roberto de los Reyes, a local attorney who occasionally wrote letters of appeal for detainees, told me he had first learned about the boat people from a local fisherman who came across some Vietnamese adrift at sea. What caught the fisherman's attention was the smell—of burning flesh. 'They were roasting human flesh. They were butchering people,' de los Reyes said. 'Later on, refugees told me stories about raffles to see who'd get eaten next. They had heard these stories themselves before they left Vietnam. So you have to think what it means that they would rather go through such an experience than stay at home.'

In the hallway of de los Reyes's home was a sign that said: 'I had no shoes and I complained until I met a man who had no feet.' A reminder to be charitable, but I wondered: does the fact of footlessness really render shoelessness acceptable? Is the economy of need such that only the most extreme cases—those, say, who must eat their shipmates in order to survive—have a legitimate claim on the world's generosity? Can a person's deprivation be his most valuable possession? If so, every form of self-improvement

becomes utterly counter-productive; the shoeless must envy the footless the authority of their complaints.

Roberto de los Reyes was a sentimental lawyer. He believed that if people felt compelled to risk cannibalism then they were entitled to 'special humanitarian consideration'. I didn't disagree with him exactly, but I don't like to be blackmailed. It is one thing to recognize one's blessings and to say of the less fortunate, 'There but for the grace of God go I.' But it is something else entirely to cave in to anyone who comes along and says, 'If I am forced to eat this person beside me, the blood is on your hands.'

If you hang around a refugee camp for a few days, your

Photo: Philip Gourevitch

Above: the Vet.

Philip Gourevitch

defences rise. Compassion fatigue, they call it. In fact, it's possible to keep your compassion intact; the greater exhaustion is political. The thoughts pile up deliriously: twenty-three million refugees in the world, a Malthusian apocalypse with everyone throwing away their shoes in order to go barefoot, then cutting off their feet—a world of quadriplegics knocking on the door of the last person with a working limb. It was essential to maintain perspective, to sheer back from the twenty-three million refugees, to the fifty thousand boat people left in the camps, to the two thousand four hundred in Palawan, to the one before me at a given moment.

And here was Vu, a seventeen-year-old who had come to Palawan alone at the age of twelve. When his mother died, his stepfather remarried and didn't want Vu around any more. He had been put on a boat and dumped on the world's doorstep. He called the camp 'my only real home'. The summer before we met, the camp administration had rounded up three or four dozen

Above: Vu. Opposite: Nguyen Thu Huong.

Photos: Philip Gourevitch

30

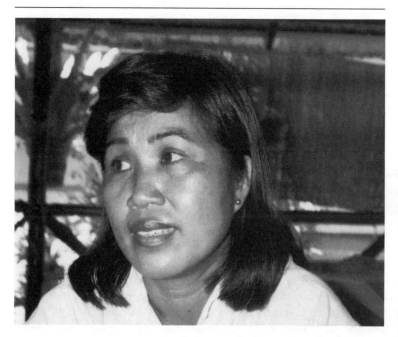

'unaccompanied minors' and shipped them back to Vietnam. Vu had eluded the sweep, and the camp administration had since agreed to let him be. They could always get him later.

I asked Vu where he hoped to go. 'Wherever is fine as long as there is the affection and love which I have been craving and could not find in Vietnam.'

Vu was an outcast, an emotional refugee. He was a very damaged, painfully shy yet very appealing kid—remarkably forthright; it intrigued me that it was Giao, the most overtly political of all the people I met, who brought him to me. By recognizing in this twitching, tender, unwanted child a person to be regarded as highly as any anti-Communist intellectual, Giao was refusing the notion that humanitarianism could be fit snugly into any strictly political scheme.

The same day that I met Vu, I also met Nguyen Thu Huong, who told me about her ten years of forced labour in a New Economic Zone, clearing virgin jungle, seeing fellow labourers blown to bits by land-mines. When she was sent there in 1975, she

31

had a one-year-old son and was pregnant with a second. In 1981, she learned that her husband, a former South Vietnamese lieutenant, had been killed four years earlier while attempting to escape from a re-education camp.

Huong escaped the New Economic Zone in 1985 and reached Palawan in 1989. On the way to the boat, she was separated from her children, who wound up with an uncle on a boat to Malaysia. The boys were accepted as refugees and now live with Huong's sister in Santa Ana, California. But Huong had been screened out in Palawan. She had not seen her sons in six years.

I thought again of Abraham bargaining for the salvation of Sodom. It seemed to me obscene to have to measure Huong's story against Vu's, to call Huong footless and Vu merely a barefoot waif. And yet, if I had to choose between them and send one back to Vietnam while giving the other onward passage to enjoy the political privileges of a life like mine, I knew I would pick Huong. I don't believe that there is room only for one of them, but Vu's troubles were something papers could not cure, and a refugee is someone who needs papers. I came to think of Vu as one of those eight innocent men who might have been destroyed in the Cities of the Plain.

There came a point at the Badjao Inn when I had to turn people away. Shortly after I was asked if I was a Congressman, I found myself standing in my room with nine Vietnamese thrusting their documents at me and talking all at once, requesting help, demanding reconsideration. None of them had been given a pass to leave the camp, and I was worried that they might get in trouble because of me. They had a faith in the power of the written word that I do not quite share; they believed that if I told you their stories, they might be saved. I asked them all to leave and made preparations to move to another hotel.

It distressed me to imagine that detainees who had considered returning to Vietnam under the Voluntary Repatriation scheme might now decide to stay in the camp just a little longer because they happened to have had a conversation with me. I was starting to think that, for many of the boat people, returning to Vietnam might be better than staying in Palawan.

I had been talking with David Derthick, an American who ran the International Catholic Migration Commission's Voluntary Repatriation programme at the camp. David had been working with boat people for more than ten years, and he supported the policy of imposing hardship to compel detainees to return to Vietnam, although he acknowledged that it didn't seem to be working.

'If you want to say the UNHCR is not an advocate for the refugees here—that's true,' David told me. 'If you want screwed-up cases, I can give you screwed-up cases. But the screening is history. The camp's closing, that's a fact, so my big interest is to see that happen as quickly and painlessly as possible. There's no future for the boat people except in Vietnam.'

If the detainees didn't return voluntarily, David expected they would eventually be returned by force. 'In the meantime, they're living in a world of dependency and learned helplessness,' he said. I asked him who's fault that was, and he said: 'Look, Palawan has been a model camp. When I was in Galang, in Indonesia, everyone weighed ten pounds less than here, and they would have these rat eradication campaigns—for every tin of rat tails you brought in you got a tin of meat. Little girls were running around with these cans of tails. Nice, right? Well, Palawan's the opposite extreme. The people who're left here like to say they'd rather die here than live in Vietnam. My job is to convince them that's absurd.'

David's biggest obstacle was the 'zero credibility' of the UNHCR. 'They're bureaucrats,' he said. 'They'll never acknowledge screwing up. If there's a big problem here, they'll cover it up. Now they're saying it'll take returnees only three to six months to get an immigration visa once they're back in Vietnam. It's a total lie. So when we tell people the truth, which is that there hasn't been a single reported case of political persecution of a returnee in Vietnam, they don't believe us.'

'They say you're playing God with them,' I told him.

'More like the devil's advocate,' David said.

On my last morning at the Badjao, someone came to tell me that two women had been caught sneaking back into the camp after visiting me. They had been put in the 'Monkey House', the camp jail, and questioned for an hour or two, then released. The person who brought me this message told me not to worry. 'We will still come,' he said. I pointed to my packed bags and said I was leaving on the next plane.

I moved to the Casa Linda Inn around the corner and sat in the garden amid the bird-of-paradise plants and coconut palms. I missed the boat people. They had come to me with hope and energy, nicely dressed; the women often wore make-up, and the men's shirts were usually carefully ironed. I regretted having lived among them for nearly a week without ever really seeing how they lived.

Twice, when David had driven me home to the Badjao, we had swung through the camp at night in his car—past the Buddhist temple and the Catholic church, into a dusty, nearly treeless village of sagging thatched huts, crammed close together. People sat around gas lanterns in front of their homes; some sold food from roadside woks—a forbidden but tolerated bit of commerce. Couples walked hand in hand in a parade of public privacy. When I recognized people, it always came as a shock: the faces, caught suddenly in the headlights, looked more raw than I remembered them, now that their owners were not sitting for their portraits. Faces that had been strictly good-humoured in my presence were slack with loneliness, and one that had wept about a missing husband was laughing with a very present-looking man.

Now, at the Casa Linda, in the close garden with its heavy vegetation, I felt as if I was the one who had been shut away, and I was glad when the bell-boy brought me a visitor.

His name was Luat, and he said David had sent him. He was thirty-two and had a high, nasal voice, an open, pock-marked face that he screwed up into a seemingly arbitrary range of perplexed expressions and a great repertoire of dismissive hand gestures. 'I haven't been to school since the age of ten,' he said, 'but I try not to show it.' He let out a most unhappy laugh, as if he were being tickled and not enjoying it at all.

'What do you want me to say?' he asked.

'Whatever you like,' I said. 'Tell me about yourself.'

Luat told me that in 1975, he was sent with his family to 'High Mountain in New Economic Zone.' After a few years there, he nearly died of malaria. He fled to Ho Chi Minh City for treatment and became a homeless person, sleeping in railroad stations and under market tents. He was arrested and sent to a plantation jail where he was put in charge of tending two oxen and three water buffalo. 'But my mind is absent,' he said. 'One ox escaped, and I was put in the Monkey House. The officer, he say, "You are not a child any more but you act like a child." I say, "Oh, I'm sorry. Oh, I'm sorry."'

Luat escaped and arranged to get on a boat. He couldn't swim, and had to wade out to the boat in water up to his shoulders. He met a woman on the shore who had two babies, and he carried one out for her. 'It was so strange to her,' he said, 'someone helpful for no reason.' He was two weeks at sea. 'After three days, no more water. Drinking urine, yes. Urine and sea water, urine and sea water. I always cry to Jesus Christ to give us a little rain, and it rained four times. But I was not afraid. I think, if I die, I was dead in Vietnam before. It's not on the sea that I die. It's on the sea I go for freedom.'

Luat's younger brother had fled to Hong Kong and was resettled. Luat was rejected. 'I don't know why,' he said. It was one of his favourite phrases, and he said it fast, as a single word. After telling me in detail about his life in Vietnam he stopped and lowered his forehead to the table. 'Take too long, my background,' he said. 'You know, my mind too bad, yah. It always absent.'

'Maybe you're thinking of something else,' I said.

'Thinking nothing,' Luat shot back. 'Many people say to me in camp, "Are you crazy? You look like mental illness." Sometimes I go and sing, Vietnamese songs or English, I don't know why. Especially I love countryside music, like "Goodbye Blue Sky" or "Lonely Blue". I love that so much. People take a glance at me—"Oh, guy, what are you doing?" I say, "Going and singing without a problem."' He grinned, looked down, turned sideways to me, and his face became a mask of sorrow. My pen stopped scratching in my notebook. He grinned again, and his hands fluttered up, swatting at nothing.

'Before,' he said suddenly, 'I know a lot of words of psychology—like, for instance, sleepwalking—but now I forget.'

Luat was a peculiar man and he knew it; he seemed always to

be listening as he spoke, his head cocked slightly to one side, as if curious to discover what he might say next. Sometimes, as though bored by what he heard, he broke off mid-sentence and said something totally unrelated.

He said: 'David's such a guy, I love him so much. He bought me teeth.' Then I remembered; David had told me about Luat. When he arrived in Palawan, his mouth was just a hideous mess of blackened stumps. He was awful to look at, and he always kept his hand up to hide his face. So David bought him dentures; seventeen teeth had to be pulled to fit them.

'David's daughters,' Luat said, 'I love them so much. When I was at their house, they saw a hunter fire down a small colourful bird. They say, "Why you kill a bird for?" The hunter say, "I kill for food." They say, "For food you can go to supermarket." They so smart, the girls. So smart,' he repeated, and then, with heavy emphasis, he added, 'And well.'

'You mean healthy?' I said.

'Healthy and doing something. Never leave a problem on the half way.' He repeated that, too. 'Never leave a problem on the half way.'

A rooster came out into the Casa Linda garden, a magnificent, picture-postcard rooster strutting to the middle of the incandescent green lawn, where he stopped to crow. Luat jumped in his chair. 'Fighting cock!' he said. 'You looking your best.' Then he turned to me and said, 'I am a first son, yah. You know, I always miss my parents. Every day. It makes me cry so much.'

I asked him if he ever considered going home.

'That's what I always think about when I lie down. Where can I go back to? When I talk to you about my situation, that makes me remember when I was young, I don't know why. I saw a local policeman tell my parents to dry a puddle up on the floor. I see my parents on the floor. In Vietnam, anybody who contradict what they want is on the floor. If I go back, will UNHCR protect me? My house is far from Ho Chi Minh City. How can UNHCR overtake the Vietnam government? They cannot. It's not fair. I really don't know how to talk about it. It's just my fate.'

One of the hotel's parrots started shrieking. 'He wants to be free,' Luat said. 'That's your fate,' he told the bird. 'Eternity in a bird cage.' Or did he say, 'A tenant in a bird cage?' I wasn't sure, and it didn't matter.

I sent a note to Mohammed Nisar, the UNHCR's Pakistani field representative at Palawan, requesting an interview. Nisar, who was, according to David, furious about my presence in Palawan, told me to talk instead to Merida Morales O'Donnel, director of the UNHCR mission in the Philippines. O'Donnel, an expensively dressed Puerto Rican-American, gave me half an hour in her Manila office, which was decorated with large, framed colour photographs of Vietnamese packed in their pathetic boats on the open sea.

'The screening process was carried out with all guarantees,' she told me. 'It was very, very fair. We are very, very pleased with the screening. If you look as an outsider, you don't have the details. The two thousand four hundred in Palawan are really looking for, dreaming of, waiting for a miracle, and anything which could give them the impression that a miracle will take place. If you help one or two, you affect two thousand four hundred. So let's be responsible and help them go home. It's not good for these people to be in a camp.'

I said I agreed: the camps were not good.

She said, 'Why should the UNHCR want to hurt refugees?'

I said, 'You tell me.'

'They aren't refugees,' she said. 'We aren't responsible for economic migrants. We would like that they go while we're here, when they get counselling, support and money. But we will pull out by the end of ninety-five. If forcible return takes place before then, we won't be involved. The population in Palawan are illegal aliens, and by international law any country can deport illegal aliens.'

I kept staring at the boat people in the photographs around the room. I wanted to ask whether they were refugees or illegal aliens, but I said nothing. I didn't want her to think that she should take the pictures down.

Hong Kong

When I met Pam Baker one afternoon in Hong Kong, she was laughing about something, and after I asked her what, she said: 'It doesn't matter. What matters is that in my business, in my line of work, if you lose your sense of humour, you're stuffed.'

Pam's business is the law, and her line of work is representing boat people. In Hong Kong, anyone who deals with boat people has to deal with Pam Baker, and I was constantly being told either that she was fantastic or that she was a terrible problem. To those who think she's a terrible problem, Pam is the primary obstacle to the speedy repatriation of the colony's twenty-four thousand Vietnamese detainees. To those who think Pam's fantastic, she is a folk hero, a feisty sixty-four-year-old Scottish grandmother running the government ragged in the courts while burning up her pension fund and a steady stream of Dunhill reds to fuel her tireless advocacy on behalf of the otherwise defenceless.

I asked Pam if she enjoyed the fight.

'It's good to win,' she said. 'There's no substitute.' But she didn't expect to win much as we knocked on the gate of Victoria Prison, a nineteenth-century stone building at the corner of Hong Kong's Chancery Lane and Old Bailey Street. We had come to see several boat people who had been transferred here in preparation for a forced repatriation flight to Hanoi.

Forced repatriation was unique to Hong Kong, and the operations in which troops capture boat people for deportation had sparked riots in the camps. In an operation at Whitehead Detention Centre in April 1994, officers fired hundreds of volleys of tear-gas, and hundreds of Vietnamese were injured. Suicides and suicide attempts—people setting fire to themselves; abdomen slashings—were common during such operations. A few days before I met Pam, I had gone to the High Island Detention Centre to see for myself how detainees were rounded up for the transfer to Victoria Prison. It was a grim place, all concrete and metal, ringed by a tall, maximum-security fence draped with coils of razor wire. Of the three thousand Vietnamese who lived there, fifty-five had been selected for deportation, but only four sought

The Boat People

to resist the nearly eight hundred Correctional Service officers who had come to haul them away. The four—three men and a woman—had climbed on to the roofs of their huts in the pre-dawn hours and hung out protest banners, one of which read DON'T COMPEL US TO THE DEATH.

One man burnt the flag of the Socialist Republic of Vietnam. After a stand-off lasting several hours, airline steps were driven over to the building, and commando teams stormed the roofs. From the press observation post about a kilometre above the camp, I watched through binoculars. One of the men held a weapon—a spike, it turned out, made from the sawn-off and sharpened aluminium shaft of a badminton racket. He thrust it at his stomach and did a little twisting dance into the arms of the commandos. As medics rushed him away on a stretcher, the man on the next roof jumped to the ground, where he was instantly captured. The third man tripped off the edge of his roof and dropped on to a giant air mattress, while the woman went limp

Photo: Philip J. Griffiths (Magnum)

Above: Vietnamese boat people in Hong Kong.

39

and allowed herself to be carried off.

Later, at a press briefing, a Correctional Service officer displayed the badminton racket spike and described the wound it had caused as 'a five-inch superficial laceration'. Brian Bresnihan, Hong Kong's refugee co-ordinator, hailed the morning's 'extremely successful, extremely smooth action' as 'proof that we are committed to bringing about the final resolution of this problem.'

But Pam had heard that some of the people slated for this round of deportation might have strong cases to appeal for last-minute reconsideration. Hoi, a young, pony-tailed, Vietnamese-Australian lawyer who had come along as Pam's interpreter, had heard the same thing. 'Could be rubbish,' Pam said, as we entered Victoria Prison, 'but we've got to make sure.'

We were taken to a visiting-room where Nguyen Thin Lan, a twenty-three-year-old woman, was ushered in by guards. She wore an orange T-shirt printed with one of those bizarre English phrases that Asian haberdashers favour: FAMOUS PURPOSIVE IMAGINATION.

Lan was engaged to a Hong Kong citizen and believed that this made her deportation illegal. But with a few quick questions, Pam established that Lan hadn't even begun the matrimonial registration formalities. She had only met 'the chap', as Pam called him, six weeks ago, and they did not share a common language.

'I'm just a girl,' Lan explained. 'So if I can find a man to marry me, that's good.'

Pam told her there were plenty of men in Vietnam, and she would have to look for one there. Lan, who had looked a bit haggard when she showed up, left seeming unaccountably cheerful.

'What nonsense,' Pam said. 'For God's sake, I've got better things to do with my time.'

She was still speaking when the door opened, and an extremely skinny man fell into the room. Hoi caught him just before he hit the floor and helped him into a chair. The man sat gripping the edge of the table. Spasms convulsed his gaunt face; his eyes were bleary, unfocused, and his lips were rimed with dry spittle. He looked as though he'd been crying for days and, after rocking in his chair for a moment, he collapsed on to his extended arms in tears, his mouth wide and noiseless.

'This is ridiculous,' Pam said. 'You should be in bed.'

Hoi didn't translate, and the man clasped Pam's hand fiercely. 'I'm so touched you came to see me,' he sobbed.

Pam started asking questions. The man called himself Nguyen; he said he left Vietnam in 1989 after writing anti-government newspaper articles. It seemed that he had been in technical college at the time, and had been told by his youth leader to write the truth, so he wrote that everyone should quit the Communist Youth League because it wasn't in the national interest. His writings, it transpired, had never been published, but he believed that they were shown to provincial Party leaders. 'I wrote the truth,' he said. 'Everyone else just wrote half the truth.'

'He's not clear,' Hoi said.

'He certainly isn't,' said Pam.

'I wrote about Communism and how in fourteen years it has led to the destruction of Vietnamese society,' Nguyen said. 'I recommended that the regime in Hanoi should adopt democratic reform because of human rights abuses. They locked me up seven days and sentenced me to re-education before I escaped.'

I wondered what he'd really written; his account sounded too pat, like something he'd read in one of the emigré journals in which he said he'd published some poems while in the camp. Nguyen was eager to talk about these poems and his political life at the High Island Detention Centre, but Pam wasn't interested. 'I need something really sensational,' she said, 'to make your case notable if you don't want to be on that plane.'

'I was on the roof Sunday,' Nguyen said. 'I tried to kill myself.' He pulled up his shirt to display a very light scratch above the navel with a little Band-Aid at one end; a fingernail could have done the damage.

'I tried to stab myself many times,' Nguyen said. 'But I didn't have time before they stopped me.'

In fact, he had had hours alone with his badminton-racket spike. Clearly, he had never intended to die, and as I realized this I became annoyed that he did not admit it. On the contrary, he persisted in his threats. When Pam asked a question, he turned to me—the note-taker: 'Rest assured that I will die on Hong Kong land only so the Hong Kong government won't treat others like me.' Or: 'I really appreciate your help, but I have tried to kill myself already and I will try again, just to show that I long for freedom and have been treated unjustly.' Or: 'It's been three days. I haven't eaten or drunk anything. I actually don't want to live.'

Perhaps Nguyen's melodrama was a strange kind of self-protection, a way of introducing a touch of grandeur to his humiliating anguish, this return in shame to a fate which genuinely terrified him.

At last he got up, wobbling, his legs stiff and uncertain. He clutched at the table, at the door, and at Hoi for support as he stumbled from the room. Both Pam and I said that, while Nguyen was completely beside himself, we did not believe he would commit suicide. Hoi was appalled. He was shaken to see 'a human being like this.' He was right: it was awful. Nguyen's stories had been rejected to the point where he could express himself only through the gestures of madness. And he must have known that he was failing even there.

The scene with Nguyen repeated itself with the next prisoner, Vo Van Thanh, the man who had burnt the Vietnamese flag at High Island and jumped from the roof. Thanh had the same tear-swollen look as Nguyen, but was not as hysterical. He was just completely depressed and, although he might have had a strong case, he no longer seemed interested in it. He had been a policeman in Haiphong and claimed to have been arrested for distributing anti-government leaflets and sentenced to six years in prison. Pam tried to draw him out, but he wanted only to talk about burning the Vietnamese flag in the camp, and about his jump from the roof. He had landed without injury, but he considered himself to have attempted suicide.

'I can only hope for the mercy of the Hong Kong government,' he said.

'The Hong Kong government,' Pam told him, 'doesn't go in for mercy.'

'I have only my life to spare,' Thanh said.

Pam said, 'It'd be great if you or your wife could let us know how it goes after you get back.'

'Tomorrow,' Thanh replied, 'is my birthday, so I believe it'll be my last day. I don't have any hope. I only have my life. That is the only weapon I have.'

'Just bear in mind,' Pam came back, 'that you have a wife and children who love you.'

'I really want to kill myself,' Thanh said.

Our visiting time was up. A guard led Thanh back to his cell, and Pam, Hoi and I walked out into the mild Hong Kong dusk. Hoi was still upset at having witnessed human beings so reduced. 'I can't stand feeling so helpless,' he said. 'It's intolerable.'

'You mustn't get cosmic,' said the unflappable Pam. 'You've got to stay practical. The minute you get cosmic, you're stuffed.'

When I left Victoria Prison, I went to a bookstore and bought *Crime and Punishment*; my encounters with Nguyen and Thanh had made me want to re-read the following scene:

At the great closed gates of the house, a little man stood with his shoulder leaning against them, wrapped in a grey soldier's coat, with a copper Achilles helmet on his head. He cast a drowsy and indifferent glance at Svidrigailov . . .

'What do you want here?' he said without changing his position.

'Nothing, brother, good morning,' answered Svidrigailov . . . 'I am going to foreign parts, brother.'

'To foreign parts?'

'To America.'

'America?'

Svidrigailov took out the revolver and cocked it. Achilles raised his eyebrows.

'I say, this is not the place for such jokes!'

'Why shouldn't it be the place?'

'Because it isn't.'

'Well, brother, I don't mind that. It's a good place. When you are asked, you just say he was going, he said, to America.'

He put the revolver to his right temple.

'You can't do it here, it's not the place,' cried Achilles, rousing himself, his eyes growing bigger and bigger.

Svidrigailov pulled the trigger.

This cryptic notion—to call one's suicide 'going to America'—suddenly made a sort of sense to me. In leaving their homeland, the boat people had taken a truly suicidal risk at sea. Luat had put it so precisely: 'I think, if I die, I was dead in Vietnam before. It's not on the sea that I die. It's on the sea I go for freedom.'

What compelled people to put to sea in small, unsafe boats was a quest for reincarnation. Bobbing over the South China Sea, they were saying, in effect, we are drowning, throw us the ring. Even if they survived, they had committed a metaphorical suicide—putting an end to their life in Vietnam—and if their bid for onward passage to the next world was denied, they felt they had been murdered. Suicide then became another kind of metaphor, enacting the death that had been imposed upon them. DON'T COMPEL US TO THE DEATH, said the banner at High Island.

Yes, I reject blackmail. But what if, behind the threats, there is a legitimate appeal to conscience?

In April 1995, the UNHCR reversed its long-standing opposition to the forced repatriation of boat people. As Southeast Asian governments prepare to ship the Vietnamese home, scenes of the kind I witnessed at High Island may become more frequent and far worse. Boat people and their advocates repeatedly showed me the hideous photo of the charred, naked corpse of Le Xuan Tho, a twenty-eight-year-old boat person who died two days after he set fire to himself at the Galang camp in Indonesia. Those who commit suicide may not be the people with the strongest claims for political asylum. But if their deaths are noticed, and the world is suddenly repulsed, and the camera crews return, then—oh, irony—once again, self-violation and macabre blackmail will have proved their own rewards.

Even if no notice is taken, even if there are no deaths, is it really necessary that it should have come to this?

Vietnam

At the Gold Cock, a western-style bar near Hoan Kiem lake, I met up with a group of young British expatriates who had settled in Hanoi. Several used to work in the camps in Hong Kong, but they got sick of it. The Vietnamese there were losers, manipulators and liars, they said; you couldn't really be friends with them, they just wanted to use you, and their fears of repatriation were insupportable. The young expats were much happier talking about life in Hanoi. Hanoi was an adventure, and the Vietnamese who returned did very well here if they had fire in their bellies and knew to keep their mouths shut.

'The people here can't be bothered about politics,' a former camp worker told me. 'They're just glad for the economic reform, and glad America lifted the embargo. It's like China in the early eighties with the opening of the market which led to the openness of Tiananmen Square.'

'Communism has its good points,' one Londoner told me. 'Literacy in Vietnam is higher than in England. And if you talk about political murder and suppression of rights, what western country hasn't done it? Now the developing countries have to go through it too. It's just another form of colonialism for the West to impose its standards of human rights on other cultures.'

'You mean individual life has a different value to the Vietnamese?' I asked.

'Well,' she said, 'why shouldn't it?'

I had noticed pirated reprints of the Penguin edition of Duong Thu Huong's novel, *Paradise of the Blind*, at book-stands around the city. I was surprised, because the book, which paints a bleak portrait of life in the Socialist Republic, had been suppressed after selling forty thousand copies in 1987. Duong herself, a former party cadre, had been jailed without trial in 1991 for exporting 'state secrets'—the manuscript of her anti-war book, *Novel Without a Name*. I was curious to know if my sightings of *Paradise of the Blind* in Hanoi meant that she had been rehabilitated, so I asked the crowd at the Gold Cock what they knew about Duong.

The ex-camp worker claimed that Duong was living in Paris, but she didn't think it was strange that *Paradise of the Blind* was on sale. Duong, this woman said, had been in jail for 'just two months'—in fact, it was seven months—and the book had only turned up recently, which was typical; every day, some previously unavailable item appeared on the market in Hanoi. 'Anyway,' she said, 'They probably don't know what they're selling.'

A man who did some translating for a local publisher said the book wasn't in print in Vietnamese. He also said Duong Thu Huong was still living in Hanoi, and when I said I'd like to meet her, he said, 'Oh, she'll still be under heavy surveillance. It would be very hard to arrange.'

'You'd just bring her trouble,' the woman said.

'Or get in trouble yourself,' the man said.

The expats told me that an American journalist had interviewed Duong for a piece on independently minded Vietnamese writers, but the piece was never published. When the government's spooks caught wind of the project, they turned the journalist out of the country and threatened to jail his Vietnamese fiancée should the article ever appear. The journalist made the sort of decision that would probably be counted as evidence against him if he were ever to wind up as a boat person applying for refugee status: he did not publish the article. And now he was back in Vietnam, married, working, no problems.

'We know we're all being watched,' said a woman who taught English at a local school. 'They have files on all of us. Our students or colleagues will let us know. Nothing official, but you'll be told people are asking about you. Someone'll mention what time you were out till the night before, or how someone left your house at three in the morning. It's nothing political—none of us is so stupid—just drinking, wild behaviour, going out dancing. We'll be reminded to take responsibility for our influence.'

All these things to get used to, I thought as I bicycled home through streets emptied by Hanoi's eleven p.m. curfew—keeping one's mouth shut, being spied on, trusting one's neighbour at one's own peril. And the subtle rhetoric of accommodation: 'nothing official . . . nothing political'.

A police state, it seems, is the closest thing to a perpetual motion machine that the inventive twentieth-century mind has come up with. Once the system is in place, the balance of the terrorizing and terrorized elements creates a perfectly self-oiling mechanism. There is little need for the terrorizer to crack the whip, since the terrorized regards the whip as incessantly cracking and reacts accordingly. Permit the terrorized to imagine that he is getting away with something—earning his living, keeping his belly full, saying good day to foreigners—and he will gratefully assume ever more of the burden of keeping himself in line.

In my own small way, I found myself accommodating the apparatus of the police state. I discovered that it was easy to get rid of chatty strangers: the word 'politics'—or, if that failed, the word 'freedom'—would send them packing. I also stopped carrying a notebook around with me. I wasn't worried about getting in trouble, but I was eager not to put anyone I might have talked to at risk, and when I did write, at the end of each day, I did so in an increasingly cryptic fashion. One evening, I wrote:

> Bananas, strong tea in a tiny pot, a cell with a mosquito
> net, a shaved head, a jail bird, and all day the watchmen
> in the windows. No phone, no mail, whispers, the post
> man comes by bicycle and the robe opens, par avion,
> and do you, ha ha, have a girlfriend?

Even now, I will obscure the details of that meeting with a Buddhist monk who invited me to tea and bananas and told me of the routine by which he prayed and meditated and studied and worked the pagoda gardens each day from three a.m. to ten p.m.. I won't say where we met, only that he approached me as I traipsed around the sanctuary with my guidebook and camera, and he was pleased that I had come alone, by bicycle. I won't say if he was young or old; only that he had recently spent four years in jail. I won't say if one or two or twenty monks lived in his pagoda; only that he named several Buddhist masters who remained in jail. I won't say all he told me, because it would identify him, and I won't even say what language we spoke, but he made a lot of small talk between mentioning that the phone was cut off, that no mail had come for a year or two now and that any of the people passing by the window could be spies. And I can't say why he trusted me, because I have no idea, but at one point he reached into his robe and withdrew an airmail envelope addressed to someone in France and asked me to mail it for him outside the country because this man did good work for human rights and Hanoi was very angry with him. He smiled and laughed and asked if I had a girlfriend and if I would like more tea.

On my last morning in Hanoi, I was strolling along Dien Bien Phu Street, and had just passed the Lenin statue across from the Citadel, when I heard someone hiss. I looked up. A soldier in a guard booth hooked his finger at me. 'Pssst!' He beckoned again, and gave a sharp nod.

I approached, and said 'What?'

He held up an index finger, and snapped: 'One dollar.'

'What for?'

He repeated his demand: 'One dollar!'

I made a face of total incomprehension and walked away slowly.

'Hey!' he said. 'Pssst! One dollar.'

I kept going, and that was that. But I wondered what I'd have done if I were Vietnamese. What if I were a boat person just back from Palawan? If I didn't deliver the dollar on demand, the soldier might ask to see my papers and, even if they were in order, he might say they weren't. To whom would I appeal? He might decide that to put my papers in order I should pay not one dollar but ten—half an average monthly income. And if this were not Hanoi, but a rural village, I might expect to pay quite regularly in order to live in peace. It was nothing official, nothing political; it was just the Vietnamese cost of living. If I were a returnee from the camps, I might, of course, report the extortionist soldier to the UNHCR monitors, if they came around, but then the UNHCR monitors were always accompanied by Vietnamese translators, and who knew their agenda? And anyway, what could I expect from the UNHCR monitors? Imagine if they offered to file a complaint. God forbid.

The French venture capitalist with a few grey hairs pasted across his sweaty forehead was on his third Johnnie Walker

Black at the terrace bar of the Rex Hotel. He waved grandly at the city lights below and narrated the happy movie he imagined himself to be a part of: 'Saigon, my boy, she was always magnificently, magnificently corrupt. These people will make business, they will make money, they will prosper in—yes, even in a vacuum. Such ripeness, good Lord, such ripeness, and now— what am I saying about a vacuum?—now we are back.'

Perhaps it was his fourth whisky or his fifth. He said: 'We are—they are—this is—the real revolution.' And then a slender Vietnamese woman half his age, with her hair piled up high and her lips painted blood red, appeared beside him in a pink silk *ao dai* and said, '*Monsieur, vraiment, venez alors,*' and he stumbled off after her.

No question about it: Vietnam was booming, and Ho Chi Minh City—as only the maps called Saigon—was the blast-off point. There was no curfew, or no enforcement of a curfew, in this city where tens of thousands of children wandered the streets at all hours, a hungry army dispatched here by their families in the

49

provinces to send home a few dollars a week. Foreign joint venturers packed the hotels that were being thrown up in a frenzy. When I checked into a guest-house at nine p.m. and was told to wait just a few minutes while my room was being prepared, I assumed the maid was plumping the pillows; in fact, the proprietor was bolting the fan to a ceiling still wet with paint.

There is a theory that economic freedom and prosperity inevitably lead to political freedom, and such subsidiary benefits as cultural, religious and intellectual freedom. This theory provides the moral-political justification behind, for instance, the United States' decision to step up trade with China following the Tiananmen Square massacre. After all, the thinking goes, why punish the good people because of the bad government?

Vietnam is the worst of both worlds, pure capitalist materialism wedded to pure communist materialism—an utterly cynical state of affairs. This, said the Frenchman at the Rex, was the real revolution. And sadly, he may be right. Life was hard, the Saigonese would tell me, but it was starting to feel like life again.

In the departure lounge at Tan Son Nhut airport, I sat amid a party of Russians returning to Moscow with bundles of cheap rattan furniture, bags of silk shirts and a few cages crowded with restless green parrots. The Russians had political freedom now, but their economy remained a shambles, and they had come to the former client state of the Soviet empire as clients themselves. Vietnam had resisted the political changes of the post-cold-war world, and now that world was coming back to Vietnam with contracts, investments, development projects, tourists; the world even gives Vietnam back its refugees, and the government has the great cunning to accept them—though not quite as quickly as the world would like. As refugees proliferate in the era of the global market-place, they have become a valuable form of international currency in the economy of unsavoury sovereignties. Vietnam controls the repatriation spigot, often exacting a price for their cooperation. Hanoi recently agreed to accept some twenty thousand rejected asylum-seekers from Germany in exchange for an aid package worth about two hundred million dollars. Why, after all, would the Socialist Republic want to be invaded all at once by a refugee army of fifty thousand? Why, especially, when the boat people's unwanted presence in the world obliges the world to oblige Hanoi?

Vietnam was the only country in history to defeat the United States at war. Now, it seemed to be busy winning the peace, and the boat people, condemned to return, were being served up as foot-soldiers in this new phase of the revolution they had fled.

Bataan

Among the street children of Saigon, there used to be a sizeable contingent of Amerasians, the issue of American troops and their Vietnamese paramours. The Amerasians were a pariah caste in post-war Vietnam—fatherless, often the children of prostitutes, reviled in a nationalist society ill-disposed to half-breeds, and doubly reviled as the monster spawn of the imperialist foe. Many had been abandoned by their mothers; they were often barred from schools, or tormented by their fellow students, and they were denied higher education and most employment opportunities. Their families, biological or adoptive, were similarly ostracized, harassed and persecuted as enemy agents. To be an Amerasian, or related to an Amerasian, was often a ticket to time in a New Economic Zone or a jail. The children, whose patrimony was conspicuous—some were black, some decidedly pink, and their hair and noses and lips and jawbones and eyes were usually give-aways as well—became street-vendors and beggars, shoe-shine hustlers and newspaper hawkers. They haunted Saigon, reminders of desertion and defeat. They slept in back alleys or railroad stations.

Eventually, word got back to the States of how badly the children of its expeditionary forces were being treated. In 1987, Congress passed the Amerasian Homecoming Act, granting blanket immigration rights to the Amerasians and their immediate families. Hanoi said good riddance, and the two governments agreed, without reference to the UNHCR or any previous resettlement conventions, that the Amerasians and their families would be speedily processed for departure to their fathers' land.

Those who left Vietnam under the Amerasian programme

51

were not asylum-seekers or refugees but immigrants, invited to come 'home'. There was to be no further screening, only a stop at the refugee transit camp on the Bataan Peninsula in the Philippines for six months of English, civics and job-skills classes in preparation for resettlement. It should have been a story with a happy ending, or at least a smooth transition between the Vietnamese and American chapters, and for the majority of Amerasian visa holders that was how it worked.

But there was a dark side to this story, too. When the word had gone out in Vietnam that an Amerasian was the equivalent of a visa, the war babies suddenly became highly prized. People who had some biological or semi-familial relationship to an Amerasian often agreed, for a price, to take on a few new family members. Others would find an unattached Amerasian and attach themselves and their real or newly assembled 'families' to him as kin. As the Vet at Palawan would have put it: needy men and women acted like needy men and women.

The United States government, however, didn't take such a lenient view of the matter. When I passed through Manila, I heard that a number of Amerasian visa holders, accused of fraud, were living as 'long-stayers' in the Bataan camp. They had been at Bataan for four, five or six years, but in the context of the overall Vietnamese migration, they were regarded as a marginal and insignificant tribe. Everyone I asked about them told me there were 'only four hundred'.

There were, in fact, 433 people in Bataan who had been brought out of Vietnam under the Amerasian Homecoming Act, and on the December morning when I arrived at the camp, most of them had been demonstrating in front of the UNHCR and camp administration offices. They had just learned that the camp was going to be closed by the end of the month, and that they would be transferred to Palawan, lumped in with the screened-out boat people and pressured, perhaps forced, to return to Vietnam. (As it turned out, hundreds of long-stayers resisted the transfer until mid-March, staging daily demonstrations, abdomen slashings and threats of mass suicide.) Wandering among the shabby, wooden huts—permeated by a whiff of latrines—I was besieged by frantic

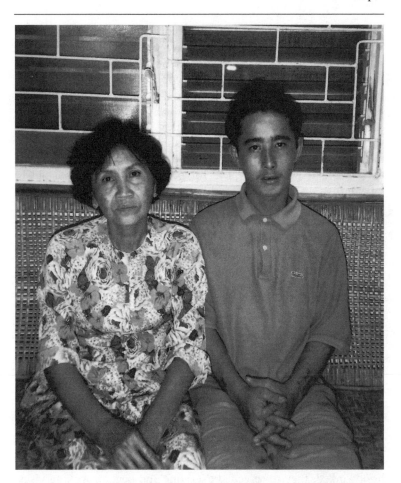

men and women who wanted to know how it was possible that the United States could bring them out of Vietnam only to turn them away.

'So what if we lied and cheated to get out of Vietnam?' one woman asked me. 'Everything in Vietnam is lies and cheating, and we wanted only to survive. America made a promise.'

Above: a Vietnamese mother with her Amerasian son in the refugee camp at Bataan.

The long-stayers' stories were incredibly complex. Living in the shadows of Vietnamese society, few of the Amerasians' families consisted of people with the same surnames. Moreover, within each family any number of people might, in order to elude problems with the authorities, have assumed several aliases. Second and third marriages spawned elaborate networks of step-siblings, and there were many children born out of wedlock. It was typical for two people with the same mother to have grown up in separate households only to be reunited for the sake of emigration. It was also typical for people with no familial ties to have grown up as brothers and sisters.

Under the circumstances, a lot of fudging had been necessary when applying for an Amerasian visa. Frequently the fudging required the un-fudging of fudgings past. How else to include mothers who had called themselves aunts; or step-brothers who lived in remote provinces and whose identities had been borrowed, on occasion, by others? Fudging was the only way.

It had hardly seemed difficult, then, to fudge complete strangers into a family when the Amerasian Homecoming Act presented the opportunity. But inevitably, in the fishbowl of the camp, many of the stories unravelled before the eyes of the erstwhile American saviours. A man would suddenly be carrying on an affair with his so-called sister. Others, having been granted their immigration visas, spoke openly about the dubious arrangements they had made to acquire those visas, naïvely happy to come clean at last. It was also common, when squabbles developed, for people to tell the camp authorities that their enemies had committed fraud.

When the Americans realized that they had been hoodwinked, they re-screened everyone and began revoking visas. The legality of the re-screening process is open to question, but the Amerasian visa holders were an unsophisticated lot without recourse to lawyers. Many claimed that they were not fraud cases; that the re-screening had been a witch-hunt; that they had been railroaded. One man explained to me that he was the step-father of an Amerasian but that the screener at his interview refused to believe that he was married to the Amerasian's mother. 'This man asked whether we slept together on our wedding night. But sleeping together can mean spending the night or having sex.

My wife said no, because that night we slept in separate homes. My parents didn't like me marrying a woman with an Amerasian son, and we could not right away have our own house. I said yes, we slept together, because we did have sex that day. For this saying no and yes, we lost our visas.'

Nobody questioned that the Amerasians themselves were, in fact, Amerasians. As such, they were often encouraged to abandon their rejected families and fly to America alone. But there were Amerasians who refused to be separated from the people with whom they left Vietnam; they had remained with their cohorts in Bataan, out of true family devotion, or out of fear of reprisal, or because these were the only people to whom they had any connection in the world.

When I interviewed the long-stayers, the first question I asked was, 'Why are you still here?'

'Because they say I did fraud,' was a frequent answer, and another was, 'Because I did drink.'

The consumption of alcohol is forbidden in Bataan, but the Filipino guards recognized a market—the same guards who would later put drinkers in the Monkey House, where, both detainees and camp staffers told me, prisoners were routinely beaten and kicked. When they were released, the offenders were referred to camp psychiatrists who diagnosed them as 'Class A'—'antisocial personality disorder and alcohol abuse'—a label which US immigration officials took as grounds for revoking visas.

The long-stayers could not comprehend this policy: drinking, they said, was no big deal in Vietnam, and they were, after all, just kids—in their late teens or early twenties—when the offences occurred. To be sure, several of the Amerasians I met at Bataan were multiple offenders, and one or two were completely loaded when they came to plead their cases before me. But if immigration was a privilege exclusive to teetotallers, America would still be Indian territory. Surely the members of Congress, when they acknowledged national paternity in the Amerasian Homecoming Act, did not imagine that they were inviting a group of socially well-adjusted children to join the family. The spirit of the law was: they're ours, and they need help.

None of the Amerasians I met knew anything about their fathers. Their mothers could rarely say more:

'His name? I called him Fella, and sometimes Darling.'

'He was a very nice black man named Johnson. We were together four months, and then he got transferred.'

'There was a man who was, I think, from Georgia. He's the one my daughter reminds me of.'

Some of these middle-aged, worry-worn women had photographs in which they appeared as lithe young beauties wearing evening gowns and, perhaps, US officers' caps, as they leaned on the arm of one or another tall, grinning American with highball in hand, his eyes narrowed to slits in the gloomy half-light of a PX dance hall. Now, once again, the Americans had beckoned, only to leave them in the lurch.

At the Buddhist pagoda in the Bataan camp, people gathered to prepare crêpe-paper decorations for a temple-closing ceremony. I sat on the porch with Tang, an eighteen-year-old from a large family whose Amerasian had left them for America.

'Buddha says this is not a real world,' Tang told me. 'You look at this table here. It's here now, but tomorrow it is nothing. This is not a real world. This life is not the real life.'

'But you're really suffering,' I said.

'Yes,' Tang said. 'It's a problem, this real suffering in a not-real world.'

New York

A few nights after my return, I was on Park Avenue at a fancy Christmas bash where writers and editors mixed and chattered over the sawing of a string quartet. When people asked what I was working on, I told them, and they said, 'Sounds like a good story.'

Small talk, benign enough, but what on earth is good about this story?

In the pocket of my jacket, I had a holiday greeting card which had come in that day's mail from Nguyen Dang Quang in Palawan, the man who had written that knowing my 'humanity

and kindness by nature' he nearly fainted when he was denied refugee status. Quang had given me a bound folder of his asylum application documents, and after the party I dug it out and read his life story.

Quang had been born in North Vietnam in 1931, the son of a militant anti-Communist, and he had served in the Allied Franco-Vietnamese Army in the early 1950s. He was a Catholic, and in 1954, after the defeat of the French at Dien Ben Phu and the partition of Vietnam, he and his family fled to the south. He served in the South Vietnamese army and worked for nine years as a clerk in the Saigon County Court, officiating at the trials and sentencings of Communists. After the fall of Saigon, Quang was sentenced to two brief stints of re-education; he was unable to find work; his children were expelled or barred from school. In 1980, he joined a secret, Catholic, anti-Communist organization

Above: Nguyen Dang Quang.

and became a courier for its leaders. Two years later, the organization was betrayed. Quang was arrested, interrogated, placed in solitary confinement, beaten, hung upside down from the rafters and threatened with decapitation. His food ration was one glass of water and two handfuls of rice a day. After about a month of this treatment, Quang was sentenced to three years in prison, a light sentence compared to the eighteen years handed down to several of his organization's leaders. Vatican intercession got his sentence reduced to one year, but when he was released, he was on probation, under constant surveillance and required to attend weekly public self-criticism meetings. He was forced from his home; he had to live in a remote hut, and could not work, or receive medical care or food rations. Quang's wife had a breakdown; he did not dare attend church; he could not move from his home without bribing officials. Quang tried to escape Vietnam sixteen times, and he was caught, detained and made to pay bribes for his release on three occasions. He finally succeeded in getting on a boat in May 1989.

Quang's screening interview in the Philippines lasted just forty-five minutes. He had no legal counsel, and he thought that the interpreter did not seem to understand much of what he said. When he was finished, the immigration officer asked him to sign a blank piece of paper. Six months later, Quang received notice that he had been rejected. The decision, which he said had almost caused him to faint, stated:

> His difficulties only started when he was involved in anti-Communist activities. He was closely watched and monitored after that, but this could not be a form of persecution. It's but normal for every state to monitor the activities of violators, in the exercise of police power, to avoid repetition of similar offences.

Quang appealed, but the UNHCR upheld the decision. In the envelope with the card, Quang enclosed a photograph of himself sitting on the concrete frame of his just-destroyed billet in the camp, surrounded by the rubble of his former walls and roof. On the back of the photograph, he had written, 'Lonely at PFAC devastated—Dec. 1, 1994.'

There are many people who have endured greater political violations than Quang claimed, and who do not flee their homelands. And there are many less violated who flee. The compulsion to abandon all that is knowable in one's existence is the quality in the story of an asylum-seeker that is most difficult to weigh. Yet we—the citizens of the end-of-the-road countries to which people flee, but from which refugees do not, right now, originate—ask: Did you really have to leave?

What we are asking, of course, is: Do we really have to take you in?

We speak of refugee protection as a looming global crisis, and we respond by seeking to protect ourselves. The cold war over, the humanitarian impulse has been stripped of its old political trappings, and is widely regarded as the last refuge of the sucker. At first, we at the end of the road found it flattering that so many Vietnamese, about whom we felt so guilty, should want to come and live with us. When the charm wore off, and especially when new Vietnamese markets beckoned, we decided that the boat people had to be protected from the risks of flight; that they were, after all, mostly undeserving of our papers; that they were a threat. So we set up a system to call them liars and put an end to the problem: send them home, close the camps and look: no more boat people.

As I write, I am in Phnom Penh, and this morning I passed a Khmer man in a T-shirt printed with the logo of the UNHCR and the legend: WHAT IF THE WORLD HAD TURNED ITS BACK ON EINSTEIN? It struck me as a rather sinister T-shirt. Einstein? Everyone knows there aren't twenty-three million Einsteins on the world's doorstep. What about the rest of us huddled masses?

THE GRANTA BOOK OF T
FAMIL

A collection of fiction, memoir, biography and reportag
inspired by those relationships thrust upon us by th
accident of birth.

Includes contributions from:

SAUL BELLOW	MIKAL GILMORE	CANDIA McWILLIAM
PETER CAREY	MICHAEL IGNATIEFF	LEONARD MICHAELS
ANGELA CARTER	IAN JACK	SUSAN J. MILLER
RAYMOND CARVER	SOUSA JAMBA	BLAKE MORRISON
HUGH COLLINS	DORIS LESSING	MONA SIMPSON
BRET EASTON ELLIS	BEVERLY LOWRY	WILLIAM WHARTON
LOUISE ERDRICH	CHRISTIAN McEWEN	GEOFFREY WOLFF
	TODD McEWEN	

HARDBACK OUT NOW, PRICED £15.99

GRANTA BOOKS

GRANTA

TRAN VU
THE CORAL REEF

28 May 1979

'So, our last night of socialism,' Dzung said as he squatted down beside me. I pulled two cigarettes out of my pocket and handed one to him, but didn't reply. Instead, I nudged my little brother, Bien, and sent him off to find somewhere to sleep in the house behind us. We had been told to assemble there and wait for the boat, the boat that was going to take us away from Vietnam.

After Bien had left, I spoke. 'When my mother gave the boat-owner her gold, he said there were going to be two hundred of us. A few days ago, there were two hundred and fifty. Now look—there are at least three hundred people on the quay, and the police are sure to try and squeeze more on at the last minute. It's going to be packed.'

Dzung sighed and lit his cigarette.

The voyage from My Tho had been postponed many times, either by the police or by Truong Hong, the boat-owner. Each time, we had returned, miserable, to Saigon. But tonight was different. Tomorrow, the MT603, claimed by Truong Hong to be the safest vessel in the region, was due to sail. No one wanted to miss it.

'Dzung, why are you leaving?' I asked abruptly, flicking my cigarette ash into the gutter.

'Same reason as you,' he said. 'I've got to get out of here, even if I have to crawl on my hands and knees.'

'I know, but *why?*'

'Why?' Dzung seemed surprised. 'That's simple. I can't stand the meetings every night of the week. I don't want to do any more irrigation work. I can't bear to see my friends being sent off to some godforsaken hole in Cambodia to die. I refuse to be condemned to a life of reading Party newspapers.'

The reasons were so obvious that no one bothered to go into them any more. People just left. Dzung and I had been born into Communism. We had had it with Marx, Lenin and the Soviet economy, and with theorizing about why we wanted to leave. We knew only that we had to.

Most of the people waiting for the boat were Chinese, or of

Photo: Michel Setboun (Rex Features)

Chinese origin, like us. Because of the border war with China, the Vietnamese government was only too happy to see us go.

That night, Dzung and I didn't sleep, and neither did anyone else. People sat on little stools, chattering in sing-song Cantonese. They hadn't read *Das Kapital* or the complete works of Lenin, but they knew, from their own wretched lives and the terror of last year's purges, that they too had to go.

29 May

Late in the afternoon, a Peugeot pulled up in front of the house, and a policeman got out. He was wearing gold-rimmed glasses and a Rolex. He had come to talk to Truong Hong.

The atmosphere in the house grew more tense. *Let's go, let's go.* Eventually, Truong Hong divided us into fifteen groups, and we set off towards the quay.

Suddenly, a shout arose from the crowd.

'Look!'

'The boat—it's there!'

Unable to contain ourselves, we broke ranks and ran towards the river. There were three large, wooden boats moored along the quay.

'Which is the MT603?'

'The red one.'

'My God, how are we going to stay afloat in that tiny thing?'

Truong Hong had disappeared. Rumours spread through the crowd: the boat was heading for Australia; it was only going as far as the South Pacific; the BBC was reporting pirate attacks in the Gulf of Siam; the Voice of America was saying Malaysia, Indonesia and Singapore were refusing to accept refugees and were towing their boats back into open sea. I didn't understand. How could our Asian neighbours send us back to our deaths?

About an hour later, Truong Hong reappeared with the policeman, who was carrying a megaphone.

'Attention! Attention! On behalf of the Party Secretary, on behalf of the police, I would like to say a few words before you leave.' He made a speech, full of exhortations to work hard in foreign lands and guard our ancient heroic tradition. Then, finally:

'These are the individuals authorized to board the MT603. Group One: leader, Mr Lam Hue; members, Truong Sieu, Dang Cam, Phung Tao—'

'That's you! Go!' Dzung elbowed me. 'Phung Tao—that's the name on your birth certificate.'

'Here!' I yelled, jumping to my feet.

One by one, we boarded the boat, sailors herding us down ramps into the hold, which was airless and gloomy, lit only by a single storm-lantern.

'Move along, ten to a bench!' the sailors yelled.

'They're packing us in like sardines,' said Dzung. 'I just heard someone say that the police have sent another hundred people.'

Bien and I, both under eighteen, were assigned places on the middle deck, with the women. At least there were portholes here, I thought: an escape route if the boat began to sink. I slipped my hand through the nearest one, then snatched it back in shock: the water was only twenty centimetres below.

It was almost midnight, and the boat was still moored by the quay. No one knew what was happening. Truong Hong and the skipper had gone back into town, presumably to split their gold with the police. I slept fitfully. Whenever I woke, I peered out of the porthole. The boat hadn't moved.

30 May

I was asleep when we set sail. Two police patrol boats escorted the MT603 out to sea, and I was woken by the police shouting through a megaphone, wishing us *bon voyage* before circling back to the harbour.

As dawn broke, I watched the muddy, red water race past on the other side of the porthole. Here, where the river met the sea, conflicting currents joined, making powerful waves that slapped against the hull, sending the boat into a drunken reel. We ploughed east, heading for the Philippines, for Australia.

After a few hours, people began to be seasick. The woman next to me was soon slimy with vomit. Old women squatted on the floor to urinate. The stench was suffocating, but the high, crashing waves made opening the portholes impossible.

I went down to the lower deck, where the situation was even worse. Stuck inside the prow, it was as though the waves were pounding at my chest, pummelling me. The hold bore the brunt of the turbulence. The storm-lantern had gone out, leaving the people there in darkness, awash in stomach-turning smells.

2 June

By the fourth day, people were beginning to feel better, though the sea was no calmer. They got out bags of rich food and ate noisily. They vomited, they ate, they pissed, they shat. The stench was so bad that I decided to try and go out on deck. I had to step over people to reach the door, accidentally kicking an old woman in the head as I went.

'Get down!' yelled a sailor on the ramp, forcing me back below.

'Just let me go and piss,' I begged, struggling to get free.

'Piss down there, like everyone else!' shouted the sailor.

'It's OK. Let him through.' Truong Doc, the boat-owner's son, was pulling me up. 'Go on, but come straight back. Understand?'

I said nothing and climbed up to the main deck. The toilets were at the back of the boat. There was no one there. My bladder was bursting. There was a hole in the floor, through which I could see the churning water below. What if a huge wave knocked me into it? The fear paralysed me. I couldn't piss. I went back outside. The wind howled around me.

'Get back here!' the sailor shouted. He tried to kick me; I seized his foot, and he went sprawling on the deck. I ran off, back towards the lavatories, the sailor lumbering after me. Suddenly, the boat keeled sharply to one side, throwing both of us off balance. There was a sound of cracking, splintering wood, and screams of terror rose from below. The sailor and I forgot our struggle; we were hypnotized by the pitching of the vessel. I could see the skipper fighting to regain control of the boat as it rolled and shuddered. Over the crashing of the waves and the roar of the engines rose the prayers of four hundred people.

'The propeller is caught in a net!' someone cried.

The skipper tried to accelerate, but the boat reeled again, tipping violently to one side, as though it was about to capsize. People began shouting.

'Rocks!'

'Reverse, reverse!'

'Turn on the back-up engines. Accelerate!'

'Throw the baggage overboard! We're overloaded!'

The boat wouldn't move forward, even with the engines at full throttle, their noise almost drowned out by the shrieking and wailing of the passengers. The sailors began to throw bags into the seething ocean.

In the cabin, the skipper and Truong Hong were arguing furiously, one convinced that the boat had run aground, the other adamant that it was snared in nets. It seemed incredible that there could be rocks here, in the middle of the sea, but clearly we had run up against something. The engines howled. The deck bucked again and again, until it seemed the boat might split in two.

The MT603 had now tipped completely to one side, its edge submerged in water. Everyone was ordered to stand to the right to restore the balance. Panic-stricken, the sailors were dumping things overboard indiscriminately: sacks of provisions, jerrycans of drinking water.

The skipper and the chief engineer tried again, hoping that now the load was lighter, we would float, but the engine had barely whined before the prow reared up and fell back on to rocks with a terrible crunch. We listened, petrified by the cracking of the beams supporting the deck as, one by one, they gave way, crushing the cabins crammed full of people below.

Arms flailed like tentacles through the portholes, trying to get a grip on the hull. People were jumping overboard. Some were struggling through the wreckage to get to the sealed cabins, where we could hear the screams of the trapped women and children. Driven by some instinct, I jumped into the sea. Before I left home, my mother had given me a US army-surplus life-jacket and made me promise to wear it throughout the voyage; I was glad now that I had kept my word. I felt the soles of my feet being shredded as I hit coral.

The sun rose, dazzling, magnificent, in the Pacific sky.

3 June

The MT603 had run aground on a coral reef. The desolate wreck lay surrounded by the glistening ocean, in limbo between sky and earth. I swam around the boat and eventually found Dzung and Bien, who had managed to smash their way out of the hold.

Under the burning sun, the sea took on different colours. At the back of the boat, the water was a deep emerald, but towards the prow it turned pale. The coral reef seemed immense, and, judging from the shade of the water, the boat had run aground about twenty metres inside it.

'We've had it,' Dzung said, paddling about. 'The boat's stuck. What can we do?'

There were about four hundred people in the water, each proposing a different solution for saving the boat. Miraculously, no one had been killed, and only nine had been injured.

The water was bracing, invigorating after days of sweat and filth. Although it was shallow, the sea was rough, and waves kept knocking us over. Razor-sharp coral clawed at our legs.

Truong Hong, brandishing a megaphone he had somehow salvaged, took charge. He ordered everyone into the fifteen groups we had been assigned to when we first boarded the boat. We were going to attempt to manoeuvre it back into the sea. The strongest men were to push the prow, while the rest of us took the sides. Women and children were told to keep out of the way, while the injured, the skipper and the engineer stayed on board.

'At the count of three, push hard. One, two, three, push!'

'Again—push!'

'One, two, three, push! Push!'

'Why aren't those bastards back there pushing?'

The men and boys braced themselves, muscles flexed, feet firmly planted on the jagged coral, pushing with all their might. But we had no lever, no fulcrum, no means of getting a purchase.

We were exhausting ourselves for nothing. The MT603 stayed put, wedged at a sixty-degree angle, waves smacking against it.

As the sun set, the tide went out, revealing an island of coral as far as the eye could see. The water receded quickly; soon it was only ankle deep. Only then did I realize the terrible truth: even when the tide was in, the water would be too shallow for the boat to float. The wreck of the MT603 would never get off the reef.

Night fell. We were cold and exhausted. Everyone's skin, pickled in salt water, was shrivelled. We clambered back on to the boat, where I collapsed, shivering.

We huddled together for warmth. I rolled up my trousers, exposing my torn legs and feet to the air; they had stopped bleeding, but the flesh was swollen and bruised violet. I no longer felt any pain, only an insistent, biting prickle.

'Bastards! They've taken all the food,' said Bien, emerging from the hold, his thin body silhouetted against the crimson sky. 'Truong Hong and the rest of them have got all the provisions. This is all I could find.'

My brother's voice was weary, bitter. He threw down two packets of rice, a pack of dried bananas and a sachet of tea. It seemed to me that his face, with its blackened skin, had aged since yesterday; he was almost unrecognizable.

'Oh, who cares,' said Dzung. 'In two weeks, we'll all be dead anyway.'

We sat cross-legged in a circle to share our meagre meal, chewing each mouthful slowly, painfully. Already, less than twenty-four hours after the shipwreck, we were utterly changed.

Emergency flares flickered in the dark, spreading an eerie light over the wreckage. By the time the moon cast its cold glow across the ocean, most of us were asleep. The wind blew all night, drowning out the sobs and moans of the children, soothing the pain of our lacerated flesh.

The next day, the fifteen groups disbanded. We Vietnamese-Chinese elected a man named Ly, a former lieutenant captain in the army, to be our leader. Most of the others remained faithful to Truong Hong; those who did not kept to themselves, refusing to help in our efforts to shift the boat. They spent their time searching the coral for the food that had been thrown overboard, and took turns guarding the bags they had managed to rescue.

Two teams of volunteers, armed with hammers, attempted to free the propellers by diving down and smashing the coral that trapped them. Ly had suggested cutting down one of the masts to use as a lever, which we propped under the boat.

'One, two, three, push!'

The wreck rose slowly, as if it were finding its balance.

'It's coming up, it's coming up—'

But suddenly the MT603 keeled back on its side, sending the men holding the lever flying on to the coral. The boat came to rest in its old position. We were up to our necks in water, and the coral had reopened the cuts on our feet.

For a moment, it seemed the boat had shifted a little, half a metre, perhaps even a whole one, but that night, as the tide receded, making the reef appear to rise like a sea monster from the waves, we realized that it was the water level that had moved, not the boat. The MT603 hadn't budged an inch.

'There'll be a big tide in a few days,' said Ly. 'Let's wait.'

He believed the reef to be one of the notorious Paracel Islands, which stretch for several hundred miles. No boat dares venture near them. He calculated that we were four or five days away from the Philippines.

When we clambered on to the boat that night, the clouds seemed darker, more threatening. Fear tightened around us like a noose.

7 June

Two days later, we found a corpse. It was a woman whose back had been broken when the main deck collapsed. I watched as some men bound the body to a piece of wood which they pushed out to sea.

In the days that followed, there were more deaths—from exhaustion, from despair. Two corpses in particular haunted me: one of an old man, whose stomach had swollen grotesquely, and one of a strangely wizened child, who had died during a seizure.

The boat-owner and his family lit incense and prayed over them, the scent from the joss-sticks wafting across the deck.

We marked the number of people left on the reef with SOS buoys which we threw into the sea each time someone died: 394, 391, 388 . . . Each day, fewer and fewer men had the strength to push the boat. Today, nine days after we had set sail, our seventh day on the reef, no one came at all.

The food and water had more or less run out. A couple of us tried to boil sea water and distil the vapour. We spent three hours hunched over a litre of oily, salty fluid, confident of our school science, but it was useless; we produced only a few drops of water we could drink. We stared into the clouds, desperate for rain. Occasionally, there were unexpected storms that blew up in minutes. We scavenged for rice in the wreck. We had to survive, so we survived.

8 June

Five of us—Dzung, Bien, the boat-owner's two sons and I—decided that we had to take our chances and get off the reef. We built two makeshift rafts—just planks bound together with rope, perched on empty water containers and kept afloat by buoys. When we sat on them, the water came up to waist level.

We tried to paddle at first, but after a while we tied our tiny rafts loosely together and let them drift, following the currents, tossing with the waves which were about to tip us into the water at any moment. We hadn't really considered the insanity of setting off on a few pieces of wood lashed together. Our only aim had been to escape the slow death that awaited us on the reef.

When it began to get dark, we grew frightened. It was very cold. Blanketed in fog, we listened to the rhythms of the current as it sucked us further into the night. The wind howled. But we were off the reef—earlier in the day, when the sun still warmed the sea, I had dived down and had seen no coral.

The sea was now calm. From time to time, we checked the knots on the ropes binding the rafts together, but otherwise we just drifted. I glanced at the Truong brothers; they were wide-eyed, pale and vacant. They evidently regretted having come with us.

I was transfixed by the immensity of the sky and the sea, unaware of anything else, when suddenly I felt an invisible force tugging at the rafts and saw a black shape sliding underneath them. At first, I thought we were running on to rocks and cried out to warn the others. But then we realized that the black shape was moving at the same speed as us.

'What is it?' whispered Dzung.

Mesmerized, we all stared, unable to take our eyes off it.

'Probably just rocks. It's nothing. Let's get out of here,' mumbled Truong Doc, clinging to the buoys, drawing his knees up to his neck.

'The sea is really deep here; it can't be a rock,' I said.

The black shape continued to slide alongside and underneath us, the white foam swirling in its wake. Then, through the fog, a triangle appeared—a huge, pointed fin, gliding towards us.

'My God, Bien, it's a shark!' I cried as the fin whipped the water less than three metres away. The waves it raised sent the rafts spinning. Panicked, I seized a paddle to defend myself. Dzung, Bien and the Truong brothers trembled convulsively, their prayers choking in their throats.

'Don't touch it!' I screamed, trying to get a grip on myself. My brother shrieked. The fin turned, moved closer, circling the rafts. It was no longer alone; there were five or six others. They plunged and resurfaced, slicing the sea and the night, scattering thousands of tiny, sparkling waves in their wake. They played at this for half an hour or so and then disappeared. It took us a long time to regain our calm.

'Probably whales,' Dzung panted.

As the danger receded, we stared ahead into the darkness, imagining fins lying in wait behind every wave. We drifted on and on, losing all sense of time. Our minds were entirely taken up by our contest with the sea. Suddenly, out of nowhere, an enormous wave raised us to its crest and hurled us back down.

'We're sinking!'

Our cries floated over the deserted sea. No echoes. Only the waves thundered in response; they seemed even more threatening in the dark.

'The waves!' Dzung shouted. 'I can hear the waves hitting the shore.'

'We must be near the coast,' I said, stunned.

'Impossible,' Bien said. 'We haven't been gone a day.'

'Maybe it's a desert island,' I said.

We watched as the silvery foam rose and fell. We were being dragged into a current. Rocks rose out of nowhere, and a strong swell threw the raft against them, almost crushing the Truong brothers.

'Push!'

'Watch out, there are more rocks on the left!'

A massive wave reared up in front of us, curling slowly inwards before crashing down on the rafts. Sucked up out of the water, we were flung backwards, clinging to the fraying rope that bound our rafts together. Then I felt my feet touch coral: we were back where we had started, run aground on the reef.

We paddled furiously, clinging to what was left of the rafts, dodging outcrops of coral, straining to gulp in air between avalanches of water. I remembered what Ly had said about the coral archipelago extending for hundreds of miles.

We fought the waves and rocks for what seemed like hours, but as the dawn came, a current swept us off the reef, and we were once again carried towards deep water. Finally, we slept, lulled by the rhythm of the waves, drifting, unconscious, kept afloat by our life-jackets and the buoys we'd tied to ourselves.

I awoke to feel my face swollen by sunburn. The sun, enormous, incandescent, scorched our skin. I roused the others, and we searched for the ten-litre water can that Truong Hong had kept hidden in the hold and then given to his sons, but it had been carried off by the waves. No more water meant certain death. Unable to bear the heat, we plunged into the sea. Bien's lips were bloated and blistered, the skin peeling off them. I began to feel weak, delirious even, as I imagined myself on dry land by a water pump. The sun pounded down. More coral, more waves, nothing but these rafts and our wrinkled bodies drifting east.

Later that day, a storm broke. In a few seconds, black clouds covered the sky. The wind howled over our heads, and rain fell, stinging our faces and whipping at the surging sea.

Clinging to the buoys, we were plunged into what seemed like a huge whirlpool. I have no idea how long the tempest lasted, but as the sea eventually grew calmer we could dimly make out, through the dense curtain of rain, the silhouette of a boat. The storm had carried us back to the shipwreck.

10 June

The MT603 was in an even worse state than it had been when we left. The main deck had collapsed further, and five people had been killed. All that remained of the safest boat in the region was the skipper's cabin, the prow and the stern.

Ly wanted to know exactly what had happened to us. Everyone else was angry and just asked about the disappearance of the ten-litre water can.

'You invented that trip just to get the water! You didn't even try to get help!'

The next morning, we tried once more to push the wreckage, without success. We threw the last emergency buoy overboard inscribed with the number of survivors: 382. Everyone watched it until it disappeared. I had lost all hope: the buoys were probably stuck somewhere in the middle of the immense coral archipelago.

Since the shipwreck, we hadn't seen a single airplane or ship. Without the Pacific rains, we would never have survived. Every day, as the tide went out, I joined the scrawny phantoms who scoured the reef in search of food, but the coral sea was a dead sea: no shrimps, no shellfish, nothing. Once, we found a starfish and a few strands of seaweed, which we boiled up with a bit of rainwater, but the seaweed was gluey and disgusting, the starfish rigid, impossible to eat.

12 June

Ly had decided to try his luck on a raft. He bound four planks together, attached them to empty barrels and covered them with a tarpaulin on which he had painted the letters SOS. He set off at noon with his wife and two young children, heading for Hong Kong.

That night, a further eighteen people, mostly sailors, left in two groups on similar rafts, taking the last of the buoys.

14 June

The big tide that Ly had predicted on the first day finally arrived. It was night, and the moon was full. Since sundown, we had been standing in the icy water, watching the horizon, waiting for a miracle. In the chill moonlight, I could no longer distinguish women from men, or adults from children: everyone looked old, shrivelled, covered from head to toe in blisters and sores. I remembered how I had promised my mother to take care of my brother, to make a man out of him. I felt plagued with guilt and regret when I thought of the gold she had handed over to buy us places on the boat.

Suddenly, a huge wave slapped me against the coral. It was the tide, the big tide.

'Push! Push!'

The sea reared up, the water rising from our waists to our chests. Seven men pushed with all their strength. The water rose to our chins. Almost totally submerged, we fought to free the boat. People with children clambered, terrified, on to what remained of the main deck. Dzung and I hung on to the sides. As the water came over our heads, I pulled myself up, landing in a heap on the deck, which was slick with oil. The boat hadn't moved.

Suddenly, we were flung to the right. I felt the boat rear and then pitch wildly to the left and back again. Then it seemed to regain its equilibrium, achieving a position we had no longer believed possible, floating in deep water.

'Skipper, turn on the engines!'

'Reverse, reverse, quickly!'

The engines sputtered, the men yelled, the women prayed, but the boat didn't move. The coral reef was no longer visible, swallowed under the black depths of the water, but still it held the boat in its grasp.

'You young people will have to get off,' the skipper ordered. 'We've got to lighten the load.'

Women took up the cry. I felt myself lifted into the air and passed from hand to hand to the edge of the boat. I struggled, resisted, but they pushed me overboard.

'We'll come back and get you when the boat is free!' the skipper shouted.

I had barely caught my breath when I felt a violent current dragging me around the wreck. The surface of the water was bleached with foam: we were being sucked towards the spinning propellers. I flailed, trying to cling to the slippery hull. I grabbed hold of someone's foot, and then a rope that hung down from the skipper's cabin. Eventually, we were pulled back on board.

I collapsed on deck, vomiting sea water. When I opened my eyes, the sky had cleared: the clouds seemed brighter, the wind more gentle. Twenty of us had been thrown into the sea; four had disappeared; one had drowned. The coral archipelago had disappeared back into the ocean. A woman began to sob.

The MT603 moved towards the rising sun.

Translated from the Vietnamese by Phan Huy Duong
and Nina McPherson

PAUL EGGERS
SAVIOURS

Mr Thanh, originally of Saigon, conducted his camp-wide rat pogrom so thoroughly that the kids were reduced to throwing rocks at each other. Some boys got beaned, and Mr Thanh, the most responsible Viet I knew in the Bidong Island refugee camp, blamed himself and went around shelter to shelter, apologizing to all their parents, more than twenty families. This was Mr Thanh's way. Before getting on a boat out of Vietnam, he had been a colonel with the South Vietnamese army. But even now, stateless and dependent, another Viet biding his time on Malaysian soil, he wore a dashing yellow scarf imprinted with the name of his old regiment.

I was the UN education adviser, the camp's English teacher. Mr Thanh was my refugee assistant. I had picked him out myself, struck by his earnestness, and would give him occasional gifts, whatever I could scrounge. Mr Thanh and I were two of a kind. I understood his need to be forgiven—he had let the camp down, he said—and I think I even understood the state of mind that made him, after a day of brush-offs from the boys' parents, walk into the island's Zone C school the next morning and root around the UN educational-supplies closet and, without asking permission, drag a filthy visual aid, a mannequin, down to the beach to wash clean. What I could not do that morning was clear his supply-closet foray with the camp's Malaysian security fucks. Mr Thanh had acted on his own. If only I had known that he was going to take the mannequin, I could have stopped refugee-camp logic from taking over.

I felt so guilty that I went to Mr Thanh that night to apologize. He told me the mannequin had been dirty. Rats had gnawed through its feet, and my predecessor, Barbara somebody, had smeared THIS IS AN ARM, LESSON 21 on one shoulder in Magic Marker. It had needed cleansing, he said—'Unclean, yeah? I can say unclean?' This was how we spoke: a kind of code, like lovers have. In the classroom, he tried hard to make me look good. He was aware of the roles we had been assigned. His was to appease, to act as factotum to the powerful forces that determined his fate. So he asked me language questions, softballs a child could hit: me,

Opposite: Vietnamese refugees at Trengganu Beach, Malaysia

the adviser, the American, the giant.

It was November 1980, and the beast was about to rise from the ocean. What was my guilt compared to that? The Malaysians were threatening to close the Bidong Island camp before the end of the year. They said the boat people weren't their responsibility alone. They said somebody, somewhere, better open their doors, or else. Since October, a battalion of Malaysian Rangers had been bivouacked on the mainland, an hour away. If they came, they would come hard and fast, with weapons. The boat people, all twenty thousand of them, would be towed back out in their leaky wrecks into the roaring water and cut adrift. Helicopters would come for us UN workers, and we would soar over the tiny island, strapped in tight, too ashamed to speak.

And still, Mr Thanh let me sit on his cardboard and scrape the mud from my sandals and correct his English. I loved him so much for it that I couldn't look him in the face.

He told me what had happened. The head fuck, Captain Rahim, had thought the mannequin a real person at first. Specifically, me. There were about eighty fucks in the camp, a hodge-podge of local militia and police, and Rahim was the nastiest: a rat-faced village boy who thought all the Viets were communist agents. That morning, he had been patrolling the Zone C beach when he saw Mr Thanh kneeling in the water, caressing what appeared to be a naked white man. Rahim didn't know squat about what we kept in the supply closet. After he rescued the mannequin, a bunch of Viets laughed at him. Rahim made a run at them, but they just disappeared and hooted from behind trees. And then he walked back and rough-talked Mr Thanh. Rahim can't have known for sure that the mannequin was a supply item—the thing could have just washed up on the beach—but he was so mad that it didn't make a difference. It was white-bastard coloured, so it must belong to Mr Thanh's white-bastard adviser.

That afternoon, Rahim fidgeted outside the wire fence of the UN compound for a while, then opened the gate and confronted me. 'No, *sir*,' I said in my best military-sarcastic voice. 'Don't know anything. I just teach English.' I was only half-lying: I hadn't seen Mr Thanh all day. I was sick and had been sleeping in my bungalow, slick with sweat. Still, I had a clear picture of the item: the stovepipe legs, the phony moustache and nose, the spooky, blank eyes. I had never touched the thing. It gave me the creeps. How, I wondered, would one teach with it?

Rahim just stood there, screwing up his little rat face, and I folded my arms. I figured that if the head fuck cared so much, I had an obligation to mess with him. The Malaysians owned the soil, but the UN paid the bills. I was jacked. I could feel my hair stand on end. I was staring Rahim down, watching his nasty little face getting rattier and rattier, while behind him, a crowd of Viets was gathering by the fence. Any time we stirred in the compound, they leaned against the wire and stared, as though they were watching a play. I saw them whispering to each other. I imagined them applauding my stand: *That Mr Joe, he's some guy.*

'Mannequin?' I said, loudly. 'What mannequin? I don't know about any mannequin.'

'How you cannot know who this is?' he said. He was holding one of its plastic fingers and waved it at me.

Who this is. I smelt victory.

'You mean, "Whose this is" or "Whom this belongs to",' I said. I towered over him. I could see the curry stains on his little bus-driver hat.

His face quivered a second, and then I sensed him withdraw. Somewhere under the hat, a decision was being made. He turned and waved for his Viet assistant, who suddenly appeared from behind the crowd, opened the gate and entered forbidden ground, dragging the rest of the mannequin behind him.

Rahim trotted back and huddled with the man. Viets were now two deep outside the wire. The assistant looked worried. But Rahim said, 'OK, OK,' and clapped him hard on the back. They set to work. They yanked off the head. They popped off the legs— Rahim holding the torso, his assistant tugging—and they bent back the hands. The crowd was laughing and pointing. Rahim couldn't get one of the arms off, so he had his assistant wiggle it back and forth until it stuck straight up.

When they were done, they just left the parts in the sand. They stood there a moment, hands on their hips, as though they were viewing something monstrous. I could see the hollow cavity where the head should have been.

The way the Viets parted for Rahim at the gate and all the way down the beach into Zone C, you could tell he was still pissed. A few hours later, Rahim accused Mr Thanh of trying to steal the mannequin. Around dinner, just as the sky was exploding with colour, the fucks rousted him from his lean-to and shaved his head and whacked him with a rattan.

Roland was the only one who accused me but, coming from him, it meant something. I admired him. He was a fat tub, a Canadian, but he kept a cool head. He was a straight arrow. On the bungalow porch, he sidled up and said, 'You're not simply you here, Joe. You're a *symbol*. You got to show some sense.'

I didn't argue.

'You piss off Rahim,' he said, 'and the fucks get on the shortwave to the mainland. The Rangers are licking their chops, just waiting for a reason to come.'

'Tell me something I don't know,' I said.

'OK, hero. Maybe we ought to have Rahim give *you* a haircut and massage.'

'Hey, look,' I said.

'This isn't your first screw-up.'

We were both quiet for a while, and he started scratching his arm, waiting for me to speak. I wouldn't. Then he gave me an example—an *example*, he said, though we both knew he was just trying to be classy. He said it was like this, it was like if someone, you know, *someone*, gave a shot of Johnnie Walker to a Viet; it wasn't just that person breaking a fuck rule, it was Uncle Sam and Aunt Geneva and Queen Victoria, the money and the arrogance of the white-bastard world. The Malaysians, he said, didn't like that.

He said it as though he was teaching me a big lesson.

'Hey,' I said. 'You got something to say to me, say it. I make mistakes, all right? I've been sick.'

'That's no excuse,' he said. 'What you feel doesn't matter.'

'I've been sick. I'm not making excuses. I'm just saying I'm flesh and blood. Now give it a rest.'

He wouldn't. 'You got to play the game right,' he said.

I looked out at the ocean. 'You see that?' I said, pointing.

'Way over there?'

He shaded his eyes and looked. Then he started shaking his head. 'I'm here to tell you, man, the Viets don't want *you*.' He pointed at me. 'Think about it. They want what you *represent*. Somebody important sent you, didn't they? That's what they want.'

'I do my job. I'm not dead weight.'

'The Viets don't love you, white boy,' he said. He held up his hand. 'You're nothing. *Nada*, yes? Zero. But what you mean to the Viets is, Hey, someone real out there gives a shit.'

'I do my job good,' I said.

'Someone real,' he said. 'Uncle Sam. God. Some cousin in California. Not you. Someone who can get them out of here. So start teaching English.'

I walked away.

He called after me. 'The Rangers come,' he said, 'then what good are we? Huh?'

I had classes to teach, and on the way I stopped in to see Mr Thanh and give him some baby milk I had taken from a shipment at the depot. He was grateful. He gave me cardboard to sit on and put a pot of brown water on the fire pit to boil. We didn't say much. He had a welt on his back, so I gave him my tube of antiseptic cream. I had some blue paper left over from a lesson, so I gave that to him too, and a pen and a Malaysian coin and a stick of gum and a paper-clip. I emptied my pockets for him. I would have given him a thousand bucks if I'd had it, and a plane ticket straight to LA. I would have shielded him with my body and taken him to the dock and hitched a ride on the supply boat all the way to the mainland. I would have jawed with the fucks and waved my passport around and screamed in their faces with a bullhorn. I would have put Mr Thanh on a bus to Kuala Lumpur and wiped his ass and cut up his meat and carried him on to the plane and flown him myself all the way across the Pacific.

Mr Thanh and I drank weak tea out of severed 7-Up cans. When you rolled up the flour-sack wall of his lean-to, all you saw was ocean. When the Rangers came, they would first appear out there, in bristling water, in a bee-swarm of engines. The whole island would stand there and stare, whispering that the beast had come. For a week now, kids had been lining the outcrop, watching the ocean, pointing. They held tightly wound palm fronds to blow like trumpets.

No one knew if the Rangers would actually come. We listened to our guts. We let the rumours hang in the air. We'd sit on someone's bunk and drink Johnnie Walker. We'd get sloppy drunk. A Viet would always be rattling something off through the camp speakers, so we'd start to talk real loud, non-stop.

This much was true: Ranger fucks had been speedboating out once a week, just walking around, scoping things. I made sure I got noticed. I wore my powder-blue T-shirt. When the Rangers saw me, my sandy hair and sunburnt neck, they saw white-bastard UNHCR. They'd nod and grin like village boys, and then they'd push through the Viets to shake my hand and show off their Form 5 English. And when they touched me, when their eyes roamed over my white skin, when they smelt my diet of meat, what was shining in their eyes was Neil Armstrong on the moon, and John Wayne, and redheads without bras, and so much money you could take an airplane ride once a week. I *was* the white-bastard world. No me, no symbol. I had power. I made the Rangers think twice. I'd say, 'It's under control here, yeah? It is *under control*,' and they'd smile like schoolgirls. 'No problem,' they'd say, and I'd grab the nearest Viet and put my arms around him. *Bye-bye*, we'd say. *Bye-bye, bye-bye.*

Roland was just the radiologist in the camp hospital, but since the doctors were always short-handed, he was allowed to join in the glory work and came to lunch with blood on his shirt. He loved to talk about how many ccs of this or that he was shooting into people's veins. Every surface in his room was covered with folders of X-rays and mysterious, smelly specimens in capped plastic cups.

But now I realized: he thought if you didn't have blood on your shirt, you weren't really there.

I said, 'That's some superior stink coming from you.'

'Burn victim,' he said. He was carrying a box of tubes and shook them at me like noodles. 'Some kid fell down a well, only it was dry, and they were using it as a fire pit. The smell gets on you.'

'*Superior* stink.'

'Mr Joe,' he said. 'Can you spell "superior"?'

'You want it?' I said. 'Come *on.*'

But he wasn't listening. A cherry was coming in on the morning supply-boat run, and he had heard it was a nurse's aide from New Zealand. He wanted the office to look sharp.

Cherries: we talked as though we were out on jungle patrol. I fantasized about it some nights, walking down the Zone C footpath, past the tarp-and-sapling shanties where the Viets slept in hammocks or on cardboard. How much would a rucksack weigh me down? How would a flak jacket feel against my stomach? I secured the perimeter, I patrolled the ville. The air smelt like mud, even when the stars were out and a nice breeze was coming in, and then I'd look up and see Viets in running shorts hustling someone, and I knew they were going to cut him for something he had done on the boat trip over.

You couldn't blame them. In the South China Sea, they could float for months. Sometimes, when the Thais pulled alongside, the women jumped in the water to drown. The sun and ocean bleached the refugees like rags. They fought over water jugs. When the boats came in, you could smell what had happened.

Those trips, they were savage. What happened on some of the boats made me so angry that I never stopped a cut-party. If I'd wanted to, I could have ploughed through the Viets and pulled the victim safe against me. Malay and white, we could do that. I could have put my arm around the man's waist, and he would have been safe as the Pope buckled up in his Popemobile. But I wouldn't. I was so angry just thinking about what he must have done, I'd say, 'You hustle his ass. You take him out and you make him *pay.*'

After lunch, a few of us waited for the cherry on the dock and said funny things to the Viet kids playing on the engine blocks sticking out of the shallow water. The monsoons had started early. On some nights, the rain was so heavy it was like rocks falling from the sky, and later we would hear the Viets in their lean-tos swearing and scooping out the mud in plastic buckets and throwing it on to the footpaths. When it wasn't raining, the sun came out and stayed there, right in your face, and after a while the Viet kids looked like they had cracks all over their bodies from where the mud had dried, so they waded out among the debris and bluegills to wet themselves up.

The cherry was Sally Hindermann. The first thing she did was point at the muddy beach and say, 'Jesus, it looks like Play-Doh.' I ignored her comment. She was tired, and by the look on her face a little scared. She had gotten seasick on the way over, she said, but had thought to bring plastic baggies and just zipped the mess up and threw it overboard.

'Good thinking,' said Roland.

I was searching for a kind response, an act of graciousness. 'Hey,' I said. 'OK. How about that.'

It turned out Roland had got it wrong: Sally was an English teacher, not a nurse's aide. She had a Masters in Teaching English as a Second Language from some college in Vermont, and from the moment the pillhouse fuck at the end of the dock waved us through and down the steps on to the beach, I could feel her watching my every move. That afternoon, I took her for an English-teaching tour in my Zone F intermediate class. I carried around an oversized lesson planner and attendance book and stood ramrod straight on the podium the Viets had built for me. I did what I knew. I had a sponge for an eraser, and I shouted over the loudspeakers, which were going most of the time. I took off my watch and one of my shoes and said, 'What's this?' and the Viets shouted their answers back at me. Then I pointed: shirt, ground, girl, boy, podium. 'What's this?' I said. 'What's this?' The class shouted back. The whole hour, Sally squatted in back, scraping mud off her ankles with a notepad and playing with her hair.

'What's your background?' she said during break.

'Peace Corps,' I said. 'Some outside teaching here and there. Hey, you're the expert. No contest.'

I thought I sounded pretty magnanimous: the *real* expert, the guy who knew the ropes, making the newcomer feel at ease. But from the way she was looking at me, I could tell the computer in her head was going full tilt.

She had a little smile that kept quivering at the ends. I knew she had another face she wasn't sure she could let out yet. That other face would accuse me soon. It would ferret out facts.

The facts: summers fishing in Alaska; two years of community college in Wassau; my friend Bud, in Records and Admissions, he of the electric eraser and drugged-out, anything-for-you access to files. I had been in Peace Corps Malaysia all right, but I had quit during training and gone north, doping around Bangkok for a couple of years, teaching coconut-head English to tour guides. I figured if I could speak it, I could teach it. I was drunk with the ease of it. The tour guides couldn't read white people. I'd laugh at nothing—T-shirts, dogs, restaurant names—and tell them it was American humour. They told me I looked like Vic Morrow on *Combat!*, and I told them I knew him. I had them read the *Bangkok Post* to me, and then I jumped all over their pronunciation. Sometimes, if they were doing too well, I'd make it up. '*Goov*-ernment,' I'd say. 'Try it again. "The American *goov*ernment".' I printed up certificates. A guy in Changmai had official seals. I made enough money; I drank ice coffee in restaurants all day and hung around the basement bar at the Opera Hotel at night.

I hung around, and the boat people came swarming into the ocean, drowning by the thousands. 'They are dr*oo*ning,' I told my tour guides. 'Say it again. Dr*oo*ning.' They scowled at the word in the *Bangkok Post* and repeated after me, chanting, and one of them, a joker, went glub-glub and shook his arms in the air, and then something came over me, some jolt, some black shame, and I smacked my hand on the table and said we were through, and everyone just filed out because they could see I was shaking. Later, I lied my way on to the island, through a Pakistani with the UN, a bar crawler. 'You,' he said, sweating with beer. 'You are teaching English, isn't it? Expert, yes?' The Opera Hotel bar had mirrors on the walls, and the black gauze netting on the ceiling was heavy with twinkling bulbs; the bar girls clicked their plastic number-tags, and in the fluorescent light my face was green. I nodded to the Paki. I knew where the conversation was going and I lied to him.

I lied because I was ashamed, but more than that: I lied because I saw what I was becoming. I was aimless, slick in a petty way, my spirit seeping out of me in small gasps. At the Opera Hotel, I got in altercations, little come-ons, mostly with Germans in cowboy hats, roustabouts from the oil-drilling platforms. They were sloppy and fat and unshaven. They ate chicken wrapped in tin foil and made the bar girls suck the bones. I'd say, 'Zo, vere ist der Führer? Ist *you* der Führer? Ist you?' Usually they just looked away. But when they were in the mood, they'd say something real insulting in German, and I'd leap up and be ready. I'd hear myself breathe like a horse and I'd have my hand tight around a bottle. 'Vere ist der Führer? Vere? Who ist he? Ist he you? You?' I'd shake and pound the counter and try to move my legs, only all I could do was sway. 'Vere ist he?' I'd say, pushing, straining, my ears popping, ready to explode, only I couldn't do anything and I just had to stand there with sweat pouring down my face until the bar girls came over and cooed they loved me until I sat back down.

Bidong was a thousand redemptions, every moment an ecstasy: a girl rubbing her gums, a man coughing into a bucket, a chainsaw whirring through plywood. In dreams, I heard Viet-talk, little musical scales, only what they were saying was *Mr Joe, Mr Joe*.

But Sally didn't know that. All she saw was me pointing and shouting, 'What's this?' Later that day, she did a lesson with my intermediate students. They sat on coconut-tree planks lashed together with pink raffia string; the sugar-bag walls billowed in the breeze. Sally had them laughing inside five minutes. She put them into groups, had them holding conversations. She did incredible things with her fingers, popping them up and down to represent words in sentences; she didn't yell in their ears. I couldn't believe how professional she was, how good.

'Mr Joe,' my students said. 'She is *very* good.'

'Very good, Mr Joe.'

'I am speaking English, Mr Joe.'

'You are very wonderful, Miss Sally,' said my best student. The man's smile was so big he didn't look like the person I saw every day. In a few weeks, they would all be looking at me with faces I didn't know.

So when we had to interview a new batch of arrivals for placements, I told Sally to ask, 'How many children do you have?' I told her the Viets love to talk about their kids, that it was the best question, that you could get a real good gauge of their English level from asking it. I told her it was the test I always used.

The first woman had iron-grey hair in a bun.

'How many children do you have?' asked Sally. The woman looked at her a moment, then at the floor.

I leaned over. 'This batch here just got in,' I said. My voice was raspy and quavering. 'Their boat was out there a couple weeks.'

Sally nodded.

'So she's tired,' I said, real nice. 'Try again.'

'I *know*,' Sally said. She smiled at the woman and locked on to her with her eyes.

'How many children do you have?' she said.

Nobody in the line moved; you could see them craning their necks to see what was taking so long. 'I have four,' the woman said, but then her shoulders were shaking. 'Thai pirate kill one.' Her voice started cracking. 'Three daughter, one son.' Then the Viets in line started whispering. They got this hard look on their faces, and one of them said, 'No,' real nasty, in Sally's direction.

Sally looked at me with fury. She didn't say a word, but she didn't have to. One of the Viets started yelling in Viet-talk. He got out of line and walked down the hill; others followed.

Later, I walked with Sally down to the Zone C beach, where the garbage was piled to your waist. At night, you could shine your flashlight and see the beach shimmer with so many rats you thought you were looking at the ocean. The *whole beach*, I said. That many rats. I said it gruffly, with authority, as if to say: This is how it is, this is what's real, get used to it. I talked like I was showing her the ropes, preparing her for life on Bidong.

Ralph the Scottish engineer came up to us, and I turned to him, grateful for the company. Ralph was responsible for sanitation, but all he had were grannies carrying wicker baskets and farmers who didn't mind moving sewage along with hookpoles. I could hear the plastic and cans rustling offshore; black clods drifted in the foam like seaweed. I started to tremble. I wanted to say, 'I am the most savage fuck on this island.'

But I didn't. There was a twitter, some little spark of *hope* that wouldn't let me. And if it were true, then what could we do? Any of us—Viet, white and fuck.

Sally and Ralph were looking at me. 'Your Garbageness,' I said to Ralph, holding my nose. 'This just stinks to high heaven.'

Sally and I split up the schools: she had Zones A to D, I had E to G. 'Why don't I come by Zone F today?' she said. It was so hot we were itchy. I was in running shorts and my powder-blue T-shirt. Sally had on a brown sundress; her arms were full of books. 'I've got some Longman Series books,' she said. 'We could do some team-teaching.'

'Is that like tag-team wrestling?' I said. 'Crossover-toe-hold, then I come in and put on the Sleeper?'

'Oh, Joe,' she said.

'I mean these Viets, they're wiry all right, but I'm the crowd favourite.'

'Oh, Joe,' she said. She held her books over her head like a parasol and squinted. 'How are you, really? And your Mr Thanh. Is he doing well?'

'I don't know about well, but he's doing Miss Thuy, I think.'

It was a good answer, a sleepy little quip to end the conversation and get on with the day. She knew I wasn't going to talk to her about Mr Thanh; what she wanted was the satisfaction of having asked and of having played her role well. She ordered people around and wore lipstick and curled her hair—she pretended it was natural, but the Viet washerwomen showed me her curlers. She did all that, and I saw she was a liar. She was playing Hotlips to my Hawkeye. That other face, the face that would accuse me, that would denounce me—I could keep it from surfacing by being Hawkeye, throwing lame one-liners her way, keeping the little smile quivering at the ends. Hawkeye was simple. He said yuck-yuck so that he wouldn't say boo-hoo, and called his cowardice black humour. Sally ate it up. Every time she put her hands on her hips and said, 'Now, Joe, that's not funny,' and pouted around, I knew she would be in her bungalow that night, the BBC on her shortwave, writing aerogrammes about how wacky we got, how tragic our smiles, how hard-nosed our love, how goddamn *good* we were.

Up the hill in my Zone F school, I saw one of the little high-keeled clinker boats come around the westward side, putt-putting. We all ran out of class and looked out; the loudspeakers started going crazy with Viet-talk, and you could hear people shouting. The planks of the boat were so beat they looked like straw. I could see arms waving. The Viets came straight from Vietnam in boats I wouldn't take around a lake. They would bring aboard cast-iron cooking pots and cases of Coca-Cola. Most didn't even know how to swim; they listened for the tide tables on the Voice of America and then took their chances.

I ran on down with everyone else, dignified as I could, but when I reached the dock I was sweaty and spattered with mud; the beach had hold of my ankles; I was as slow as a swimmer, one stroke at a time. The beach was already thick with Viets. They were still running in from the tree-line behind our compound, and kids were standing on the engine blocks, cheering. All I could see was black hair and brown legs; a rippling brown, T-shirted sea, but I wanted to be there when the boat putt-putted to the dock, so I stuck out my white arms to let everyone see who was coming and cut through the crowd.

Mr Thanh was waving to me a stone's throw away. I pushed closer. 'American, American,' I said, and people turned sideways to let me through. I waved back to Mr Thanh, shouting greetings, but then we were stuck. The beach was so packed up front, there was no room to move. Up around the dock steps, I heard splashing. People were being pushed by the crowd into the water.

'Ever been in a riot?' said Roland. He rammed me from behind with his elbow, but it wasn't his fault; we were all holding on to the shoulders of the person in front, leaning forward with the crowd and drawing back, just trying to keep our balance.

I couldn't see much. The fucks were out in force, but they were just going through the motions, banging truncheons on the pilings to let everyone know they were there. Two of them stood on the dock steps holding their M-16s. Some other fucks and Vietnamese security with special white bracelets were milling around. A Viet was lashing the docking rope around a pillar. The boat was rocking, bumping against the dock, and the pilot-house window had been smashed. One of the fucks dragged a portable ladder and a blanket from the pillhouse and started helping people off, single file. They were dirty and scared. Captain Rahim, wearing his little bus-driver hat, chivvied them along. The last one off, a woman, was wearing a blanket. Her hair was wild; she was trembling so hard she stumbled a little on the last rung, and for a moment you could see she was naked.

'Now we know,' said Roland.

I didn't say anything. I was chewing the inside of my cheek.

'Thai pirates got her,' he said.

'I *know*.'

The way he said *got her* made me shout it.

One of the fucks ran up and lent her his arm, which seemed to me really decent, except that Roland then pointed to him and shouted, 'The fuck has a hard-on.'

I looked, but couldn't see. 'Where?'

'Right *there*,' he said, pointing. 'What do you mean, "where"? You think it's on his head?'

'You're full of it,' I said. 'He's helping her.'

'You don't want to see, OK.'

I stooped my shoulders and frowned, zeroing in on the fuck. He was snapping his fingers at one of the Viet security guys, who ran into the pillhouse and came out with another blanket.

'He doesn't have one,' I said.

'Hey,' he said, cupping his hand. 'You want to defend him, go ahead.'

'If it's not there, it's *not there*,' I said. 'And it's *not there*.'

The naked woman collapsed, and a couple of the Viets in line started walking over to her, while the fucks clapped their hands like they were commanding genies to disappear and chased them back.

Some Viet security ran into the pillhouse and came out with a stretcher.

Mr Thanh squeezed over and greeted me politely, but I could tell he was agitated. He was pinched and raspy, like he was about to get the dry heaves.

'Mr Joe,' he said, touching my arm. 'The woman is very afraid, yeah. You can do? Yeah.'

You can do, as in, Why can't you get out there and summon

white jinns and make this go away?

I held on tight to the shoulders of the man in front. 'Mr Thanh. I'm sorry. I would if I could.' I could hear my heart pounding; I was shouting over the crowd.

'The stretcher's there,' I said. 'They're lifting her now.'

'You're not looking right,' said Roland.

'He *doesn't have one*,' I said.

'No?' said Roland. He paused a moment. 'OK. OK. I was wrong.' He grabbed hold of my shoulders. 'Who does? Maybe it's you, huh?'

'Shut up,' I said, and I looked down, just for a moment, not even moving my head. I looked down just to make sure.

Roland and Mr Thanh followed my eyes and then looked at me.

'My mistake,' said Roland. 'Sorry.'

Mr Thanh's face clamped shut. His shoulders hunched.

The crowd was shouting out questions in Vietnamese: 'What province are you from?' 'How many days did you sail?' 'Do you know my town?' Roland put his hand on my shoulder and talked into my ear. He said he didn't mean it. He said he was just upset. He was asking me to forgive him. Mr Thanh's elbow jabbed me hard in the ribs, but when I looked over he was drifting away, caught from behind in a current of people. He didn't look back. The current caught me, and I could hear people yelling, snapping at each other, and we all stumbled forward, closing in on the dock, where I could see the fucks raising their truncheons, warning people away from the steps. I would ride the current, feel the hands pushing from behind, and at the last second I would grab one of the fucks by the arm, I would shout in his face and start pulling at his shirt until he brought his truncheon down and made me bite my tongue and tumble into the water, splashing, blood speckling my shirt, and I would sink to my knees, yelling from my gut.

But that's not what happened. What happened was, the pushing stopped. Just like that. We all held on to each other's shoulders, breathing hard, just waiting. The Viets started talking softly, whispering, calming each other down. You could hear the little clinker boat creaking in the water. Roland was breathing behind me, rubbing my shoulders. Captain Rahim had his bullhorn out and started yelling at the crowd and waving his bus-driver hat around. I smelled a whiff of Mercurochrome; one of the Viet security men was dabbing a cotton ball on the naked woman's head. I heard seagulls, and in front of me, the tiny waves rolled on to the sand. I saw Mr Thanh and sidled my way around until I was staring him hard in the face and told him I had something wrong inside. I pointed to my chest and screwed up my mouth. I roared at him.

Later, after the crowd had disappeared, Mr Thanh and I walked down the beach. He stopped to wash the dirt off his arms and looked at me with a question on his face, and I told him I would just have a bucket bath in the compound. I told him Miss Sally would be teaching the lessons tomorrow. I stood a few paces back, a decent distance, while he frothed the water. When he was finished, he was clean.

BAO NINH
SAVAGE WINDS

The sun had not yet risen, but above the grassy plain, the mist was already starting to drift away. The village of Diem—a cluster of shacks along the highway—was emerging from the night.

The war was almost over. On the other side of the plain, the enemy artillery base lay silent; no reconnaissance plane had yet appeared on the horizon. At the edge of the village, the last clandestine supply truck crossed the A Rang river, using the stone ford built to replace the iron bridge that had been lost in the bombing. Ripples fanned out from the truck in concentric circles and died away, leaving the water still.

A voice rose lightly from somewhere in the fog, floating away with the night's last murmur, moving further and further along the banks of the river, singing:

I wander through life, not knowing where I've come from.
I am the shore that awaits the touch of your feet.

Beyond the jagged foothills that bordered the plain to the east, a shimmering red sun rose. The mist gave way to translucence, and the sky turned blue. Across the plain, drops of dew sparkled in the light like diamonds on the grass. The singing grew louder, at once sombre and ethereal, vibrant and savage.

The voice belonged to Dieu Nuong. She had been killed months ago, years even; no one really knew. But now, as day was breaking, the people of Diem, half-asleep, heard the singing and murmured, 'It's her.'

From the other side of the village, in the entrenched artillery camp, watchmen trained their binoculars on the village.

Oh moon, how wretched I am,
My beloved has gone, and will never return.

'Look! You see, there she is!' a soldier cried, pointing.

Behind the groves bordering the village, he thought he could see the shadowy figure of a woman advancing, singing, a slender figure with a graceful, swaying walk, long ebony hair cascading down her back. In the dawn, dream and reality mingled. Perhaps she was a mirage born of the song. A ghost. A lascivious, seductive, blithe phantom.

In the trenches, a captain and a political officer passed the

Photo: Marc Riboud (Magnum)

binoculars back and forth. The legend of Dieu Nuong, a singer from Saigon who had been trapped in the liberated zone, was much discussed in the battalion, and embellished with every telling.

The political officer dropped the binoculars. 'If we can't shut that whore up, she'll destroy the soul of this company. They'll all follow her.'

'But how can you prevent a ghost from singing?' asked the captain.

'By forbidding it! It's yellow music, anti-military. And why does she start yowling at exactly the same time every day? It might be a signal. Or maybe she's trying to seduce our men, lure them into her bed so she can infect them with diseases, sap their fighting strength. That's probably what she's after.'

'But she sings so beautifully.'

A group of infantrymen was crossing the plain. A straggler stopped and looked towards Diem. Mist rose in curls off the green water of the river. A breeze swept over it, carrying off the song. The soldiers felt the voice shiver through their bodies, its melody caressing their hearts. Clear, luminous, pure as the dawn air, the song swelled with the sadness of the vast, free forests lost beyond the horizon, ignoring the frontiers, the front lines, mocking the battlefields, the bombs, the killings.

When my own battalion arrived in Diem in 1973, Dieu Nuong was still alive. We knew almost nothing about her: only that she had come here the previous summer, after the offensive of the Armed Forces of Liberation and the débâcle of the Saigon troops. Those who claimed to know more told conflicting stories.

'They say that she wasn't wearing a stitch of clothing when she wandered over here.'

But during that summer of flames, she would not have been the only one suffering. Thousands had been killed, and there were corpses everywhere, lining the roads, piled up in the fields, floating in the rivers. Those who had survived were often more dead than alive. The village had been almost completely destroyed; only prickly underbrush, heaps of shattered bricks, broken tiles and splintered beams remained. Here and there, makeshift houses, half-shack, half-trench, rose from the debris.

Dogs scavenged in the rubble, retrieving the remains of the vanished past: tattered pieces of clothing in garish colours, hats, leather and plastic objects, bits of wood and glass, household goods—and human bones, which the dogs fought over.

Before that summer, Diem had been a thriving community under the protection of the Americans. The men had lived off their army wages; the women had worked in small businesses. But then the village was attacked. Day after day, the planes came, raining bombs on the houses and the fields. The riches of the American days were over.

The following year, my company, Artillery Battalion No. 17, arrived in Diem to defend the A Rang river against the air force. We were stationed at the edge of the ghost village.

The inhabitants of Diem were destitute, almost wild. The few remaining men, the blind, crippled remnants of the puppet army, no longer received rations. Only the women dared venture outside, gaunt and dazed, dressed in rags, surrounded by swarms of hungry children.

Most of these people were refugees from the towns, villages and military camps of the region who, in trying to escape the previous summer, had run up against the tanks of the Liberation Army. One night that summer, at around midnight, there was a massacre. It was said that the refugees, hearing the rumble of an airplane far away, lit thousands of torches and formed a huge, flaming cross right in front of the church. In the darkness, they screamed, waving to the pilots. No one heard the first salvos, no one saw the first flashes from the horizon. For hours on end, people fell under a hail of shells. Wave after wave of American planes flew over until dawn, showering the mass grave with bombs. Dieu Nuong was among the few survivors.

Diem was plunged into misery and hunger. Everyone had to work the land, bending over the rows of manioc, toiling in the rice paddies. Everyone had to submit to the Revolution. Those who protested were persecuted, and many were shot.

Dieu Nuong herself was imprisoned. They locked her up in an underground dungeon for three days as punishment for singing her yellow songs, but this didn't cure her; she continued to live in her own world, free. Every day, at dawn and at dusk, she would sing. People whispered that at night, soldiers visited her dilapidated hut on the riverbank, knocking at her door, scratching at the bamboo walls. They brought their rations: rice, a packet of cigarettes, a bit of cloth, some thread, a needle, a mirror, a comb, matches, salt—anything that could be traded for sex. Her reputation as a madwoman and a prostitute spread among the villagers.

The story went that she had been a singer in a musical troupe in Saigon. Her troupe had agreed to perform for a unit of special forces stationed in Tan Tran. The performance started just as the tanks of the Liberation Army invaded the city. Dieu Nuong fled, following a stream of refugees through blazing fields to Diem, where she found herself trapped. On the night of the massacre, she was buried under a mountain of corpses in the churchyard. For an entire day she breathed in their stench. When she was pulled out from under the pile, her body, drenched in blood, looked like a block of red lacquer. It was said that the terror of that night had finally driven her mad.

Our battalion grew accustomed to her singing; day after day, like a savage wind, her bewitching, startling voice drifted across the plain. She sang odes of longing, of yearning for the homeland, of nostalgia for a life devoted to her art, to the audiences and the limelight. She sang of lost youth, lost beauty, of everything that was gone:

> *Oh, for the time when we knew love,*
> *When we too had a homeland.*

The people of Diem still hum this lament, the song Dieu Nuong first sang the night a convoy of prisoners crossed the village shortly after the massacre. Hundreds of wretched men in camouflage uniforms, bound together in pairs, dragged themselves along the road. Frightened villagers watched furtively from inside their shacks, searching for relatives among the prisoners. No one dared venture out to the roadside. But then, from behind the trees, at the end of the village, a figure appeared—Dieu Nuong. It was twilight, the hour of apparitions.

Muttering, a wild look in her eyes, she slashed at the undergrowth, following the prisoners. The men, hunched over, dragging their feet along the road, didn't notice her, until she began her unearthly singing. Her voice was feeble, and she kept stopping to catch her breath. One of the prisoners raised his voice along with hers. Another joined him. Then another. Dieu Nuong's voice seemed to touch each man's lips like a kiss. The prisoners became a choir, and their singing drowned out the noise of their marching. The guards tried to impose silence, but soon lowered their bayonets.

The villagers swarmed to the edge of the road, staring, silent and petrified, as the procession disappeared into the vastness of the forest. Amplified by the chorus of wretched men, Dieu Nuong's song echoed through the night.

> *. . . In this war where brother kills brother,*
> *we are nothing but worms and ants.*
> *Oh, for the time when we knew love,*
> *When we too had a homeland.*

Dieu Nuong has no tomb. She lies somewhere on the plain, a mound of earth among many mounds of earth.

At the river's edge, all that remain of the anti-aircraft fortifications today are pock-marked walls shaped like horseshoes. Time has filled most of the gaping craters from the cluster and phosphorous bombs. The footpath that once linked our artillery unit with the village is now a faint white trace twisting in and out of the tall grasses along the river. But the soldiers, now scattered, can't have forgotten this path. Back then, twice a day, the army cooks used it to transport meals for the combatants. And at night, especially when there was no moon, the soldiers would secretly sneak off along the path to 'win the hearts of the people,' plunging into the silent grasses, moving towards the river, piling into junks the moment the shadow of the guerrilla patrols appeared.

In those days, contact with the population of the liberated zones was forbidden. Those who had no mission there were under orders to stay out of the village. People who disobeyed could expect punishment, expulsion from the Communist Party and every other imaginable misfortune. But a soldier near the people is like fire near straw.

Relations between between the soldiers and the inhabitants of the village's dilapidated straw huts were not close, but a path through the grass had silently been etched. By day, no one but the cooks and their suppliers dared use it. But at night, it was the road to love.

In my battalion, a soldier's supreme ambition was to become a cook's helper under the orders of Cu—the only man who was permanently assigned to the the village.

The kitchen had been built next to the church. Cu had chosen the plot because he thought it an unlikely target for the bombers, and because it was near a well that contained the clearest water in the village. Cu wasn't happy to be sharing the well with the priest, but the priest was accommodating, and more reasonable than the other villagers, whom Cu regarded as a bunch of good-for-nothings. They lived among fields, but ever since they had been forced to become farmers they had lost all desire to work the land. They had probably become too accustomed to living off American aid and were nostalgic for the golden age when men enlisted and women prostituted themselves to the Americans and their collaborators. Cu believed they were all in league with the enemy, secretly waiting for an opportunity to rejoin them, hiding their true loyalties behind a façade of patient resignation.

Cu couldn't understand why his companions lost their heads over the village women. The fifty men in the company had been living peaceably in the depths of the forest for years, but as soon as they were stationed on the plain, under an open sky, near a river, a village and women, the quarrels started. Yet the women here were completely different from those in the North; they weren't obedient, faithful, courageous, ingenious and responsible; nor were they heroines of the resistance. The entire village, Cu thought, was teeming with female microbes.

'Female microbes spread gonorrhea and syphilis,' he would warn his helpers.

Cu wouldn't accept just anybody as a helper. He ruthlessly eliminated the playboys, the fast talkers, the crafty ones—any man whose talents might attract the village women. 'When you're a cook, when you work all day with food for the unit,' he said, 'you've got to keep your hands clean. They must not touch anything dirty or rotten, and it's *absolutely* forbidden to plunge them into the bodies of women.'

The villagers were terrified of Cu, and didn't dare come near his well or his kitchen. When they became friendly with the cook's helpers and wanted to beg or trade things, they waited for Cu to take supplies to the front.

Twice a day, at dawn and at dusk, Cu and one of his men would leave the house under the guard of another helper and take meals to the company. Nich, a tiny, pure-breed Laotian dog who was particularly sensitive to smells, would lead the way. They went via a short section of the highway, turned towards the village and then zig-zagged through the huts. They forged ahead, their bodies tilted slightly forward, their hands on their rumps to support the enormous baskets hoisted on their backs, which gave off warmth and the fragrance of cooked rice.

The village dogs fled at the sight of Nich. They watched, famished, from behind the rubble, but dared not bark. Only the children in rags, drawn by the warm smell of the rice, chased after Cu and his helper, grasping at their baskets.

'Uncle Cook, oh, Uncle Cook,' they pleaded.

'Dirty little beggars, get away from me!' shouted Cu.

Nevertheless, when a particularly brave kid followed the procession to the village limits, Cu would stop and beckon him. Then he would pull a bit of grilled manioc, or an ear of steamed corn, or sometimes even a dried fish out of his basket, and say: 'Here. That's all there is. There's nothing to eat for the *bo doi*. No more manioc and no more rice. All they get is salted bindweed and a bit of ginger. That's it. The Revolution frees you, but you'd better learn to deal with misery. Learn to dig and work hard to feed yourself. Tell that to your mother. It's going to take a long time, this Revolution. It's going to take our generation and yours as well.'

Today, they say that you can still see Nich come and go along the footpath. He sniffs at the rusted, greenish casing of the 35mm cartridges, climbs over the weed-covered trench where they once kept anti-aircraft batteries and dolefully watches the river.

'Uncle Cook, Uncle Cook!' One of the children from back

then, now grown up, still calls out when he sees the little dog wandering miserably along the footpath. Behind the dog, he thinks he can make out the shapes of two figures carrying large baskets on their backs.

The dog seems unable to leave the footpath. He always returns at dawn and at dusk. Nothing can distract him from his sleepwalker's trajectory. No one dares lay a hand on him.

'That's the dog that killed Dieu Nuong.'

At least that's what they say. Even those who know nothing about the tragedy are afraid of this dog. Perhaps they sense that in this painful, rhythmic promenade, there is a blindness, a madness that is almost human.

Cu's two helpers were changed every month, but one day, when a changeover was due, he announced that he did not want to lose Tuan, one of the previous month's assistants. 'He's well trained now. He's hardworking and meticulous. I'd like to keep him on,' Cu said.

Tuan had started as an infantryman, although no one knew exactly where he had fought before he joined our battalion. He had been seriously injured and, under normal circumstances, would have been invalided out of the army, but he yielded to the Party's exhortations and volunteered to remain on the battlefield. Instead of being sent back to his unit, he was assigned to my artillery battalion, taking up the post of third gunner. He was tall, thin and gaunt. His Adam's apple stuck out. A horrible scar from a rifle blow gashed his face from one temple to the corner of his lip, twisting his mouth. The other artillerymen liked to fool around, but Tuan never joined in. He remained silent, neither laughing nor becoming angry.

He ignored the planes that nosedived towards our positions, the bombs that exploded close by and the rockets that ripped into our defences; he didn't care. This coldness, this indifference towards everything, meant that he made a perfect third gunner. His only duty was to turn the handle of his gun and regulate the shooting according to orders.

'Artillery combat is really monotonous,' he once said to me. 'It's like typing. There's nothing theatrical about it. It's nothing compared with hand-to-hand combat.'

'That's because you've only been third gunner,' I replied. 'If you want, I'll ask the chief to move me back to your position. You can be number two and pull the trigger.'

'Oh, I don't care. I'll go wherever I'm sent. It's all the same to me.'

'If you feel that way, why didn't you go back North when you had the chance? Why did you stay?'

Tuan shrugged.

'Was it your love life? Had your wife been sleeping with the militia? Was that it?'

Tuan grunted, but said nothing.

In fact, no one knew if he was married or had children. And no one had ever seen him read or write a letter. Even the political officer knew no more than the few lines written in his file. Tuan never confided in anyone.

Aside from this unusual discretion, Tuan was also known for his talent as a guitarist. He was the best in the company. But he didn't play like a soldier, thumping out the rhythm with his foot, swinging his shoulders; he didn't whistle or sing as he strummed. He played distractedly, neither for his own entertainment nor ours.

'What are you playing there, Tuan? What strange music.'

Tuan didn't reply. He took off his guitar—an old one, its body ready to fracture—and went into the kitchen. He had brought the guitar with him when he joined the army, and you wondered by what miracle he had kept it intact through all that had happened.

At first, Cu was irritated by Tuan's taciturn nature, but he got used to it. Discretion, after all, was not a fault. And the kitchen was always busy, and Cu and his helpers spent their day running around, rushing to complete some job; there wasn't really time to talk.

It wasn't until late at night, after the unit had been fed, that Cu and his helpers found a moment to exchange a few words before they slumped into their hammocks. Cu would get out a bottle of wine, and the helpers would drink while he assigned the next day's tasks. On quieter days, Cu and another helper, Binh, would play cards, and Tuan would take his guitar down from the wall, gently adjust the strings and play softly. Binh would whistle, accompanying the music. And Cu, letting his cards fall, would turn towards Tuan, listening. One night, he recognized the tune; he had heard it every day, at dawn and at dusk: *I wander through life, not knowing where I've come from.* Was this when Cu guessed Tuan's secret?

Outside, the rain fell, relentlessly. A dank, humid atmosphere hung over the cabin. The lamp cast a yellowish glow. The sad life of soldiers. Like a long sigh.

The priest's house, next door to Cu's hut, was half-buried, surrounded by four slopes of earth. It was sparsely furnished: a bamboo bed covered with straw, a wooden pillow, a table, a bookshelf and some holy pictures. A basket hung over the entrance. In the morning, the village faithful would leave food in it for the priest, who seldom left his room and never ventured further than the garden. He was a wise old man, aloof from the world. He disappeared the day Dieu Nuong was killed.

The year before, on the night the Americans showered the refugees with bombs, the priest and Dieu Nuong had found themselves lying side by side, and it was he who had pulled her from under the mountain of corpses. He had revived her, saved her life, and from that day on, had taken care of her. For a time, Dieu Nuong had lived in the church, by the priest's side, like a sister. It wasn't exactly a suitable arrangement, but in those chaotic times many taboos were broken; no rule survived without compromise.

Later, when Dieu Nuong went to live in her hut at the edge of the village, she often returned to the church to see the priest— perhaps to make her confession, or to pass on the gifts the soldiers gave her daily, things they had saved from their meagre rations, or pilfered from the stores, or looted from somewhere.

I don't think I am alone in saying this: I never thought Dieu Nuong wicked. She gave me happiness I had never known back North. Many years have passed, but I cannot forget her, nor do I want to. I see her walking alone, on a deserted road, graceful, lithe, swaying; I see her seated on the riverbank, wistful, silent.

'Come here, soldier, honey. Don't be afraid. I'm alone.'

My heart racing, I would sweep back the curtain that was her door and enter her room. Taking a step forward, I brushed against something wonderful and warm, something that trembled, something impossible to describe, then sank into an inferno of softness.

'What's your name, my love? Is this the first time you've come?'

Even the hard life of the liberated zones hadn't destroyed Dieu Nuong's body; there was something intensely feminine about it, making her seem more womanly than any other woman. It wasn't just her caresses, nor the moments when she suddenly let go, consumed by tenderness, moaning and thrashing about; nor the times she panted silently, collapsing, exhausted, exuding wave after wave of sinful female desire.

'Are you going so soon?' She would hold me back. 'It's a long time until dawn. Stay a while. I have something to tell you. One thing, only one thing—'

But few men dared stay, and fewer still dared listen to what Dieu Nuong had to tell them. No one wanted to hear it, because no one could help her. It was too dangerous. No doubt Dieu Nuong believed that there were still men in this world crazy enough to risk their lives for love, to betray everything for love.

We were all anxious to see her again and so we lied to her, promising the impossible, even though we knew there was no way we could help her escape. But once, a year ago, there had been a man who promised to help her, and this man had kept his word.

I learned afterwards, when it was all over, that when Tuan was in the infantry he had passed through Diem many times.

During the summer of flames, after the massacre, the village had been struck by famine; the meagre stocks of food donated by the *bo doi* at the time of Liberation were gone. The authorities called for increased production, and even the priest had to fend for himself.

Dieu Nuong was living with the priest at this time, and since her guardian didn't till the earth, she tried to do the work of two people, felling trees and planting manioc. But she wasn't used to the hard labour, to the mud, and after each thrust of the hoe she would bury her face in her hands and weep. At the end of the day, her field would still be covered with trees and undergrowth.

Nearby, a group of soldiers lounged in their hammocks. They jeered at her, contemptuous of this little woman, lazy, frail as tissue paper, who had known only the good life and who was learning for the first time what human existence was all about. But little by little, they took pity on her suffering and offered to help. They spent the entire night felling trees, clearing her field. One man introduced himself. His name was Tuan. He promised to come back in a few days to help Dieu Nuong burn the land. And he kept his word.

Dieu Nuong's field was perfect, the clearest in the village. Not a tree stump remained. When he left, Tuan promised to come back to help sow the manioc. And he kept his word.

The first rains came. In a few days, the manioc Tuan had planted covered the burnt patch with a thick carpet of green. All around, Tuan sowed a hedge of squash. On the strip of land behind the church, he helped Dieu Nuong plant vegetables. Every five days or so, Tuan crept away from the front line near the town and crossed the fields to come to Diem.

It was about this time that Dieu Nuong left the church and made her home in a hut that Tuan had built for her on the riverbank. Thanks to him, she lost her desperate expression; her eyes sparkled and she started to smile again.

Sometimes, Tuan brought his guitar with him to Dieu Nuong's hut. He would play softly, and Dieu Nuong would sing in a murmur. Back then, she sang only for him.

No doubt they made promises to each other. No doubt Dieu Nuong told Tuan that she dreamed of leaving her harsh life, scratching at the earth in this godforsaken village; that she was looking for a man worthy of her trust, who would help her cross the front line and return her to the calm, comfortable life she had known before Liberation.

Tuan was confident they could cross the line—those ten kilometres riddled with mines, patrolled by guards—for those were the days following the the peace talks. Intoxicated with love, transported by the hope of peace, he promised to help her. And no doubt he meant it. But, suddenly, he disappeared. Days passed, then months; no one in Diem spoke of him.

Like the rest of us, Dieu Nuong never mentioned Tuan. The memory of him and his promise had probably dissolved along with her mind. But her yearning for freedom survived, surfacing from time to time in the songs she sang every day at dawn and at dusk. Night after night, she extracted promises from the soldiers who visited her, promises that grew emptier with each passing day as the war became more brutal, as bombs and shells pounded the village, crushing all hopes of peace.

One rainy night, as she walked along the footpath to the priest's house, through the vegetable garden near the cook's cabin, Dieu Nuong heard the strains of a guitar. She approached soundlessly, peering into the hut. An oil lamp flickered. She couldn't make out the guitarist's face, but she recognized the familiar melody of her nights with Tuan. Frantic, she approached the door. Nich, the dog, bounded out of a corner of the cabin, barking. 'Who is it?' Cu shouted, climbing out of his hammock, seizing his rifle.

Dieu Nuong jumped back. The guitar stopped, and she ran off.

Cu flung open the door.

'A spy!' he shouted. 'Stop!'

He caught sight of Dieu Nuong's silhouette.

'Ah it's you, you whore! Stop, or I'll shoot!' Cu shouted, running into the rain, slipping in the mud and falling flat on his face. Pulling himself up, furious, he fired a volley of shots in Dieu Nuong's direction.

Tuan rushed out after him and grabbed the machine-gun. 'You idiot!' he shouted, his voice choked. Wildly, he punched Cu in the face, threw down his gun and ran off into the blackness in pursuit of Dieu Nuong. The village rang out with alarm sirens.

Binh helped Cu up and brought him back to the cabin. 'When people ask, you're going to tell them that it was nothing,' Cu murmured painfully, wiping the blood and rain off his face with his sleeve. 'Tell them that I had a nightmare, that I shot without thinking. Go and see what's happened.' He sighed. 'But why did she run off?'

Later, when Binh told me what had happened that night, he

said mournfully: 'If Dieu Nuong hadn't been wounded, they might have made it.'

Thinking about it now, Cu's actions seem to me incomprehensible. He was the only one who knew something of what had happened between Tuan and Dieu Nuong. Why did he shoot her?

Binh told no one about Cu firing on Dieu Nuong, or about the fight between Cu and Tuan, nor even about the mysterious relationship between Tuan and Dieu Nuong. All anyone knew was that both of them had disappeared.

At the edge of the village, weeds began to grow around Dieu Nuong's deserted hut. Rumour had it that she had fled, or been killed—drowned in the river, blown up by a bomb.

The rains seemed interminable, but little by little I understood why I felt so sad. I missed Dieu Nuong's singing; I missed *her*. I wasn't the only one; the whole company seemed depressed. There no longer seemed any reason for our presence here.

Then, on a sunny day at the beginning of the dry season, we learned that she and Tuan had been hiding in the church, waiting for the rains to stop and for Dieu Nuong's wounds to heal. Now, they had gone for good.

It was the priest who told us. He came to the trenches at dawn, his cassock damp with mist. 'Last year, one of your men seduced the girl. The man with the scar and the sullen face. And then he came back. Not only has he betrayed you, but it was he who led the girl to betray God.' He told us he had alerted Cu the night before, as soon as he discovered that Tuan and Dieu Nuong had fled, but Cu hadn't told the rest of us.

'If you really want to catch them, it's not too late. She's wounded and can't walk very fast,' he said. 'You could take the dog.'

I had the honour of participating in the operation, joined by Cu and two scouts. We left immediately. Nich led the way, moving quickly, pulling at the leash which Cu held.

We followed him in silence, fanning out, rifles at the ready. We had orders not to let them get away with their secrets about the unit's next campaign.

The traces that Nich followed led us along the river, rising towards the densely forested plain.

We quickly lost our enthusiasm. We advanced reluctantly. Dust swirled under our feet. The hours passed. Relentless, Nich followed the fugitives' invisible, zig-zagging trace. But just as we had decided to turn back, we came across a lone *knia* tree in the middle of a field of grass higher than our heads. Here, we could see that Tuan and Dieu Nuong had lain down to rest. An army of ants was dragging away grains of rice. There was a cigarette butt, a bit of rough tobacco rolled in a piece of newspaper, on the ground. But the clearest sign was a shape, pressed upon the grass—a reclining, human form, a woman's silhouette.

We caught up with them just before dusk.

Exhausted, we stopped by a stream. Nich had lost the scent in the water, and we sat down to rest. Our silence hung in the intense red of the sunset.

Suddenly, over the murmuring of the stream, came a thin, unexpected sound.

'The guitar!' cried Cu.

We listened, holding our breath. A voice began to sing.

We forded the river, creeping towards the place from where the song seemed to rise. It was a pine forest. Sparse trees reached for the sky. A thin curl of smoke evaporated in the evening.

A twig snapped. The song stopped.

I hid myself behind a tree trunk, staring, wide-eyed. A pot hung over a tiny fire. Nearby lay a guitar. A hammock had been strung between two pines. Our prey had hidden in the bushes.

Silence. For a long time. Mechanically, I cocked my rifle.

'Friends, brothers!' It was Tuan's voice. 'We haven't harmed anyone. Let us go!'

'Quiet!' shouted one of the scouts. 'Stand up! Hands up! Come out of there!'

One minute. Minutes. Still silence. Cu suddenly let go of Nich's leash. The dog ran off, and I heard him barking in the bushes. Frantic yelps of joy. The bush trembled.

'*I am wandering*,' sang the voice.

'Crazy woman!' someone shouted. 'Whore!'

Four rifles spat bullets in the same instant. Flashes merged, ripping through the night.

We emptied four cartridges. The guns stopped at the same moment. All four of us ran forward and then stopped, petrified.

Behind the shattered bush, two figures lay entwined. Our bullets seemed only to have locked them more tightly together. The man had tried to protect the woman with his body, but the bullets had pierced both of them. The firelight flickered on their naked backs.

We stood paralysed for a long time. Night fell. It was as if we were chained to each other, captive to something invisible but overpowering. The smell of gunpowder, the only trace of our frenzy, had evaporated.

Cu started to sob.

I knelt next to Tuan and Dieu Nuong and parted them.

Two days later, we received orders to march south. We left Diem forever. I pulled myself together, as did Cu. There was a battle ahead of us, the only salvation left for our souls. We would fight and forget.

We didn't know it then, but we had reached the last dry season of the war. We had shot the messengers of peace, and yet, in spite of everything, peace returned.

On the plain, all through the dry season, winds howled. Peaceful winds; savage winds.

Adapted from a novella translated from the Vietnamese by
Phan Huy Duong and Nina McPherson

ED GRAZDA
HANOI, 1994

GRANTA

REDMOND O'HANLON
UPRIVER

Brazzaville

'As far as I can see,' announced Lary, 'every law of nature is suspended in this goddamn country.'

I realized, with a twinge of disquiet, that Lary Shaffer, the emphatically rational specialist in animal behaviour at the State University of New York at Plattsburgh, was not responding to our circumstances as I thought a scientist should. But then it dawned on me how presumptuous I had been. You haven't seen him since you were at university together twenty years ago, I thought: you hardly know him.

'Lary, what is this? What's up?'

'Well, when we were in the plane and the lights of Brazzaville and Kinshasa came up in the dark with the black river between them, and the pilot started circling, and there I was sitting with that sucking plastic bag on my knees containing more film than I've ever carried in my life, and over the Tannoy the pilot announces that he thinks he just ought to remind passengers unwise enough to be disembarking in Brazzaville that anyone caught taking photographs in the city goes straight to prison and is never seen again, and I said what do you estimate they'll actually do to me? and you said, "Oh, nothing much Lary, they'll just tap you about with the odd swagger stick;" and when we got across the tarmac and into that brown cage of a shed with the naked light-bulbs sure as hell there were enough soldiers to start a medium-sized war and they were all carrying swagger sticks and Kalashnikovs and hand-grenades and Christ knows what and taking people apart in booths and robbing them stupid, I suppose you thought that was funny?'

'It was funny. Ish.'

'It wasn't a bit funny. And if you're going to suspend the laws of nature, that airport is a good place to start. Besides, I've been doing some reading.'

He reached into his shirt-pocket, pulled out two crumpled paperback pages and smoothed them flat on his knee.

'The latest warning from *Africa on a Shoestring*: "Depending

Photo: Lary Shaffer

Opposite: a Congo pygmy boy with a hunting net on his head.

on your nationality and where you apply for your visa, you may be given only five days, though fifteen days is the usual with a fixed date of entry. It will be hard going to get through the country in that time. *Visa extensions are not available.*" And just in case you're planning to go in there without permission, perhaps you should get this too: "There are police checkpoints every twenty-five to thirty kilometres in the countryside where you will be stopped and asked for your passport and vaccination certificates." Now we all know what that means—the white American capitalist spy Lary Shaffer will be cut in half with a burst of Kalashnikov fire, and some bastard will nick his boots.'

'Spy? What are you talking about?'

'It may have escaped your notice, Redso, but this is a Communist state. This was the base from which the Russians and Cubans won the war in Angola. Three hundred and fifty thousand Africans dead. The CIA and South Africa bankrolled Unita. They don't like Americans here.'

'But that's part of the point. This is the most difficult equatorial African country to get into, the least explored, the most interesting. We'll see gorillas, chimps, guenons, forest elephants, swamp antelope, pythons, three species of crocodile.'

'They'll kick us out. We'll see that shithole of an airport again in precisely thirteen days. This is a great mistake.'

'Everything depends on tomorrow,' I said. 'Everything. Jean Ngatsiebe, the Cabinet Secretary to the Ministry for Scientific Research, and Dr Serge Pangou, his adviser, are coming to dinner. We'll wear our suits. We're going to be a scientific expedition. We've got to get them to give us a *laissez-passer*. I've worked on this for a year.'

'I know. I know. When I think of the money and effort it's cost you to get here, I could cry.'

'So could I.'

'And I can't think of a single reason why they should want to let you in.'

'Neither can I.'

'This whole project is insane. And what is it you *really* want to see?'

'The pygmies. And something else. Before the war, my father

Every issue of Granta features fiction, travel writing, autobiography, reportage and more. So don't miss out — subscribe today and save up to 40% on the £7.99 cover price.

Don't miss out on major issues. Subscribe now to Granta and save up to 40%.

Don't let your friends miss out either. One year gifts (4 issues) are only £21.95.

GRANTA

FREEPOST
2-3 Hanover Yard
Noel Road
London
N1 8BR

FREEPOST
2-3 Hanover Yard
Noel Road
London
N1 8BR

was an Anglican missionary in Abyssinia. He wrote a book on the
Coptic Church. He got out when the Italians invaded, taking the
Emperor's Bible with him, and he gave it back when Haile Selassie
went into exile and came to live in Bath. Anyway, he had a
wonderful collection of books on Africa in his big dark study in
the Wiltshire vicarage where I grew up. When he was visiting his
parishioners or at choir practice or evensong or bell-ringing, I'd
creep in and take down a volume of Bannerman's *Birds of Tropical
West Africa* from the second shelf on the right behind the door,
and lay it out over the papers on his table. I must have been eleven
or twelve. I want to see a pennant-winged nightjar. There's a
drawing in volume three of a pennant-winged nightjar trailing its
twenty-eight-inch plumes across the moon. I thought it was the
oddest, the most desirable bird in the air. I still do.'

'Strange but true,' muttered Lary, with a profound sigh.
'He's left his family, risked everything, spent his last penny and
come all this way . . . to see . . . a bird.'

Jean Ngatsiebe, Cabinet Secretary to the Ministry of Scientific
Research, overweight, domineering, dressed in a perfectly
tailored Parisian suit, put his enormous fist on the white tablecloth.

'Mr O'Hanlon, I hear you have written a book on Darwin,'
he said in French. 'Is that so?'

I nodded.

'Good. Then you can tell me, if you will—in your opinion,
do you think that you and I are the same species?'

Dr Serge Pangou, his adviser from the university, bearded,
wearing a suit which, like mine and Lary's, might have fitted him
ten years ago, embarrassed, looked into the night beyond the large
plate-glass window of the hotel dining-room, at the lights round
the swimming-pool.

Lary's eyes bulged.

'I'm sure of it,' I said, taken aback. 'Our ancestors evolved in
Africa around a hundred thousand years ago. Maybe not far from
here.'

Jean Ngatsiebe put his black hand next to my pink one.

'You're sure?'

'Of course he's sure,' said Lary, butting in. 'Skin colour is a

very superficial affair. A matter of a mere ten genes or so in tens
of thousands.'

'Good. Then that's settled. I, too, am an admirer of Darwin.
I believe everything that Darwin says. At first I was sceptical, but
now I am convinced—because Darwin's fish diet is certainly
whitening my skin.'

He turned his hand palm-up.

'I may be wrong,' I said, 'but I don't remember Darwin
prescribing a diet for anything.'

'You mustn't bother about Redmond,' said Lary quickly,
with a forced smile. 'He's always arguing. Darwin's his thing. Of
course Darwin worried about his diet. He was a sick man.'

'Whereas I am in the best of health,' said Jean Ngatsiebe,
ordering another bottle of white wine.

We talked about the appalling price of French cars; about the
dastardly way the French had kept their factories in France, so
that when the Marxist-Leninist revolution happened there were no
means of production for a decent Communist to seize; about the
ozone conference in London, and how the People's Republic of the
Congo actually contributed ozone to the atmosphere, whereas the
hypocritical industrial countries had long ago cut down all their
own forests and were even now fouling the upper air and 'So what
is it exactly,' said Jean Ngatsiebe over the cognac, 'that you wish
to do in my country? I do not understand. Why are you here?'

'We want to see the birds and mammals and reptiles in the
jungles of the north,' I said.

Jean Ngatsiebe was silent.

'I am fascinated by the People's Republic of the Congo,' I
said lamely, and then, without thinking, 'I've been writing to
Marcellin Agnagna at the Ministry for the Conservation of
Water and Forests. He says he'll come with us.'

'Two different Ministries?' said Ngatsiebe, displeased. 'You
wrote to two different Ministries?'

'Jopop!' said Dr Serge Pangou. 'But I know him!'

'Jopop?' said Jean Ngatsiebe, with distaste.

'I was at university with him in Havana. Jopop! He knew all
the songs of Otis Redding. He was always dancing with the girls
of Cuba. He's a pharmacist. He studied crocodile growth rates at

Montpellier. He wants to be a crocodile farmer. And he says he's seen the sauropod dinosaur at Lake Télé.'

'So, Mr O'Hanlon,' said Jean Ngatsiebe, his voice full of hostility, 'you have come to investigate some kind of dinosaur? To make fun of us? To mock the African?'

'Of course not,' I said. 'I'm interested in the wisdom of old men. I always have been. I want to learn about the history of the many different Bantu groups who live in the far interior. I want to learn about the history of your people.'

Jean Ngatsiebe leant back in his chair. He smiled for the first time. 'Then I may be able to help you,' he said, placing his huge hand briefly on my shoulder. 'My father was himself a great provider, a great sorcerer. Everyone respected him. He knew all the plants of the forest. He would lay special leaves along the paths round our village—and the next morning hundreds of poisonous snakes would be lying on them, dead.'

'Look,' I said, growing desperate, 'I am a Darwinian Marxist with a deep interest in sorcery.'

'In that case,' said Jean Ngatsiebe, with a violent bark of laughter, slapping his thigh, 'I will give you a six-month visa for your travels in my country. You may collect it from my office tomorrow morning. Dr Serge Pangou will call for you at nine.'

Drunk, we all embraced by the black Mercedes, and Serge Pangou whispered in my ear: 'Jean Ngatsiebe is not a man of science: he is a relation of the President.'

The next day, directed by Serge Pangou, we moved hotels. 'You can't afford to stay at the M'Bamou Palace,' he said. 'That's for people who are frightened of Africa. I know why you're there—you thought it would impress us, the locals, that we'd think you were rich and so let you into our country. Well, believe me, brothers,' (he grinned) 'we're not fooled. No rich man in his right mind would be seen dead in suits like yours.'

We had just lugged everything into our forlorn little room when there was a loud knock on the half-open door: a very tall, fit-looking man stood in the doorway; he was perhaps in his mid-thirties, with a sharp chin, a slightly hooked nose and the darkest skin-tone I had ever seen. His face was velvet black, the kind of black which, as you look at it, appears to absorb all the surrounding light. 'Marcellin Agnagna!' he said in a high-pitched shout, 'I'm hungry! I have a taxi! We must eat!'

I grabbed Serle and Morel's *Birds of West Africa* from the side-pocket of my pack and locked the door. Lary and I followed Marcellin up the path. In his wake, the tang of aftershave overwhelmed the smell of fish-frying from the hotel kitchen; his white shirt was dazzling in the heat; his blue jeans were freshly laundered. In one smooth athletic movement, a double flash of white trainers, he disappeared into the back of the taxi. I got awkwardly into the front, turned round, and was surprised to see that he was not alone: a young girl, her pupils dilated with admiration and desire, was massaging the back of his neck with one hand and his right inside leg just above the knee with the other; her breasts so stretched her meagre white T-shirt that its hem barely reached her navel; her red cotton skirt curled half-way up her slim black thighs.

Lary, his mind on some previous train of thought, got into the back beside Marcellin, noticed the girl and extended an arm to shake hands: 'Madame Agnagna?'

'She's not my wife!' shouted Marcellin, pushing Lary's hand away, 'And she doesn't speak English!'

'Is your wife joining us?' said Lary, fuddled with embarrassment.

'Of course not!' Marcellin yelled into Lary's ear. 'She's pregnant!'

'Pregnant?'

'She's having a baby!' explained Marcellin, slightly louder.

'Congratulations,' said Lary, bemused. 'Well done.'

Marcellin sat up. The girl withdrew her hands as if he had slapped her. 'Look!' he shouted, his chin jutting forward, 'Let's get one thing straight, shall we? Right at the start. This is not England! This is not small-town America! This is Africa! My wife is pregnant. So we can't have sex. So here is Louise, who finds it hard to stop having sex. OK?'

Marcellin ordered the taxi to a café with a terrace overlooking a little tributary of the Congo river. In the middle of the tributary was a sandbank, and in the middle of the sandbank was a hippopotamus, and under the middle of the hippopotamus was his extraordinarily long, thin, tremblingly erect penis.

'Muh muh muh,' said the hippopotamus.

'That's right,' said Marcellin. 'See? He needs sex too. Only his wife's not pregnant. The army shot her and ate her.'

'Of course,' said Lary.

We ordered fish and Primus, the Congo beer, and I opened Serle and Morel at the grey-wash plate, number twenty-six, where an overstuffed museum specimen of the pennant-winged nightjar sits on the ground, lined up with five other equally lifeless species of nightjar, and Marcellin, not surprisingly, shook his head at them. My pennant-winged nightjar, I told myself—it didn't look like that, either.

After lunch, on Marcellin's instructions, we stopped outside a shack with rooms for hire. He disentangled himself from Louise and leant forward. 'You'll pay my government salary. Thirty pounds a day.'

'But we've already slipped Ngatsiebe a thousand pounds for our visas,' I said, with reflex annoyance.

'Was that all? You got a bargain. He must have liked you.'

'It's bribery,' said Lary. 'It's corruption.'

'It's Africa,' said Marcellin. 'How else is he to make up his salary? Those jobs don't last long. They're just a political favour. In and out every four years. Even I can't count on my salary, as a government employee. Some months I'm paid, some months I'm not. At least with you, Redmond, I know I'll get my money.'

'How do you know?' I said stupidly.

'Because you'll pay me every franc in advance,' said Marcellin, getting out of the car.

With ten days to wait until the steamer returned from upriver, we settled into a routine—or rather, the methodical Lary showed me how a life with a routine might be constructed.

On our first morning, we set off to Marcellin's office. The Ministry for the Conservation of Fauna and Protected Areas lay down to the left, behind the zoo, and its chef de service, Marcellin Agnagna, sat at a table in one of an L-shaped row of offices. Wearing a pink-striped shirt, white trousers and smart brown shoes, he was writing in biro on a block of foolscap, a blue diary open in front of him. Otherwise the hot little room was almost empty—just a pinboard of photographs on the right-hand wall, and an issue of *The Journal of Cryptozoology* by Marcellin's left elbow.

'I am preparing the official report of my forest elephant survey,' he said, looking up. 'We estimate that the total forest elephant population in the Congo has been reduced by fifty per cent in the last ten years. It's the Muslims, it's the traders from Sudan and the Central African Republic—they lend the pygmies high-powered rifles, they pay them a few packets of cigarettes and they come back later to collect the ivory. No one can guard a jungle border. It's not possible.'

'You're sure that's the main problem?' said Lary. 'It's not logging, land-clearance, population pressure?'

'You'll understand when you get there, my friend. The huge swamp forest between the Oubangui and Sangha rivers—it's the last untouched jungle in Africa. The population density is 0.9 per square kilometre—and even they are confined to the banks of the rivers. They fish, they work in their plantations, but they never venture far into the swamp forest. You'll see why that is, too.'

'Why?' asked Lary.

'It is hard, Dr Shaffer. You may be in water up to your waist. You'll be attacked by bees. There'll be leopards round the camp at night. You'll get ulcers on your legs. You'll develop body fungus. You must take care with vipers and cobras. And along the waterways—the tsetse flies are truly terrible.'

'Thanks,' said Lary, hunching his shoulders.

'In any case, my Director is pleased I have the opportunity to make this journey with you. I will be able to inform the chiefs and the Vice-Presidents of the People's Party Committees in the villages of the far interior that we now consider the hereditary chiefs, rather than the government of the People's Republic of the Congo, to be once more the direct guardians of their traditional areas of the forest—it is now their job to help us stop the poaching, by warfare, if necessary. We'll be an official expedition.'

'Right,' said Lary, appalled.

'Besides,' said Marcellin, standing up and moving towards the door, our audience at an end, 'it's safer for us that way. I think, on balance, that a government expedition is slightly less likely to be speared, or cut with machetes, or shot.'

For the next few days, we woke to the alarm at six, took a shower, drank our coffee and crumbled our croissants at a café table in the garden of the hotel, watching a pair of grey-headed sparrows cheep-cheep-cheeping about their nest beneath the roof of the bungalow, familiar and busy and craning their necks to look round at us, just like the sparrows in Oxford. Then we went for a walk (at a cyclist's pace, it seemed to me, in the enveloping heat) until Lary decided that he had had his morning's quota of exercise, when we would return to the hotel garden, read, eat fried Congo-river fish for lunch, take a siesta, wash one set of sweat-soaked clothes in the basin, hang them to dry on the wardrobe, change, walk downtown to eat, drink a litre of cheap red Spanish wine each (eight pounds per ten-gallon drum), wrap up in our tarpaulins and fall asleep. And eventually I got a hangover.

It was worse than any hangover I had ever had (but then so was the red wine). Returning from one of our walks, I realized that it hurt just to touch the hair on my head. The back of my neck locked rigid. My intestines seemed to uncoil and move beneath my stomach like a sidewinder. Contorted on the lavatory-seat, I said aloud, 'You'd better lie down;' but my body spun itself round and threw up so violently into the diarrhoea-filled pan that I thought the lining of my throat and oesophagus might rip loose and hang from my mouth like an inverted sock.

'Christ,' said Lary, as I regained the room, 'you'd better lie down.' His head detached itself from his shoulders and loomed over me. 'Christ,' it said. 'If you ask me, that's no hangover.'

Hours later, or so it seemed, I was back on a family holiday in the west of Ireland, on top of Croagh Patrick, in a sudden blizzard, only my mother and father and elder brother had abandoned me, and I lay in the gathering snow, just beside the cairn, wearing nothing but my scratchy grey school shorts.

'They've left me,' I said. 'I'm cold.'

'But it's ninety degrees in here,' said Lary from the bottom of the mountain.

'Please. Get me some clothes.'

There was a rattling noise in my inner ear, the sound of hooves on the scree, and Lary emptied my spare trousers, shirts and pants, a sweater and two blankets over me. He covered the corpse with a tarpaulin.

'Your pack's a mess,' he said, kneeling down by my head. 'Why don't you have a system? It's all just shoved in any old how. Crammed into plastic bags. It's truly horrible. First off, you should differentiate between the main load-bearing sack and the side-pockets. Second off, you should put the maps flat in the map-pocket, properly folded. They're precious. And why's the whole thing stuffed with socks?'

'The SAS Major in Hereford said that's what you do. You s-stuff the c-crannies with s-socks.'

'You could breed rats in here,' said Lary. Then: 'Found it. John Hatt, *The Tropical Traveller*. Enlarged and updated. I should hope so. Let me see. Page ninety-five.'

There was a silence.

'Just as I thought,' he said. '"Remember that however careful you have been about taking the tablets, *there is no guaranteed prophylactic against malaria* . . . Usually only falciparum malaria will kill you . . . Vomiting and diarrhoea may be the more obvious symptoms."'

'J-Jesus.'

'So there's nothing to worry about,' said Lary. 'You've got the only strain of malaria that kills you.'

'I'm a named p-patient,' I said, trying to take control of my jaw muscles. 'There's a new drug in the medicine p-pack. It's called Lariam.'

'You made that up,' said Lary.

'Professor D-David Warrell at the t-tropical diseases research unit in Oxford gave it to me. He says it may make you dizzy.'

'Dizzy!' said Lary, crackling through the heavy-duty plastic bags.

It sounded as if he was walking in his big boots, very slowly, over a ploughed field in the frost.

'Here you are,' he said, handing me three big white pills and a refilled black water-bottle. 'Three more in six hours' time. Side effects unknown. Slight dizziness suspected.'

So I lay still. I closed my eyes. I was eight years old, flying my grandmother to America on the contraption I had built of planks and tins and bits of bicycle in the little copse above the front lawn, behind the high stone wall, where I kept my bantams; I was paddling with my father in his two-seater canvas canoe on a Wiltshire stream; I was dumb with fear, sitting in the back seat of his Riley, halfway across a desolate Salisbury Plain, being taken away to a prep school in Dorset; but the involuntary memories kept snapping, the images broke up and disappeared into a nausea of yawning, deep groaning yawns that felt as if they must unhinge my jaw.

The next morning I awoke, cured, temporarily over-charged with mental energy, euphoric.

'Did you give me the rest of the pills?' I said.

'Of course I did. I set the alarm clock. Not that I needed to—how could I possibly sleep with you banging your teeth together and steaming like a kettle all night?'

After breakfast (which I couldn't eat), Marcellin arrived, and we took a taxi down to the main market to buy supplies.

In the press of narrow alley-ways, lined with little wooden stalls roofed with tarpaulins or corrugated iron, we bought sacks of rice (because it would be twice as expensive upriver in Impfondo, said Marcellin); manioc flour (a better quality in Brazzaville); two five-gallon plastic drums of cheap red wine and five bottles of Johnnie Walker Red Label (for the Chiefs—so he said—and the Vice-Presidents of the People's Party Committees in the villages of the interior); twenty-five cartons of cigarettes (for the pygmies); tins of sardines, brown sugar, powdered milk, tea and coffee (because Impfondo might not have any); packets of salt, flaked onions and chicken-flavoured stock-cubes (essential, apparently, to mask the taste of the giant Gambian rat); soap in big red bars (for clothes) and soap in small white bars (for armpits); knives, forks, spoons, aluminium plates, machetes and disposable lighters; and one small blue camping-gas cooking-stove with retractable legs (because Marcellin couldn't resist it).

'Marcellin,' I said, the euphoria wearing off, feeling weak and giddy as we lugged the booty into the hotel and filled every one of the spare kitbags, 'I've had malaria.'

'Of course you've had malaria,' said Marcellin, without the slightest interest, hiding the stove deep inside the rice sack. 'This is Africa. You'll get it again upriver. You'll both get it. We all will.'

'But,' said Lary, 'there's no more Lariam.'

Marcellin re-tied the neck of the sack, felt round the waist for any tell-tale metallic bulge and, satisfied, turned to go. 'I'll be here at six tomorrow morning. Make sure you're ready. If we miss the steamer—it's another two weeks' wait, maybe more. And I start counting off my salary, Redmond, from tomorrow, whatever happens. OK? Understood?'

'Understood,' I said, sitting on the manioc sack.

Marcellin paused in the doorway. 'The steamer calls at Mossaka. There is a cholera outbreak at Mossaka. Many people are already dead. Perhaps we will get that, too, and then—just for the chance to earn thirty pounds a day—I will never see my daughter, Vanessa Sweet Grace, again.'

We heard him slam the outer door.

The steamer was delayed upriver; but two mornings later, much to Lary's surprise ('All we do here is wait to die'), Nicholas called to take us to the port.

Under the grey sky, in the heavy gathering heat of the early morning, people fanned out from the high, steel-grilled gates of the dock-shed, down the pavements, across the wide road, up against the warehouse opposite. Marcellin was nowhere to be seen.

We dumped the packs and kitbags on the tarmac. A Berliet troop-carrier, its air brakes whistling, slewed to a halt beside us. The soldiers, in their black fatigues, jumped down as if going into battle. Nicholas grabbed a couple of porters, loaded them with three kitbags apiece—one on the head, one in each hand—and we followed close behind the soldiers, the invisible shock wave in front of them parting the crowd right up to the steel entrance.

'That's the only way,' said Nicholas, pleased with himself, dropping a pack on the olive-drab pile. 'It's against the law to touch a soldier.'

The queue reformed around us. The guard on the gate, swinging it open to let the soldiers pass, re-padlocked the chains at head- and ankle-height, restoring the one-man-wide slit.

'It's my brother!' said Nicholas.

'It's that mournful little twisted-Nickers, the fly in my palm wine, the dog turd in my doughnut!' (or something of the sort) said the guard in Bateké. They yelled and laughed at each other, through the grille, above the noise of the crowd, in their ancient, semi-private language.

'Have you noticed,' Lary said to me, 'that we're the only honkies going on this trip?'

Nicholas turned to us. 'My brother says, Redmond, that he will let you through to clear your papers with Security. And now—I have to go! It is sad! You are the most sympathetic man I have ever had in my taxi!'

'Where's Marcellin?' said Lary.

'No idea.'

'He's saying goodbye to that girl. Or maybe—maybe it was a mistake, paying him all that money in advance. Perhaps he's going to keep the cash? Have done with us?'

'You guard the baggage.'

'How do I do that?'

'Sit on it.'

Nicholas's brother let me through the gap in the gate, shook my hand, laughed, slapped me on the back and pointed me into the dim interior. To the right, at the end of the warehouse-sized hall, a crowd pressed up against a brown metal grille.

Someone sidled out of the shadows and tugged at my sleeve. A very thin young man in blue jeans and a white T-shirt stood at my elbow. 'William Ipemba,' he said. 'Secret agent.'

'How do you do,' I said, nonplussed.

'Very well,' said William Ipemba. 'You need help?'

'I expect so.'

He took my arm and towed me into the semi-circular crush of subdued, anxious-looking men and women, each one holding an identity card.

'We ought to wait in the queue,' I said.

'There is no queue,' said William Ipemba, dragging me up to the grille. Behind it, a row of officials sat at a long table, examining papers, tickets, identity cards, checking lists, sweating, exchanging shouts with their supplicants through the bars.

William Ipemba took my ticket and passport, leafed the one inside the other and, with a backflip of the wrist, sent them spinning under the grille, across the table (scattering other people's papers as they went) into the lap of a clerk on the end of the row. The clerk, middle-aged, tired, was holding his spectacles in one hand and rubbing his eyes with the other. He replaced his spectacles and looked up, annoyed. We pushed our way down to him.

He scrutinized me and my passport and said, 'You are a big problem.'

'I know,' I said, attempting a smile.

'This is not funny,' he said, leaning back in his chair and handing my passport to an office boy, who disappeared with it through a door to the right.

'No!' I said, the smile jammed half-open.

'Security!'

A guard opened a narrow steel gate against the wall and beckoned us inside.

'The foreigner will see the Chief of the Port Police,' he said. He ushered me into a side-room and knocked twice at a black door. 'Enter!' came an uninviting shout. The guard pushed me in and shut the door at my back.

The Chief of the People's Port Police was wide and squat and wore a Sten gun. He sat facing me, my passport open on his desk.

'You have nothing,' he said. 'Nothing but an entry visa.'

I leaned forward, repossessed my passport, turned two pages, unfolded the precious taped-in document from the Ministry of Scientific Research and laid it in front of him. 'Look—here is my permission to journey in your country. I have the full authority of the Ministry of Scientific Research. Jean Ngatsiebe himself has signed it.'

The Chief of the People's Port Police stood up. I revised my initial impression: he was still wide and wearing a Sten gun, but only his top half was squat. His legs had towered him way above six feet. He unslung his Sten gun; he cocked it; he clattered it down on his papers, the stub of the barrel towards me. He ripped the stencilled form out of my passport.

'Ministry of nothing! Ministry for nothing of the least

importance! This is a piece of lavatory paper!' (He rubbed the form between his fingers.) It's not even quality lavatory paper!' (He took a deep breath.) 'Now get out, and come back with a proper visa.' (He looked at his gold watch.) 'You have five hours—and it takes ten days! Minimum!'

'We must go to Immigration,' said William Ipemba. 'But I warn you, our government does not encourage visitors. It is not easy.'

I gave him ten thousand CFA. William Ipemba at once lost his slight stoop; he hauled me through the crush of pectoral muscles and biceps and thrusting breasts and jamming buttocks with a sweaty, brutal dedication. Outside, Lary sat on the bags, encircled, two deep, by small boys, who stared at him, soundlessly.

Immigration was a two-storey building next to the town hall, opposite Brazzaville's main barracks. We squeezed up to a counter in a narrow room. 'There is no hope for you,' said the young girl facing me, with an incredulous laugh. 'None whatever.' William Ipemba, whom she obviously knew, pleaded; she ripped a square from her official notepad and scrawled, 'This is to certify that William Ipemba and his client called here. Anita.'

We took a taxi back to the port. The crowd had grown larger. Lary's light-blue denim shirt, I noticed, as I was swept past him and his incomprehensible shout, was now dark with sweat. 'So what is this?' said the Chief of the People's Port Police, taking a rabbit-chop at the chit in his palm; the square of paper, transformed into a V, butterflied down and settled on the floor; he put his boot on it. 'Out! You need a visa! It takes ten days! You have four hours left! You have wasted one hour! Ten days minimum! Out! Out!'

Outside, Marcellin had arrived. William Ipemba explained our problem.

'Redmond!' shouted Marcellin, his voice at its highest pitch, 'All this time—what the hell have you been doing?'

'I thought the Ministry permission was enough,' I said, feeling like a schoolboy.

'Idiot!' shouted Marcellin. 'Idiot!'

The depth of his anger was comforting; he cared; Marcellin would do something.

Back in Immigration, Marcellin let himself into offices marked PRIVATE, he was charming, his laugh was almost genuine, he knew everybody. Clean-shaven, in his long-sleeved white cotton shirt, his pressed jeans, his washed-white trainers, he really was a chef de service. I congratulated myself on picking companions made of the right stuff. 'I have informed this taxi-driver,' said Marcellin as we careered across the city, 'that you will pay him exactly double his normal fare, because he will drive at exactly double his normal speed.' Back at the port, we forced Lary to hand over his passport, inoculation certificates and return ticket (he gave it a frantic goodbye kiss). In the centre of the city, we found a photocopying shop (the manager insisted on trimming each piece of paper with a pair of nail-scissors); we drove to a shack in Poto-Poto to have our pictures taken; and in the poor quarter, down behind the railway-line, off a courtyard, in a building with no sign as to its present function, in the fourth concrete stall on the right sat a very old woman at a very small table, and in the middle of the table lay one book of the stamps required for the visas of long-stay visitors to the People's Republic of the Congo.

The Boat

Out in Malebo Pool, the Captain set his engines on slow ahead. Standing under the bridge, Lary and I watched a flotilla of ten small white tugs come out from the shore, form into a line, tie up down the port side of the barges and cut their engines. They were timber tugs, said Marcellin, they were hitching a lift upriver to collect their log-rafts.

Further up, by wide flat sandbanks covered with reed-grass, grey boats were waiting, plank-built, high-sided, upturned at the prow, squared off at the stern, some with flimsy roofs on gunwale struts and each one with an outboard motor—*baleinières*, said Marcellin, whaleboats; they, too, were going to ride upriver with us.

At every fold in the slow-moving hills, a stream supported a meagre twist of gallery forest, and by its outlet to the great river the huts of a fishing village would shelter beside a few giant cotton trees. Through the binoculars we sometimes saw women working in the plantations. Upstream, hanging in the current, paddling their dugouts standing up, were their menfolk. They thrust toward the floating city as we passed, and grabbed the fender of a timber-tug, the gunwale of a whaleboat, a rope thrown from the lower deck of the steamer or, most precarious of all, the side of another already-tethered dugout emptied of its crew and cargo and slewing, bucking, lashing its tail, frantic in the slipwaves from several thousand tons of kinetic energy.

The moment they tied up, bargaining began with the merchants on the steamer and the barges. The fishermen handed or threw up or carried aboard stacks of smoked fish; big, fresh, whiskery catfish; and zinc bowls full of little fish like whitebait. The booty would disappear into a pushing, shouting, gesticulating chaos of people. It was a relief to contemplate the young mother whose patch we stood beside: she filled a white enamel pail with brown river water; she undressed her timid little girl (yellow frock over the head), took a bar of white soap, washed her all over and rubbed her down with a red tea towel. She cupped out a handful of palm oil from a blue plastic jerrycan and worked it slowly into the little girl's skin, attentive to every crease and to the spaces between the toes. Satisfied, she lit a stove in an empty paint can and began to boil up a saucepan of drinking water. The child, lustrous, wearing nothing but a tin bracelet on her left tiny wrist, sat down heavily in the middle of her washing-puddle and, absorbed, with her right index finger she began to draw secret, watery, toddler symbols on the iron deck.

'Redmond,' came a familiar high-pitched shout. 'Where did you get to? Come and buy us a beer!'

Marcellin, triumphant, was holding the hand of a young girl.

'Her name's Marie,' he said. 'We'll go to the bar.'

'The bar?'

'Of course!'

As we jostled down the stairwell to the lower deck there was a long broken scream, shouting, beneath us, from outside. We pushed up to the rail: six empty dugouts were tied to the *Impfondo* in a quarter-fan, their painters attached to a single loop of cable, their sterns swinging free. An overloaded dugout was attempting to dock alongside the outermost hull: the bow-paddler, a teenage boy in red nylon shorts, pigeon-chested, his shoulders thin, had somehow lost his paddle overboard. He was half-kneeling, his left hand on the gunwale, his right lunging for the paddle—just out of reach, spinning, disappearing, gathering speed in the current. The canoe rocked; the fisherman at the stern dug his own paddle into the water, trying to propel the boat forward against the wake of the *Impfondo* and the force of the current; the men and women around us yelled instructions; in the dugout, an old woman, naked to the waist, sitting amidships behind a humped pile of belongings—pots, pans, buckets, a yellow cushion, a net, a foam mattress, a stack of smoked fish—held a baby to her wrinkled breasts and screamed.

The stern of the furthest canoe in the fan swung out and clipped the bow where the boy crouched: still clutching the gunwale with his left hand, he pitched into the water. The dugout rolled over. The long, narrow, upturned hull glistened wet in the sunlight; the *adze*-marks, the hundreds of hours of patient work, were clearly visible on the burned-black wood.

The foam mattress, the baby and the grandmother, the yellow cushion and the fisherman surfaced, in that order. The upturned hull jarred against the sterns of the inner dugouts, smacked into the steel side of the *Impfondo* and was sucked beneath the ship. The grandmother, her lungs obviously in prime condition, held the baby's head above water and screamed.

Two young men in an approaching dugout, loaded with fish, abandoned their own attempt to dock (and so any chance of trade for another two or three weeks) and, with a virtuoso display of balance and control, they pulled the grandmother, the baby and the fisherman from the water. Everyone cheered. The young men waved, dropping back in the current, heading for the distant shore.

I trained my binoculars on the boy—he was moving downriver at speed, well ahead of the chopped-up sections of dugout splintered by the steamer's screws, the paddle still just out of reach. I thought: was it a last present from his dead father? Did he borrow it from a sorcerer? Or is he just not quite right in the head?

And then, as he was swept past the only remaining dugout that might have saved him, I realized that he and the paddle were simply caught in the same current, midstream, in the deep fast waters of Le Couloir. A long way back, his black head bobbed in and out of focus in the white light, the glare of the river—and disappeared.

'He's gone!' I shouted. 'Tell the captain! He's gone!'

Marcellin put his free arm hard round my shoulders and pulled me against him like an errant child. 'Quiet,' he said. 'You're the only person who saw it. You and the Captain are the only people on this ship who possess binoculars. You're a foreigner. Why should anyone believe you? The story goes like this: everyone lost overboard is picked up by fishermen. OK?'

'But he's gone! I saw his head—it disappeared!'

'That's enough,' said Marcellin sharply, releasing his grip. 'You keep calm. There's nothing to be done. This ship never turns back. It can't. You can't turn around with three or four thousand people on barges in this current. It can't be done.'

'But he's drowned!'

'So he's drowned,' said Marcellin, looking out across the water at a village on the opposite bank. 'This is the best-governed country in Africa, our people are the best educated. There's no war, no famine. But it's still Africa. Where we're going—you'll hear wailing women all day long. If you make a fuss like that every time someone dies, my friend, you won't last. You'll be wasting my time. We won't complete our mission.'

That night, under the Southern Cross, Marcellin, Marie, Lary and I sat in colonial chairs, drinking whisky from our plastic mugs, the steamer's lights reflected in the water alongside us, the deck-plates juddering to the engines.

'It's that oxtail we had at dinner,' said Lary, as I handed out a couple of codeine-phosphate diarrhoea-blockers apiece and poured everyone a second quarter-mug of Johnnie Walker. 'Why should we have to eat the rotting ass-end of some animal when this whole boat is flapping with fresh fish? And the way that purser grins when he serves it up! You can bet your butt he wouldn't touch that stuff himself.'

'Meat like that is a luxury,' said Marcellin. 'The company provides it. First class. Besides, the purser has a family. He buys all the fish he can and stores it wherever he can and then he'll sell it in Impfondo. He needs money. He has a family.'

'Most everyone has a family.'

'No, no, my friend, not your kind of family, with two children and a car and a dog and a house full of machines. I mean an African family. It's hopeless. It's the cause of all our problems. Lary Shaffer—I've heard you talk about corruption. You call it corruption but that is not the case. The true explanation is this: the African family. I myself—I have a wife and two children just like you do in the West, but my mother, she has fifteen children, six from my own father and nine from Kossima, the husband she took when my father left her in Impfondo and moved to Brazzaville. I am the eldest son. I went with him. I studied hard. We were poor. We had no electricity. I did my homework under a street-lamp, and when it rained I put a sheet of polythene over my book and my head. I sat for my secondary studies exam in 1966, when I was fifteen, and I did well—I did brilliantly!—I went to the best school in Africa, the Lycée Savorgnan de Brazza in Brazzaville. I was taught by famous Frenchmen, terrible strict men who cared about you, who really made you learn things; I got my *baccalauréat* in natural science and I won a scholarship to Cuba, to Havana, to university. I got away! I escaped!'

'Well done!' said Lary, excited at the prospect himself, 'Well done! Good for you!'

'Then I won a scholarship to go to France! To the Montpellier International Centre of Advanced Tropical Agronomic Studies and Forestry Studies, and I presented a scientific paper on the conception and management of a zoological park, a protected area. And I am still working for my doctorate on the biology of crocodiles with the Natural History Museum of Paris. So I'm telling you, it's obvious, isn't it? I do not deserve to be poor. I am a scientist. I am highly educated. I speak French, Spanish and English. Yet I return home—and what happens? I have become a Big Man! The head of the family! Now I don't want to be a Big Man or the head of anybody's family, but that makes no difference—the moment I get my job in the Ministry of Water and Forests and earn some money and rent a house, then any one of my mother's fifteen children and their wives and their relations by marriage, any one of my father's new family, all those cousins, they can all just turn up and sit on my new chairs and eat all the food in my fridge before I come home from work—and then it's Dr Marcellin this and Dr Marcellin that and do look at the holes in my shoes I need some new trainers and if only I had a big leather briefcase from that shop I'd be sure to get a job in an office—you wouldn't believe it! One of them wanted me to buy him a taxi! A taxi! So I thought—why bother? Why bother to work or be successful or try harder when you're expected to share out everything you have? But I outwitted them. I fooled them. I stopped it. I moved to a really small house with three tiny rooms, and in the first of those rooms, by the door to the compound and the street, I dug a shallow pit, and in that shallow pit I put two crocodiles. They trust no one but me. I promise you—they can tell if you're frightened. They're fierce!'

'But your wife,' said Marie, 'do they trust your wife?'

'No!' shouted Marcellin, committing himself. 'They hate her! They snap at her! They lash their tails! At mealtimes—she has to stand right back and throw their fish to them! Besides,' he said, scooping Marie up in his arms, sitting down again and placing her sideways on his lap, 'when a man owns crocodiles, it means something.'

'What does it mean?' I said, overeager.

'You'll find out,' said Marcellin languidly, his right hand on Marie's left breast. 'Whereas for you, Marie, my crocodiles—they wouldn't snap at you. I think they'd start here' (with his free hand he eased off her left sandal) 'your toes—the first nibble—it's always at your toes' (she sighed) 'they have all these teeth, you see, rows and rows of teeth, with lots and lots of others waiting to replace them, pushing up hard from underneath . . . '

'It's time to go,' said Lary to me sharply, gathering up the plastic mugs; and we walked forward to our cabin along the companion-way, stepping over sleeping bodies as we went.

The next day, collapsed in our bunks, halfway through our early afternoon, ninety-five-degree-heat-exhaustion siesta, we were woken by a hammering knock on the cabin door.

'We've been buzzed!' came Marcellin's shout from outside.

'Quick! Quick! We've been buzzed!'

'Buzzed?' said Lary, opening the door, letting in the blinding light. 'Buzzed?'

'The Zairois! A Zairean military helicopter! It flew right over us, really low, like that'—he skimmed the flat of his right hand over his left—'We thought we'd be machine-gunned. The Captain—he has radioed for more soldiers. The Marines are coming!'

'Oh God,' said Lary.

And an hour or so later, as we watched from below the bridge, a timber-tug and a speedboat from the Marxist-Leninist bank joined the *Impfondo*. Twenty-five marines began to search the ship and the barges (for fifth columnists? Spies? Weapons? 'For beer,' said Marcellin); and an hour or so after that, from the second barge up on the port side, there came a bang and a scream loud enough to be heard above the thumping of the diesels.

Marcellin, squaring his shoulders, straightening his back, becoming an official of the People's Republic, ordering us to stay where we were, ran down to investigate—and returned just as four marines, a fifth holding a saline drip, carried one of their number to the speedboat, yanked the outboard to life and set off downriver.

'Drunk,' said Marcellin. 'Shot himself in the leg. He was standing up, bending forward. The bullet travelled down his thigh, re-entered via the calf muscle, came out at his ankle and ricocheted overboard. I saw him lying on the deck. He was screaming—he lay screaming in a pool of blood. The medic injected him with morphine. He had a lot of blood, a great deal of blood. Kalashnikovs—they're powerful. Myself—I don't think he'll live.'

I decided that the time had come to give Marcellin his presents—a pair of binoculars (hidden in the medicine kitbag), a briar pipe from Savory's in Oxford, a tin of Balkan Sobranie, a machete in its scabbard, a floppy jungle-hat, a webbing belt and two attachable water-bottles.

'Thank you,' said Marcellin with his biggest smile, placing the hat on his head, the binoculars round his neck, the pipe and tobacco in his pocket. 'But don't expect anyone else to say thank you' (he snapped on the belt-kit) 'because this is Africa. There is no word for thank you in Lingala. Here you give someone a present because they've earned it, or because they're part of your family, or because you expect something from them.'

'Quite right,' I said.

Lary and I found a spare patch of deck against the mess-cabin and settled down to read. Marcellin joined us, still wearing his hat, binoculars and belt-kit but with a Walkman clipped to the webbing and earphones under the hat.

There was a long ululating wail from the deck below, screams, a rhythmic chanting.

'Marcellin,' I said, shaking his shoulder, 'What's that?'

'What's that?' yelled Marcellin; then he pushed his headphones back from his ears and listened.

'I forgot to tell you,' he said. 'A baby died this afternoon. The mother gave it unboiled water to drink. Diarrhoea. It's a boy. The mother cries out for her husband—but he is in Impfondo. The father does not know that his son is dead.'

We were silent.

'Go on,' said Marcellin, readjusting his headphones. 'Go and pay your respects.'

The baby was lying on a mattress, face up, wrapped in a white sheet. Two benches flanked the little body: on one the mother sat, rocking from side to side, held by two friends, her eyes shut; on the other, six women sang their sad songs and beat time with gourd-rattles full of seeds.

Impfondo

Outside our cabins, Marcellin swung his small blue rucksack on to his shoulders and Lary and I struggled into our packs. We made our slow way down the gangplank and along the line of barges.

On the ramp, a soldier inspected our papers—and pocketed our passports.

'It's OK,' said Marcellin. 'I know all the soldiers, all the officers. Trust me.'

'Trust my aunt,' muttered Lary, reaching for the soldier's pocket.

'Don't touch!' shouted Marcellin, grabbing Lary's wrist.

The soldier smiled.

'Lary, Redmond,' said Marcellin, pointing to the low, yellow-painted wall of the dock-building, 'pile the packs over there. Sit on them. Guard them. Impfondo is full of thieves. I'll be back. I must see Joseph. I must get the truck.' And he disappeared into the crowd.

'Truck?' said Lary, intoning the magic word. 'Truck?'

A little swallow was criss-crossing the air fifty feet above us, the crowd, the sweat, the noise. Its delicate tail was deeply forked, its white breast lined with black speckles, its head chestnut, its wings grey beneath, dark blue above. It should have been named, I thought, the untroubled, the perfectly happy whizz-diving swallow, and not, as Serle and Morel boringly told us, the lesser striped; and it appeared to be hunting the same insects as the pair of another species, the absolutely ordinary comforting European house martin.

'Lary,' I said, 'do you realize we've seen four species of swallows and martins already? Without even trying! But I'm sorry, I'm really sorry we missed the African river martin—that's the strangest of them all, confined to the Congo and Oubangui rivers with a few on the Gabon coast. It's all black with a big round head and red eyes. It hovers, it runs like a pratincole, it nests in burrows, it tunnels into the flat sand bars in the middle of the rivers. It's bizarre.'

'Look,' said Lary, swotting a small green fly on his cheek. 'I realize that for you the real journey is only just beginning. But for me that boat trip was the most extraordinary, and also the grimmest experience of my life. The dead baby, the people drowned, all for nothing. And pratincole, what's that? A rude word. Birds, sure, I like to see them around. But when they're that size, they're off my map, they're just too small, they're LBJs.'

'LBJs?'

'Little Brown Jobs.'

'But those are blue! And the African sand martin—that's black!'

'Correction,' said Lary. 'Little Blue Jobs. Little Black Jobs.'

JULIAN BARNES
GNOSSIENNE

L et me make it clear that I never attend literary conferences. I know that they're held in art deco hotels close to legendary museums; that sessions on the future of the novel are conducted with *camaraderie, brio* and *bonhomie*; that the impromptu friendships always endure; and that after the work is done you may savour hard liquor, soft drugs and a fair slither of sex. Taxi-drivers in Frankfurt are said to dislike the annual Book Fair because literary folk, instead of being shuttled to prostitutes like respectable members of other convening professions, prefer to stay in their hotels and fuck one another. I also know that literary conferences are held in mafia-built blocks whose air-conditioning throbs with typhoid, tetanus and diphtheria; that the organizers are international snobs seeking local tax write-offs; that delegates covet the free air ticket and the chance to bore their rivals in several different languages simultaneously; that in the presumed democracy of art everyone acknowledges and therefore resents their place in the true hierarchy; and that not a single novelist, poet, essayist or even journalist has ever left that mafia hotel a better writer than he or she entered it. I know all this, as I say, because I have never attended a single literary conference.

My replies are sent on postcards free of my own address: 'Sorry, no'; 'Don't do conferences'; 'Regret travelling elsewhere in the world'; and so on. The opening line of my reply to French invitations was not perfected for some years. Eventually it became: *'Je regrette que je ne suis pas conférencier ni de tempérament ni d'aptitude . . . '* I was rather pleased with this: if I pleaded mere incapacity it might be read as modesty, and if I pleaded temperamental unsuitability alone, conditions might be improved until it would be too difficult for me to refuse. This way I had rendered myself invulnerable to any comeback.

It was the sheer amateurishness of the invitation to Marrant that made me read it twice. Perhaps I don't mean amateurish; more old-fashioned, as if it came from a vanished world. There was no municipal seal, no promise of five-star accommodation, no menu-list for S&M devotees of literary theory. The paper was unheaded, and though the signature looked original, the text above it had that faded, blurry, purply look of the Roneo machine or pre-war carbon paper. Some of the letters on the

Photo: B. Barbey (Magnum)

original typewriter (clearly an old manual, with sticky-up keys for a single-finger operator to peck at) were cracked. I noted all this; but what I most noted—what made me wonder briefly if I might for once have the temperament or the aptitude—was the sentence which stood by itself above the signature. The main text explained that the conference would take place in a certain small village in the Massif Central on a particular day in October. My presence would be welcome but a reply was not expected; I merely had to arrive by one of the three trains listed overleaf. Then came the second paragraph, which consisted of the following statement of intent: 'The point of the conference consists in being met at the station: attendance is performance.'

I checked the letter again. No, I wasn't being asked to give a paper, sit on a panel, fret about Whither the Novel. I wasn't being wooed with an A-list of fellow *conférenciers*. I wasn't being offered my fare, my hotel bill, let alone a fee. I frowned at the looping signature untranslated into type. There was something familiar about it, which I eventually located, as I did the insouciance and cheeky familiarity of tone, in a particular French literary tradition: Jarry, pataphysics, Queneau, Perec, the OULIPO group and so on. The official unofficials, the honoured rebels. Jean-Luc Cazes, yes, surely he was one of that gang. A bit of a surprise that he was still alive. What was that definition of pataphysics? 'The science of imagining solutions.' And the point of the conference consisted in being met at the station.

I didn't have to reply: this, I think, was what enchanted me. I didn't have to say whether I was going or not. So the letter rose and fell among that sticky scatter of bills and receipts, invitations and VAT forms, proofs, begging letters and PLR print-outs which is to be found on most writers' desks. One afternoon I got out the appropriate yellow Michelin map: no. 76. There it was: Marrant-sur-Cère, thirty or forty kilometres short of Aurillac. The railway line from Clermont-Ferrand ran straight through the village, whose name, I noticed, wasn't underlined in red. So no listing in the Michelin guide. I double-checked, in case my yellow map was out of date, but there was no entry, nor one in the *Logis de France* either. Where would they put me up? It wasn't a part of the Cantal I was familiar with. I grazed the map for a few minutes, making it work like a pop-up book: steep hill, *point de vue*, hikers' trail, *maison forestière*. I imagined chestnut groves, truffle-hounds, forest clearings where charcoal-makers had once practised. Small mahogany cows jigged on the slopes of extinct volcanoes to the music of local bagpipes. I imagined all this, because my actual memories of the Cantal reduced to two items: cheese and rain.

The English autumn succumbed to the first spiky prod of winter; fallen leaves were sugar-dusted by early frost. I flew to Clermont-Ferrand and stayed the night at the Albert-Elisabeth (*sans restaurant*). At the station the next morning, I did as I had been told: I booked a ticket to Vic-sur-Cère without mentioning to the clerk that my actual destination was Marrant. Certain trains—the three listed on my invitation—would stop at Marrant, but they would do so exceptionally, and by private arrangement with certain individuals connected with the railway. This touch of mystery pleased me: I felt a spy's relish when the departures board showed no intermediate stop between Murat and Vic-sur-Cère. I had only hand-luggage anyway: the train would slow as if for a routine red light, would pause, squeak, exhale, and in that moment I would make a goblin disembarkation, shutting the door with a sly caress. If anyone saw me get off, they would assume I was an SNCF employee being done a favour by the driver.

I had been imagining some old-fashioned French train, the ferrovial equivalent of the Roneoed invitation, but I found myself in a smartly-liveried, four-carriage job with driver-controlled doors. I updated my descent at Marrant: I would rise from my seat as we left Murat, stand casually close to the door, wait for the conspiratorial humph of compressed air and be gone before the other passengers could miss me. I managed the first part of the manoeuvre without trouble; ostentatiously casual, I didn't even look through the glass as the anticipated deceleration finally took hold. The train stopped, the doors opened and I got off. To my surprise I was hustled from behind by what I logically took to be other *conférenciers*—except that they were two broad-hipped, headscarfed women of uplands rubicundity whom you would expect to see behind a trestle table selling six eggs and a rabbit rather than signing copies of their latest novel. My second surprise was to read the words VIC-SUR-CÈRE. Shit! I must have been dreaming—my station must be after Vic, not before. I scooted back between the humphing doors and pulled out my invitation. Shit again! I'd been right before. So much for private arrangements with certain individuals. The bloody driver had gone straight through Marrant. Obviously no taste for literature, that fellow. I was swearing, and yet in a remarkably good mood.

At Aurillac I hired a car and took the N126 back up the Cère valley. I passed through Vic, and began looking out for a D-road east to Marrant. The weather was closing in, a fact I noted with benign neutrality. Normally I'm intolerant of fuck-ups: I find that enough things go wrong at my desk without more going wrong in all the contingent aspects of the literary life. The inert microphone at a public reading; the self-erasing tape-recorder; the journalist whose questions fail to fit any of the answers you might be capable of fabricating in an entire lifetime. I once did an interview for French radio in a Paris hotel room. There was a sound-check, the recordist pressed the switch and, as the spools began to circle, the interviewer shaved my chin with the microphone. 'Monsieur Clements,' he asked, with a kind of intimate authority, *'le mythe et la réalité?'* I stared at him for quite some time, feeling my French evaporate and my brain dry. Eventually, I gave him the only answer I could: that such questions and their appropriate responses no doubt came naturally to French intellectuals, but that since I was a mere pragmatic English novelist, he would get a better interview out of me if he perhaps approached larger matters by way of smaller, lighter ones. This would also, I explained, help warm up my French for me. He smiled in concord, the engineer wound back the tape and the microphone was placed again like a tear-glass to catch my drops of wisdom. 'Monsieur Clements, we are sitting here in your hotel room in Paris one afternoon in April. The window is open, and outside is unrolling the daily life of the city. Opposite the window is a wardrobe with a tall mirror in the door. I look in the wardrobe mirror and in it I see reflected the daily life of Paris which is unrolling outside the window. Monsieur Clements, *le mythe et la réalité?'*

The D-road climbed sharply towards a barrier of high mist or low cloud. I switched on my windscreen wipers in anticipation; then twisted the headlights to full beam, prodded the fog-lamp, wound the window down a little and chuckled. What an absurd idea to escape from an English October to one of the wettest parts of France: like the American who saw the Second World War coming and relocated to Guadalcanal. Visibility was no more than a few metres, the road was narrow, and on the nearside the ground dropped away into the unknown. Through my half-open window I thought I heard cowbells, a goat and the squeal of bagpipes, unless it was just a pig. My mood continued to be one of cheerful certainty. I didn't feel like an anxious tourist groping for a destination; more a confident writer who knows where his book is going.

I came out of wet mist into sudden sunlight and a sky of Ingres blue. The village of Marrant was deserted: the shops had their shutters down; the trays of vegetables outside the *épicerie* were covered with sacking; a dog snoozed on a doorstep. The church clock showed two-fifty but creakily struck three as I looked. The *boulangerie* had its opening hours engraved into the glass of its door: 8h–12h, 16h–19h. It made me feel nostalgic: those old-fashioned timings ruled when I first came to France. If you hadn't bought your picnic lunch by twelve you went hungry, because everyone knows that in French villages the *charcutier* has to take four hours off to sleep with the baker's wife, the baker four hours to sleep with the owner of the *quincaillerie* and so on. As for Mondays: forget it. Everything would shut down from Sunday lunchtime to Tuesday morning. Now the pan-European commercial impulse had reached everywhere in France, except, oddly, here.

The station also had a lunch-time look as I approached it. The booking-office and newsagent's kiosk were both closed, though for some reason the public-address system seemed to be broadcasting music. An amateurish brass band oompahing away: Scott Joplin by the sound of it. I pushed open a grimy glass door, turned on to an unswept platform, noticed thistles growing between the sleepers and saw, to my left, a small welcoming party. A mayor, or at least a man looking like a mayor, from sash of

157

office to chinstrap beard. Behind him was the most peculiar municipal band I had ever seen: one cornet, one tuba and a serpent, all going hard at the same bit of ragtime, music-hall or whatever. The mayor, young, plumpish and sallow, stepped forward, grasped my upper arms and gave me a ceremonial two-cheek kiss.

'Thank you for meeting me,' I said automatically.

'Attendance is performance,' he replied, smiling. 'We hope you are pleased to hear the music of your country.'

'I'm not American, I'm afraid.'

'Nor was Satie,' said the mayor. 'Ah, you didn't know that his mother was Scottish? Well. The piece is called "Le Piccadilly". Shall we continue?'

For some reason unknown to myself yet approved by the mayor, I fell in directly behind him and kept step as he led the way. Behind me the *ad hoc* trio struck up 'Le Piccadilly' again. I got to know the piece pretty well, since it lasts just over a minute and they played it seven or eight times as we processed down the platform, over an unguarded level crossing and through the sleeping town. I expected the *charcutier* to protest that the brassy blast was affecting his sexual concentration with the baker's wife, or at least an inquisitive urchin to speed out of a shady alley-way, but we passed only a few sleeping pets, who behaved as if this three o'clock concert was normal. Not a shutter stirred.

The village petered out by a lilting *lavoir*, a humpy bridge and a spread of immaculate but untenanted allotments. An old Citroën appeared from nowhere and suavely overtook us. You don't see many of those cars any more: you know, the black ones that sit wide and hippy on the road, running boards at the side, Maigret at the wheel. But I didn't spot the driver as he disappeared in a dusty curve.

We passed the cemetery, with my backing group still pomping out 'Le Piccadilly'. A high wall, only the steeply tops of a few tombs visible, then a quick view through a chained gate. Sun flashed on glass: I had forgotten the custom of building little greenhouses over and around the tombs. Is it symbolic protection for the departed, self-interest for the mourners or simply a way of ensuring fresh flowers for a longer season? I never found a gravedigger to ask. In any case, you don't really want answers to every question. About your own country, perhaps. But about others? Leave some space for reverie, for amical invention.

We halted outside the gates of a small manor-house of proportions laid down by God. Biscuity stone, thunder-grey slate roof, modest pepper-pot towers at each corner. A venerable wisteria in a miraculous second flowering hung over the front door, which was reached by double-sided steps which no doubt once doubled as a mounting block. The mayor and I now walked side by side across the gravel, our feet inciting a distant, unthreatening bark from the stables. Behind the house were some rising beech woods; to the left a shaded pond with several varieties of edible wildlife; beyond it a sloping meadow eased towards the sort of lush valley that the British would convert into a golf-course. I stopped; the mayor propelled me forward by an elbow. I climbed two steps, paused to inhale the wisteria blossom, climbed six more, turned and saw that he had disappeared. I was not in the mood to be surprised—or rather, what would normally have surprised me struck me as perfectly understandable. In ordinary, pedantic life I might have asked myself at what precise point the band had stopped playing, whether the Citroën was garaged in the stables, why I hadn't heard the mayor's feet on the gravel. Instead, I merely thought, I am here, they are gone. Normally, I would have tugged on the bell-pull which hung down through a rusty, iron ring; instead I pushed the door.

Part of me expected a bobbing chambermaid in black with a gauffered mob-cap and an apron tied with a floppy double bow in the middle of her arching back. Instead, I found some more purply Roneoed words informing me that my room was at the top of the stairs and that I would be expected in the *salon* at seven-thirty. The boards creaked, as I knew they would, in a comforting rather than sinister fashion. The shutters of my room were propped half-open, giving enough light for me to take in the jug and bowl on a marble washstand, the brass bedstead, the curvy armoire. A Bonnard interior, lacking only a cat, or perhaps Mme Bonnard sponging herself in the bathroom. I lay on the bed and hovered half-way to sleep, untempted by dreams, unperturbed by reality.

How can I describe the sense of being there, in that village, in that room, the familiarity of it all? It was not, as you might think, the familiarity of memory. The best way I can explain it is to make a literary comparison, which seems fair enough in the circumstances. Gide once said that he wrote in order to be reread. About ten years ago I interviewed Michel Tournier, who quoted me this line, paused and added with a certain smiling complacency, 'Whereas *I* write to be reread on the first occasion.' Do you see what I mean?

Downstairs at seven-thirty, I was greeted by Jean-Luc Cazes, one of those old-fashioned, Left-Bank, anarcho-rock characters in a tired leather blouson and with a pipe wedged in the corner of his mouth; the sort of genial zinc-bar philosopher you suspect has an alarming success rate among women. Handing me a *vin blanc* so viscous with cassis that you suspect Canon Kir must have had a lot of inferior white wine on his hands, he introduced me to the other guests: a Spanish poet, an Algerian film-maker, an Italian semiotician, a Swiss crime-writer, a German dramatist and a Belgian art critic. Cazes was fluent in all our languages, though we each spoke French more or less approximately. I meant to ask the others about their invitations, their arrivals, their receptions, their tunes, but somehow it never came to that; or if it did, I have forgotten.

Dinner was served by a shy peasant girl with high, nasal vowels, her *a* moving towards *i*: '*Si vous n'ivez pas suffisimint, vous n'ivez qu'à deminder,*' she told us with nervous authority. A thick, cabbagy, ham-bony soup which I imagined snoring gently in a large copper for five days or so. A tomato salad with a vinegary dressing. An omelette *aux fines herbes* which ran *baveuse* when you put the spoon into it. A plate of pink *gigot* with gravy. Round, big-beaned *haricots verts* cooked until floppy, and drenched in butter. Salad. Four types of cheese. A fruit bowl. Wine in unlabelled litre bottles with a row of stars across the shoulder like an American general. Cutlery handed down from course to course. Coffee and a *vieille prune.*

We talked easily: this was not, after all, a conference, and M. Cazes was less *animateur* than encouraging presence. The others . . . you know, I can't remember what they said, though at the time it made sense to me, especially in the light of what I knew, or thought I knew, about their reputations. For myself, I discovered an improbable spontaneity when my turn came to address the table. I had, of course, prepared nothing, secure in the promise that attendance was performance; yet I eased into a confident *tour d'horizon* of various French cultural topics, and managed strangely well. I talked about *Le Grand Meaulnes*, *Le Petit Prince*, Greuze, Astérix, the *comédie larmoyante*, Bernardin de Saint-Pierre, pre-Great War railway posters, Rousseau, Offenbach, the early films of Fernandel and the semiotic significance of the yellow triangular—nay, tricornic—Ricard ashtray. You should understand that this is not how I normally behave. I have a poor memory and little capacity for generalization. I prefer to discuss a single book, or better still a single chapter, or best of all a single page which I happen to have in front of me.

I told them a story to illustrate what I meant by Gallic charm. I once appeared on *Apostrophes*, the television book programme, with a French novelist who had written the autobiography of his cat. He was a well-known writer who had unhooked several domestic literary prizes. When the host asked him about the composition of his latest work, he replied, 'I did not write the book, my cat wrote the book.' This response irritated the host, who began attacking the novelist. 'I did not write the book,' he replied every time, a Gauloise smokescreening his white polo-necked sweater and mustachioed smile, 'My cat wrote the book.' We all chuckled at this example of whimsical provocation.

I'd better warn you that there was no *coup*. No sudden electrical storm across a midnight sky, no *feux d'artifice* or irruption of mime artists. No one walked towards a full-length mirror, arm mythically extended, to vanish into and beyond it; there were no *visiteurs du soir*. Nor was there a *coup* in the French sense: no flamboyant episode with svelte *conférencière* or tangy servant-girl; Mme Bonnard did not get out of her bath for me. We went to bed early after shaking hands all round.

Cheese is supposed to provoke bad dreams, but the combination of Brie, Saint-Nectaire and Pont-l'Evèque (I had declined the Bon Bel) had the opposite effect. I slept eventlessly, without even one of those tranquil episodes in which someone whom I knew to be me but was not me moved across landscapes both strange and familiar towards a reward both surprising yet predictable. I woke clear-headed to the sound of a late-season bumble-bee butting against the peeling slats of the shutters. Downstairs, I dipped my still-warm baguette into my bowl of hot chocolate and set off for the station before the others were up. Dewy spiders' webs caught the early-morning sun like Christmas decorations. I heard a clattering behind me and was overtaken by one of those itinerant butcher's vans made from silvery corrugated metal. At the station I picked up my car and drove through the village which seemed dormant, though I could see that the pavement in front of the shops had already been sluiced and broomed. It was seven-forty, and the creaky church clock struck the three-quarter.

When I started the car, my headlights and wipers came on, and I soon needed both as I headed down through damp morning mist to rejoin the N126. At Aurillac, another smart, four-carriage train was ready to take me to Clermont-Ferrand. There were few passengers, and my view was unimpeded; at times, I could even see the N126, which helped locate me. We stopped at Vic-sur-Cère and thereafter I paid particular attention. I was apprehensive about that misty cloud, but the soft October sun must have burnt it off. I watched, I switched my head regularly from side to side, I listened out for the train's warning whistle, and all I can say is that we didn't pass through the station of Marrant-sur-Cère.

As the plane ended its first curving climb, and the levelling wing erased the Puy-de-Dôme, I remembered the name of the French writer who had written the autobiography of his cat. I also remembered my reaction as I sat next to him in the studio: you pretentious twat, I thought, or some such words. The French writers I am loyal to run from Montaigne to Voltaire to Flaubert to Mauriac to Camus. Does it need saying that I am unable to read Le Petit Prince and find most of Greuze nauseating? I am sentimental about clarity of thought, emotional about rationality.

When I was an adolescent I used to come to France with my parents for motoring holidays. I had never seen a Bonnard. The only cheese I would eat was Gruyère. I despaired of the way they ruined tomatoes with vinaigrette. I could not understand why you had to eat all your meat before you got your vegetables. I wondered why they put grass-clippings in their omelettes. I loathed red wine. Nor was it just the alimentary apprehension: I was nervous about the language, the sleeping arrangements, the hotels. The absorbed tensions of a family holiday played on me. I was not happy, to put the matter simply. Like most adolescents, I needed the science of imaginary solutions. Is all nostalgia false, I wonder, and all sentimentality the representation of unfelt emotions?

Jean-Luc Cazes, I discovered from my encyclopedia, was a writer invented by the OULIPO group and used as a front for various promotional and provocational enterprises. *Marrant* is the French for funny, which of course I had known before I set off: where else would you expect a pataphysical encounter to take place? I have not seen any of my fellow-participants since that day, which isn't surprising. And I have still never been to a literary conference.

MICHAEL PYE

THE DROWNING ROOM

THE STORY OF GRETJE REYNIERS,
FIRST WHORE OF NEW YORK

IN THE SEVENTEENTH century, when the Dutch first established a
settlement on Manhattan, Gretje Reyniers—moneylender and pelt-dealer
—was the town whore. She's there in the records: whom she slandered and
sued; who sued and slandered her back; debts welshed on; debts demanded;
minor assaults; charges of lewdness. But nothing more is known of her.

In this remarkable novel, Michael Pye has conjured a life for Gretje
and created a heroine of indomitable spirit and strength.

Hardback £13.99
Published 25 May 1995

WILLIAM BOYD
NEVER SAW BRAZIL

On one of the sunniest of bright May mornings, Senator Dom Liceu Maximiliano Lobo needlessly ran his comb through his neat goatee and ordered his chauffeur to pull into the side of the road. On mornings like these he liked to walk the remaining five hundred metres to his office, which he maintained, out of sentiment's sake and because of the sea breezes, in Salvador's *Cidade Alta*. He sauntered along the sidewalks, debating pleasantly whether to linger a moment with a coffee and a newspaper on the terrace of the hotel, or whether to stop off at Olimpia's little apartment, which he kept for her, at very reasonable expense, in an old colonial building in a square near the cathedral. She would not be expecting him, and it might be an amusing, not to say sensuous, experience to dally an hour or so this early before the day's work called. How bright the sun was this fine morning, Senator Dom Liceu Maximiliano Lobo thought as he turned towards the cathedral, his heels ringing on the cobbles, and how vivid the solar benefaction made the geraniums. Life was indeed good.

* * *

The name was a problem, he saw. The problem lay there, definitely. Because . . . Because if you were not happy with your name, he realized, then a small, but sustained, lifelong stress was imposed on your psyche, your sense of self. It was like being condemned to wear too-small shoes all the time: you could still get about, but there would always be a pinching, a corn or two aching, something unnaturally hobbled about your gait.

Wesley Bright. Wesley. Bright.

The trouble with his name was that it wasn't quite stupid enough—he was not a Wesley Bilderbeest or a Wesley Bugger; in fact, it was almost a good name. If he had been Wesley Blade, say, or Wesley Beauregard, he would have no complaints.

'Wesley?'

Janice passed him the docket. He clicked the switch on the mike.

'Four-seven? Four-seven?'

Silence. Just the permanent death-rattle of the ether.

Four-seven answered. 'Four-seven.'

Photo: David Hoffman

167

'Parcel, Four-seven. Pick up at Track-Track. Going to Putney as directed.'

'Account?'

Wesley sighed. 'Yes, Four-seven. We do not do cash.'

'Oh, yeah. Roger, Rog.'

He could always change his name, he supposed. Roger, perhaps. Roger Bright. Wesley Roger . . . No. There was that option, though: choose a new moniker, a new handle. But he wondered about that too: hard to shake off an old name, he would guess. It was the way you thought of yourself, after all, your tag on the pigeon-hole. And when you were young, you never thought your name was odd—it was a dissatisfaction that came with ageing, in his case a realization that he didn't really like being a 'Wesley Bright' sort of person at all. For him, it had started at college, this chafing, this discomfort. And it would not go away. He often wondered about these fellows, actors and rock musicians, who called themselves Tsar, or Zane Zorro, or DJ Sofaman . . . He was sure that, to themselves, they were always Norman Sidcup or Wilbur Dongdorfer in their private moments.

'Wesley?'

Janice handed him the phone receiver. 'It's your Pauline. Wants a word.'

* * *

Colonel Liceu 'o Falcão' Lobo opened his eyes and he saw the sun had risen sharp and green through the leaf mass outside his bedroom. He shifted and stretched and felt the warm flank of Nilda brush his thigh. He eased himself out of bed and stood naked in the green-bright gloom. He freed his sweaty balls, tugging delicately at his scrotum. He rubbed his face and chest, inhaled, walked quietly out on to the balcony and felt the cool morning on his nakedness. He stood there, the wooden planks rough beneath his bare feet, and leaned on the balustrade, looking at the beaten-earth parade-ground his battalion had spent two weeks clearing out of the virgin jungle. There was nothing like a new parade-ground, Colonel Liceu Lobo thought with a thin smile of satisfaction, to signal you were here to stay.

He saw Sergeant Elias Galvão emerge from the latrines and

amble across the square towards the battalion mess, tightening his belt as he went. A good man, Galvão, a professional, up this early too.

'Morning, Sergeant,' Colonel Liceu Lobo called from his balcony. Sergeant Elias Galvão came abruptly to attention, swivelled to face his naked colonel and saluted.

'Carry on,' Colonel Liceu Lobo instructed. Not a flicker on the man's impassive face: excellent. Sergeant Galvão's lieutenant's pips could not be long away.

'Liceu?' Nilda's husky, sleepy voice came from the bedroom. 'Where are you?' The colonel felt his manhood stir, as if of its own accord. Yes, he thought, there were some compensations to be had from a provincial command.

* * *

Wesley, trying not to inhale, walked with his business partner, Gerald Brockway, co-owner of BB Radio Cars, through the humid fug of the 'bull pen' towards the front door. There were three drivers there waiting for jobs and they were naturally talking about cars.

'How's the Carlton, Tone?' Gerald asked.

'Diamond.'

'Brilliant.'

'Cheers.'

Outside, Wesley opened the passenger door of his Rover for Gerald.

'You happy with this?' Gerald asked. 'I thought you wanted a Scorpio.'

'It's fine,' Wesley said.

'Noel got five grand for his Granada.'

'Really?'

'They hold their value, the old ones. Amazing. Years later. It's well rubbish what they did, restyling like that.'

Wesley couldn't think of what to say. He thought a shrill ringing had started in his inner ear. Tinnitus. He lived in constant fear of tinnitus.

'Change for the sake of change,' Gerald said, slowly, sadly, shaking his head.

Wesley started the engine and pulled away.

'Look at Saab.'

'Sorry?'

'They've had to bring back the 900. You can't give away the 9000.'

'Can we talk about something else, Ger?'

Gerald looked at him. 'You all right?'

'Of course. Just, you know.'

'No prob, my son. Where are we going to eat?'

'Everyone has heard of samba and bossa nova, sure,' Wesley said. 'But this is another type of music called *chorinho*—not many people know about it. Love it. Play it all the time. I can lend you some CDs.'

'See, I'd like to give him a break, Wes. But something in me says "fire the bastard." Why should we, I mean, why should we help him, Wes? Why? Big error. "No good deed goes unpunished," that's my personal philosophy. Is there any way we can turn this down? What the hell is it?'

'*Chorinho.*'

'You cannot diddle major account customers. Two hours' waiting time? I mean, what does he take us for? Couple of merchant bankers?'

'It means "little cry".'

'What is this stuff, Wesley? You got any English music?'

Wesley watched Gerald mash his egg mayonnaise into a creamy pulp. He dribbled thin streams of olive oil and vinegar on to the mixture, which he stirred, and then freely sprinkled on pepper and salt.

'That's disgusting,' Wesley said. 'How am I meant to eat this?' He pointed his knife at his steak.

'I haven't had a steak for two years. You should have my teeth problems, Wesley. You should feel sorry for me, mate.'

'I do feel sorry for you. I'd feel more sorry for you if you'd been to a dentist. You *can* be helped, you know. You don't have to suffer. A man of your age. Jesus.'

'Dentists and me, Wes. Not on. Actually, it's very tasty.'

He ate some of his mixture. Wesley looked round for a waitress and saw Elizabetta, the plump one. She came over, beaming.

'Pint of lager, please. Ger?'

'Large gin and tonic.'

Wesley lowered his voice. 'Is, um, Margarita in today?' he asked Elizabetta.

'This afternoon she come.'

He shifted his shoulders round. Gerald was not listening. 'Tell her I'll phone. Say Wesley will phone. Wesley.'

'Wesley. OK.'

G erald pulped his apple crumble with the back of his spoon. 'Nice little place this, Wes. Worth the drive. What is it, Italian?'

'Sort of. Bit of everything.'

'Your "international cuisine", then.'

Wesley looked around the Caravelle. There was no nautical theme visible in its pragmatic décor, unless you counted the one seascape among its five reproductions on the wall. He and Gerald sat in a row of booths reminiscent more of—what was the word? Seating arrangements in libraries—carrels, yes. Maybe the name was a malapropism, he thought. An asparagus on the banks of the Nile. Someone had blundered: it should have been called the Carrel Café & Restaurant. Names, again . . . He stopped thinking about it and thought instead about Margarita.

Mar-gar-it-a. Not Margaret.

He rolled the 'r's. Marrrrgarrritha.

She was dark, of course, very Latin, with a severe, thin face which possessed, he thought, what you might call a strong beauty. Not pretty, exactly, but there was a look about her that attracted him, although he realized she was one of those southern European women who would not age well. But now she was young and slim, and her hair was long, and, most important of all, she was Portuguese. *Uma moca bonita.*

Gerald offered him one of his small cigars.

* * *

Doctor Liceu Lobo put down his coffee cup and relit his *real excelente*. He drew, with pedantic and practised care, a steady, thin stream of smoke from the neatly docked and already nicely moist end and held it in his mouth, savouring the tobacco's dry tang, before pluming it at the small sunbird that pecked at the crumbs of his pastry on the patio table. The bird flew off with a shrill *shgrreakakak*, and Doctor Liceu Lobo chuckled. It was time to return to the clinic; Senhora Fontenova was due for her vitamin D injections.

He felt Adalgisa's hand on his shoulder and, as he leaned his head back against her firm midriff, her finger trickled down over his collar-bone and tangled and twirled the dense grey hairs on his chest.

'Your mother wants to see you.'

* * *

Wesley swung open the gate to his small and scruffy garden and reminded himself yet again to do something about the clematis that overburdened the trellis on either side of his front door. Pauline was bloody meant to be i.c. garden, he told himself, irritated at her, but then he also remembered he had contrived to keep her away from the house the last month or so, prepared to spend weekends and the odd night at her small flat rather than have her in his home. As he hooked his door keys out of his right pocket with one hand, he tugged with the other at a frond of clematis that dangled annoyingly close to his face, and a fine confetti of dust and dead leaves fell quickly on his hair and shoulders.

After he had showered, he lay naked on his bed, his hand on his cock, and thought about masturbating but decided against. He felt clean and, for the first time that day, almost relaxed. He thought about Margarita and wondered what she looked like with her clothes off. She was thin, perhaps a little on the thin side for his taste, if he were honest, but she did have a distinct bust, and her long, straight hair was always clean, though he wished she wouldn't tuck it behind her ears and drag it taut into a lank, swishing pony-tail. Restaurant regulations, he supposed. He realized then that he had never even seen her with her hair down and felt, for a moment, a sharp, intense sorrow for himself and his lot in life. He sat up and swung his legs off the bed, amazed that there was a shimmer of tears in his eyes.

'God. Jesus!' he said mockingly to himself, out loud. 'Poor little chap.'

He dressed himself brusquely.

Downstairs, he poured himself a large rum and Coke and put Milton Nascimento on the CD-player and hummed along to the great man's ethereal falsetto. Never failed to cheer him up. Never failed. He took a great gulp of chilled drink and felt the alcohol surge. He swayed over to the drinks cabinet and added another slug. It was only four-thirty in the afternoon. Fuck it, he thought. Fuck it.

He should have parked somewhere else, he realized crossly, as unexpected sun warmed the Rover as he waited outside Pauline's bank. He didn't have a headache, but his palate was dry and stretched, and his sinuses were responding unhappily to the rum. He flared his nostrils and exhaled into his cupped hand. His breath felt unnaturally hot on his palm. He sneezed three times, violently. Come on, Pauline. Jesus.

She emerged from the stout teak doors of the bank, waved and skittered over towards the car. High heels, he saw. She *has* got nice legs. Definitely, he thought. Thin ankles. They must be three-inch heels, he reckoned, she'll be taller than me. Was it his imagination or was that the sun flashing off the small diamond cluster of her engagement ring?

He leaned across the seat and flung the door open for her.

'Wesley! You going to a funeral or something? Gaw!'

'It's just a suit. Jesus.'

'It's a black suit. Black. Really.'

'Charcoal grey.'

'Where's your Prince of Wales check? I love that one.'

'Cleaners.'

'You don't wear a black suit to a christening, Wesley. Honestly.'

* * *

Professor Liceu Lobo kissed the top of his mother's head and sat down at her feet.

'Hey, little Mama, how are you today?'

Oh, I'm fine. A little closer to God.'

'Nah, little Mama, He needs you here, to look after me.'

She laughed softly and smoothed the hair back from his forehead in gentle combing motions.

'Are you going to the university today?'

'Tomorrow. Today is for you, little Mama.'

He felt her small, rough hands on his skin at the hairline and closed his eyes. His mother had been doing this to him ever since he could remember. Soothing, like waves on the shore. 'Like waves on the shore your hands on my hair . . . ' The line came to him and with it, elusively, a hint of something more. Don't force it, he told himself, it will come. The rhythm was fixed already. Like waves on the shore. The mother figure, mother earth . . . Maybe there was an idea to investigate. He would work on it in the study, after dinner. Perhaps a poem? Or maybe the title of a novel? *As ondas em la praia.* It had a serene yet epic ring to it.

He heard a sound and looked up, opening his eyes to see Marialva carrying a tray. The muffled belling of ice in a glass jug filled with a clear fruit punch. Seven glasses. The children must be back from school.

* * *

Wesley looked across the room at Pauline trying vainly to calm the puce, wailing baby, Daniel-Ian Young, his nephew. It was a better name than Wesley Bright, he thought— just—though he had never come across two Christian names thus conjoined before. Bit of a mouthful. He wondered if he dared point out to his brother-in-law the good decade of remorseless bullying that lay ahead for the youngster once his peers discovered what his initials spelt. He decided to store it away in his grudge-bunker as potential retaliation. Sometimes Dermot really got on his wick.

He watched his brother-in-law, Dermot Young, approach, two pint-tankards in hand. Wesley accepted his gladly. He had a terrible thirst.

'Fine pair of lungs on him, any road,' Dermot said. 'You were saying, Wesley.'

'—no, it's a state called Minas Geraes, quite remote, but with this amazing musical tradition. I mean, you've got your Beto Guedes, Toninho Horta, the one and only Milton Nascimento of course, Lo Borges, Wagner Tiso. All these incredible talents who—'

'—HELEN! Can you put him down, or something? We can't hear ourselves think here.'

Wesley gulped fizzy beer. Pauline, relieved of Daniel-Ian, was coming over with a slice of christening cake on a plate, Wesley's mother in tow.

'All right, all right,' Pauline said, with an unpleasant leering tone to her voice, Wesley thought. 'What are you two plotting? Mmm?'

'Where did you get that suit, Wesley?' his mother asked guilelessly. 'Is it one of your dad's?'

There was merry laughter at this. Wesley kept a smile on his face.

'No,' Dermot said, 'Wes was telling me about this bunch of musicians from—'

'—Brazil.' Pauline's shoulders sagged, and she turned wearily to Wesley's mother. 'Told you, didn't I, Isobel? Brazil, Brazil. Told you. Honestly.'

'You and Brazil,' his mother admonished. 'It's not as if we've got any Brazilians in the family.'

'Not as if you've even been there,' Pauline said, a distinct hostility in her voice. 'Never even set foot.'

Wesley silently hummed the melody from a João Gilberto samba to himself. Gilberto had taken the traditional form and distilled it through a cool jazz filter. It was João who had stripped away the excess of percussion in Brazilian music and brought bossa nova to the—

'Yeah, what is it with you and Brazil, Wes?' Dermot asked, a thin line of beer suds on his top lip. 'What gives?'

* * *

WHUCHINNNNNNG! WHACHANNNNG!! Liceu Lobo put down his guitar and, before selecting the mandolin, he tied up his dreadlocks back behind his head in a slack bun. Gibson Piacava played a dull roll on the *zabumba*, and Liceu Lobo began slowly to strum the musical phrase that seemed to be dominating 'The Waves on the Shore' at this stage in its extemporized composition. Joel Carlos Brandt automatically started to echo the mandolin phrases on his guitar, and Bola da Rocha plaintively picked up the melody on his saxophone.

Behind the glass of the recording studio, Albertina swayed her hips to and fro to the sinuous rhythm that was slowly building. Pure *chorinho*, she thought, sensuous yet melancholy, only Liceu is capable of this: of all the great *choroes* in Brazil, he was the greatest. At that moment, he looked round and caught her eye and he smiled at her as he played. She kissed the tip of her forefinger and pressed it against the warm glass of the window that separated them. Once Liceu and his fellow musicians started a session like this, it could last for days, weeks even. She would wait patiently for him, though, wait until he was finished and take him home to their wide bed.

* * *

Wesley stepped out into the back garden and flipped open his mobile phone.

'Café Caravelle, may I help you, please?'

'Ah. Could I speak to, ah, Margarita?'

'MARGARITA! *Telefono.*'

In the chilly dusk of a back garden in Hounslow, Wesley Bright listened to the gabble of foreign voices, the erratic percussion of silverware and china, and felt he was calling some distant land, far overseas. A warmth located itself in his body, a spreading coin of heat, deep in his bowels.

'Hello?' That slight guttural catch on the 'h' . . .

'Margarita, it's Wesley.'

'Ghello?'

'Wesley. It's me—Wesley.'

'Please?'

'WESLEY!' He caught himself from shouting louder and repeated his name in a throat-tearing whisper several times, glancing round at the yellow windows of Dermot's house. He saw someone peering at him, a silhouette.

'Ah, Weseley,' Margarita said. 'Yes?'

'I'll pick you up at ten, outside the café.'

Pauline stood at the kitchen door frowning out into the thickening dusk of the garden. Wesley advanced into the rectangle of light the open door had thrown on the grass.

'What're you up to, Wesley?'

Wesley slid his thin phone into his hip pocket.

'Needed a breath of fresh air,' he said. 'I'm feeling a bit off, to tell the truth. Those vol-au-vents tasted dodgy to me.'

Pauline was upset. She had been expecting a meal out after the christening but she was also concerned for Wesley and his health. 'I thought you looked a bit sort of pallid,' she said when he dropped her at her flat. She made him wait while she went inside and re-emerged with two sachets of mint infusion 'to help settle your stomach,' she said. She took them whenever she felt bilious, she told him, and they worked wonders.

As he drove off, he smelt the pungent impress of her perfume or powder or make-up on his cheek where she had kissed him, and he felt a squirm of guilt at his duplicity—if something so easily accomplished merited the description—and a small pelt of shame covered him for a minute or two as he headed east towards the Café Caravelle and the waiting Margarita.

Her hair was down. Her hair was down, and he was both rapt and astonished at the change it wrought in her. And to see her out of black, he thought, it was almost too much. He carried their drinks through the jostling, noisy pub to the back, where she sat on a high stool, elbow resting on a narrow shelf designed to take glasses. She was drinking a double vodka and water, no ice and no slice, a fact he found exciting and vaguely troubling. He had smelt her drink as the barmaid had served up his rum and Coke, and it had seemed redolent of heavy industry, some strange fuel or new lubricant, something one would pour into a machine rather than down one's throat. It seemed definitely not a drink of the warm south either, not at all apt for this taciturn Latin beauty, more suited to the bleak cravings of a sheet-metal

worker in Smolensk. Still, it was gratifying to observe how she
put it away, shudderless, in three pragmatic draughts. Then she
spoke briefly, brutally, of how much she hated her job. It was a
familiar theme, one Wesley recognized from his two previous
social encounters with Margarita—the first a snatched coffee in a
hamburger franchise before her evening shift began, and then a
more leisurely autumnal Sunday lunch at a brash pub on the
river at Richmond.

On that last occasion, she had seemed out of sorts, cowed
perhaps by the strapping conviviality of the tall, noisy lads and
their feisty, jolly girls. But tonight she had returned to the same
tiresome plaint—the mendacious and rebarbative qualities of the
Caravelle's manager, João—so Wesley had to concede it was
clearly something of an obsession.

They had kissed briefly and not very satisfactorily after their
Sunday pub tryst, and Wesley felt that this allowed him now to
take her free hand (her other held a cigarette) and squeeze it. She
stopped talking and, he thought, half-smiled at him.

'Weseley,' she said and stubbed out her cigarette. Then she
grinned. 'Tonight, I thin I wan to be drunk . . . '

There you had it, he thought. There. That was it. That
moment held the gigantic difference between a Pauline and a
Margarita. A mint infusion and an iceless vodka. He felt his
bowels weaken with shocking desire.

He returned to the bar to fetch another drink for her and
ordered the same for himself. The tepid alcohol seemed all the
more powerful for the absence of chill. His nasal passages burnt,
he wrinkled his tear-flooded eyes. Made from potatoes, hard to
believe. Or is it potato peelings? His teeth felt loose. He stood
beside her. Someone had taken his stool.

Margarita sipped her drink with more decorum this time. 'I
hate that fackin job,' she said.

He raised his knuckles to his lips and dabbed at them.

'God, I've missed you,' he said, then took a deep breath.
'Margarita,' he said softly, '*tenho muito atracão para tu.*' He
hoped to God he had it right, with the correct slushing and nasal
sounds. He found Portuguese farcically difficult to pronounce, no
matter the hours he spent listening to his tapes.

She frowned. Too fast, you fool, you bloody fool.

'What?' Her lips half-formed a word. 'I, I don't—'

More slowly, more carefully: *'Tenho muito atracão—muito, muito—para tu.'*

He slipped his hand round her thin back, fingers snagging momentarily on the clip of her bra, and drew her to him. He kissed her, there in the hot pub, boldly, with noticeable teeth clash, but no recoil from Margarita.

He moved his head back, his palm still resting on her body, warm above her hip.

She touched her lips with the palp of her thumb, scrutinizing him, not hostile, he was glad to see, not even surprised. She drank some more of her grey, flat drink, still looking at him over the rim of her glass.

'Sempre para tu, Margarita, sempre.' Huskily, this. Sincere.

'Weseley. What you saying? *Sempre*, I know. But the rest . . . '

'I. I am speaking Portuguese.'

'For why?'

'Because, I—because I want to speak your language to you. I love your language, you must understand. I love it. I hear it in my head, in your music.'

'Well . . . ' She shrugged and reached for her cigarettes, 'then you must not speak Portuguese at me, Weseley. I am Italian.'

* * *

Marta shucked off her brassière and had hooked down her panties with her thumbs within seconds, Liceu Lobo thought, of his entering her room in the bordello. He caught a glimpse of her plump fanny in the light cast by the bathroom cubicle. She was hot tonight, on fire, he thought, as he hauled off his T-shirt and allowed his shorts to fall to the floor. As he reached the bedside, he felt her hands reaching for his engorged member. He was a pretty boy, and even the oldest hooker liked a pretty boy with a precocious and impatient tool. He felt Marta's hands all over his *pepino* as if she were assessing it for some strumpet's inventory. *Maldito seja!* Liceu Lobo thought, violently clenching his sphincter muscles as Marta settled him between her generous and welcoming thighs, he should definitely have jerked off before coming here tonight. Marta always had that effect on him. *Deus!* He hurled himself into the fray.

* * *

It had not gone well. No. He had to face up to that, acknowledge it squarely. As love-making went it was indubitably B-minus. B double-minus, possibly. And it was his fault. But could he put it down to the fact that he had been in bed with an Italian girl and *not* a Portuguese one? Or perhaps it had something to do with the half-dozen vodkas and water he had consumed to keep pace with Margarita?

But the mood had changed, subtly, when he had learned the truth, a kind of keening sadness, a thin draught of melancholy seemed to enter the boisterous pub, depressing him. An unmistakable sense of being let down by Margarita's nationality. She was meant to be Portuguese, that was the whole point, anything else was wrong.

He turned over in his bed and stared at the faint silhouette of Margarita's profile as she slept beside him. Did it really matter that much, he urged himself? This was the first non-British girl he had kissed, let alone made love to, so why had he been unable to shake off that sense of distraction? It was a sullenness of spirit that had possessed him, as if he were a spoilt child who had been promised and then denied a present. It was hardly Margarita's fault after all, but an irrational side of him still blamed her for not being Portuguese, for unconsciously raising his hopes by not warning him from their first encounter that she didn't fit his national bill. Somehow she had to share the responsibility.

He turned away and dozed, and half-dreamed of Liceu Lobo in a white suit. On a mountain top with Leonor or Branca or Caterina or Joana. A balcony with two cane chairs. Mangoes big as rugby balls. Liceu, blond hair flying, putting down his sunglasses, offering his hand saying, 'My deal is my smile.' Joana's slim, mulatto body. The sound of distant water falling.

He half-sat, blinking stupidly.

'Joana?'

The naked figure in his doorway froze.

'Joana?'

The figure moved.

'Vaffanculo,' Margarita said, weariness making her voice harsh. She switched on the light and began to get dressed, still talking more to herself than to him. Wesley's meagre Portuguese was no help here, but he could tell her words were unkind. He hadn't fully awoken from his dream, that was all, but how could he explain that to her? She was dressed in a moment and did not shut the door as she left.

After she had gone, Wesley pulled on his dressing-gown and walked slowly down the stairs. He sat for a while in his unlit sitting-room, swigging directly from the rum bottle, resting it on his knee between mouthfuls, coughing and breathing deeply, wiping his mouth with the back of his hand. Eventually, he rose to his feet and slid Elis Regina into his CD-player. The strange and almost insupportable plangency of the woman's voice filled the shadowy space around him. *Nem uma lagrima.* 'Not one tear,' Wesley said to himself, out loud. His voice sounded peculiar to him, a stranger's. Poor tragic Elis, Elis Regina, who died in 1982, aged thirty-seven, tragically, of an unwise cocktail of drugs and alcohol. 'Drink 'n' drugs,' the CD's sleeve-notes had said. Tragic. A tragic loss to Brazilian music. Fucking tragic. He would call Pauline in the morning, that's what he would do. In the meantime, he had his *chorinho* to console him. He would make it up with Pauline, she deserved a treat, some sort of treat, definitely, a weekend somewhere. Definitely. Not one tear, Elis Regina sang for him. He would be all right. There was always Brazil. Not one tear.

RICHARD FORD
THE SHORE

Nowadays I end up driving over once a week to pass a jolly-intimate evening on the Jersey Shore with Sally Caldwell. We often attend a movie, later slip out to some little end-of-a-pier place for an amberjack steak, a pitcher of martinis, sometimes a stroll along a beach or out some jetty, following which events take care of themselves. Though often as not I end up driving back to Haddam in the moonlight alone, my heart pulsing regularly, my windows wide open, a man in charge of his own tent stakes and personal equipment, my head full of vivid but fast-disappearing memories and no anxious expectancies for a late-night phone call full of longing and confusion, or demands that I spell out my intentions and come back immediately, or bitter accusations that I have not been forthright in every conceivable way. (I may not have, of course; forthright being a greater challenge than would seem, though my intentions are always good if few.) Our relationship, in fact, hasn't seemed to need more attention to theme or direction but has proceeded or at least persisted on autopilot, like a small plane flying out over a peaceful ocean with no one exactly in command.

Sally is the widow of a boy I attended Gulf Pines Military Academy with, Wally 'Weasel' Caldwell of Lake Forest, Illinois; and for that reason Sally and I sometimes act as if we have a long, bittersweet history together of love lost and fate reconciled—which we don't. Sally, who's forty-two, merely saw my snapshot, address and a short personal reminiscence of Wally in the *Pine Boughs* alumni book printed for our twentieth Gulf Pines reunion, which I didn't attend. At the time she didn't know me from Bela Lugosi's ghost. Only in trying to dream up a good reminiscence and skimming through my old yearbook for somebody I could attribute something amusing to, I chose Wally and sent in a mirthful but affectionate account that made fleeting reference to his having once drunkenly washed his socks in a urinal (a complete fabrication; I, in fact, chose him, because I discovered from another school publication that he was deceased). But it was my 'reminiscence' that Sally happened to see. I barely, in fact, had any memory of Wally, except that back in the sixties he was a fat, bespectacled boy with blackheads who was always trying to smoke Chesterfields using a cigarette holder—a character who, in spite of a certain likeness, turned out not to be Wally Caldwell at all but somebody else, whose name I could never remember. I have since explained my whole gambit to Sally, and we have had a good laugh about it.

I learned later from Sally that Wally had gone to Vietnam about the time I enlisted in the Marines, had come damn close to getting blown to bits in some ridiculous Navy mishap which left him intermittently distracted, though he came home to Chicago (Sally and two kids waiting devotedly), unpacked his bags, talked about studying biology, but after two weeks simply disappeared. Completely. Gone. The End. A nice boy who would've made a better than average horticulturist, become forever a mystery.

Sally, however, never remarried. Finally, for IRS reasons, she was forced to obtain a divorce by having Wally declared a croaker. But she went right on and raised her kids as a single mom in the Chicago suburb of Hoffman Estates, earned her BA in marketing administration from Loyola while holding down a full-time job in the adventure-travel industry. Wally's well-heeled Lake Forest parents provided her with make-ends-meet money and moral support, having realized she was not the cause of their son's going loony and that some human conditions are beyond love's reach.

Years went by.

But as quick as the kids were old enough to be safely lumped out of the nest, Sally put into motion her plan for setting sail with whatever fresh wind was blowing. And in 1983, on a rental-car trip to Atlantic City, she happened to turn off the Garden State Thruway in search of a clean rest room, stumbled all at once upon the Jersey Shore, South Mantoloking and the big old Queen-Anne-style double-gallery beach house facing the sea, a place she could afford with her parents' and in-laws' help, and where her kids would be happy coming home to with their friends and spouses, while she got her feet wet in some new business enterprise. (As it happened, as marketing director and later owner of an agency that finds tickets to Broadway shows for people in the later stages of terminal illness but who somehow think that seeing a revival of *Oliver!* or the original London cast of *Hair* will make life—discolored by impending death—seem brighter. 'Curtain Call' is her company's name.)

I luckily enough got into the picture when Sally read my bio and reminiscence about ersatz Wally in *Pine Boughs*, saw I was a realtor in central New Jersey and tracked me down, thinking I might help her find bigger space for her business.

I came over on Saturday morning almost a year ago, and got a look at her—angularly pretty, frosted-blonde, blue-eyed, tall in the extreme, with long flashing model's legs (one an inch shorter than the other from a freak tennis accident, but not an issue) and the occasional habit of looking at you out the corner of her eyes as though most of what you were talking about was mighty damn silly. I took her to lunch at Johnny Matassa's in Point Pleasant, a lunch that lasted well past dark and moved over subjects far afield of office space—Vietnam, the coming election prospects for the Democrats, the sad state of American theatre and elder care, and how lucky we were to have kids who weren't drug addicts, young litigators-to-be or maladjusted sociopaths. And from there the rest was old hat: the inevitable usual, with a weather-eye out for health concerns.

At Lower Squankum I turn off then slide over to NJ34, which becomes NJ35, the beach highway, and head into the steamy swarm of Fourth of July early-bird traffic, those who so love misery and wall-to-wall car companionship that they're willing to rise before dawn and drive ten hours from Ohio. (Many of these Buckeye Staters, I find, are Bush supporters, which makes the holiday spirit seem meanly expropriated.)

Along the beach drag through Bay Head and West Mantoloking, patriotic pennants and American flags are snapping along the curbside, and down the short streets past the seawall I can see sails tilting and springing at close quarters on a hazy blue-steel sea. Though there's no actual feel of shimmery patriot fervor, just the everyday summery wrangle of loud Harleys, mopeds, topless Jeeps with jutting surfboards, squeezed in too close to Lincolns and Prowlers with stickers saying TRY BURNING THIS ONE! Here the baked sidewalks are cluttered with itchy, skinny, bikini'd teens waiting on line for saltwater taffy and snow cones, while out on the beach the wooden lifeguard stands are occupied by brawny hunks and hunkettes, their arms folded, staring thoughtlessly at the waves. Parking-lots are all full; motels, efficiencies and trailer hookups on the landward side have been booked for months, their renter-occupants basking in lawn chairs brought from home, or stretched out reading on skimpy porches bordered by holly shrubs. Others simply stand on old, thirties shuffleboard pavements, sticks in hand, wondering: Wasn't this once—summer—a time of inner joy?

Though off to the right the view inland opens behind the town toward the broad reach of cloudy, brackish estuarial veldt, wintry and sprouted with low-tide pussy willows, rose hips and rotting boat husks stuck in the muck; and, overseeing all, farther and across, a great water tower, pink as a primrose, beyond which regimented housing takes up again. Silver Bay, New Jersey, this is, its sky fletched with darkened gulls gliding to sea behind the morning's storm. I pass a lone and leathered biker, standing on the shoulder beside his broken-down chopper just watching, taking it all in across the panoramic estuary, trying, I suppose, to imagine how to get from here to there, where help might be.

Sally's rambling dark-green beach house at the end of narrow Asbury Street is, when I hike up the old concrete seawall steps alongside the beach-level promenade, locked, and she surprisingly gone, though all the side-opening windows, upstairs and down, are thrown out to catch a breeze. I am still early.

I, for a while, have had my own set of keys, though for a moment I simply stand on the shaded porch (plastic wine sack in hand) and gaze at the quiet, underused stretch of beach, the silent, absolute Atlantic and the gray-blue sky, against which more near-in sailboats and windsurfers joust in the summer haze, and farther out a dark freighter inches north on the horizon. It is not so far from here that in my distant, postdivorce days I set sail for many a night's charter cruise with the Divorced Men's Club, all of us drinking grappa and angling for weakfish off Manasquan, a solemn, hopeful, joyless crew, mostly scattered now, most remarried, two dead, a couple still in town. Back in '83 we'd come over as a group, using the occasion of a midnight fishing excursion to put an even firmer lock on our complaints and sorrows—important training for the Existence Period, and good practice if your resolve is never to complain about life.

On the beach, beyond the sandy concrete walk, moms under beach umbrellas lie fast asleep on their heavy sides, arms flung over sleeping babies. Secretaries with a half day off to start the long weekend are lying on their bellies, shoulder to shoulder, chatting, winking and smoking cigarettes in their two-pieces. Tiny, stick-figure boys stand bare-chested at the margins of the small surf, shading their eyes as dogs trot by, tanned joggers jog and elderlies in pastel garb stroll behind them in the fractured light. Here is human hum in the barely moving air and surf-sigh, the low scrim of radio notes and water subsiding over words spoken in whispers. Something in it moves me as though to a tear (but not quite): some sensation that I have been here, or nearby, been at dire pains here time-ago and am here now again, sharing the air just as then. Only nothing signifies, nothing gives a nod. The sea closes up, and so does the land.

I am not sure what chokes me up: either the place's familiarity or its rigid reluctance to act familiar. It is another useful theme and exercise of the Existence Period, and a patent lesson of the realty profession, to cease sanctifying places—houses, beaches, hometowns, a street corner where you once kissed a girl, a parade ground where you marched in line, a courthouse where you secured a divorce on a cloudy day in July but where there is now no sign of you, no mention in the air's breath that you were there or that you were ever, importantly you, or that you even *were*. We may feel they *ought* to, *should* confer something—sanction, again—because of events that transpired there once; light a warming fire to animate us when we're well nigh inanimate and sunk. But they don't. Places never cooperate by revering you back when you need it. In fact, they almost always let you down. Best just to swallow back your tear, get accustomed to the minor sentimentals and shove off to whatever's next, not whatever was. Place means nothing.

Down the wide, cool center hall I head to the shadowy, high, tin-ceilinged kitchen that smells of garlic, fruit and refrigerator freon, where I unload my wine into the big Sub-Zero. A 'Curtain Call' note is stuck on the door: 'FB. Go jump in the ocean. See you at 6. Have fun. S.' No words about where she might be, or why it's necessary to use both the 'F' and the 'B'. Perhaps another 'F' lurks in the wings.

Up the heavy oak stairs, I make straight for the brown-curtained and breezy bedroom on the front of the house. It has become a point of policy with Sally—whether she's here or in New York with a vanload of Lou Gehrig's sufferers seeing *Carnival*—that I have my own space when I show up. (So far there's been no quibbling about where I sleep once the sun goes down—her room on the back.) But this small, eave-shaded, semi-garret overlooking the beach and the end of Asbury Street has been designated mine, though it would otherwise be a spare: brown gingham wallpaper, an antique ceiling fan, a few tasteful but manly grouse-hunting prints, an oak dresser, a double bed with brass rainbow headboard, an armoire converted to a TV closet, a mahogany clothes-horse, serviced by its own small, demure forest-green and oak bathroom—perfect for someone (a man) you don't know too well but sort of like.

I draw the curtains, strip down and crawl between the cool blue-paisley sheets. Only when I reach to turn off the bedside lamp, I notice on the table, conspicuous, a set of gold cuff links engraved with the anchor, ball and chain of USMC, my old service branch (though I didn't last long). I pluck up one cuff link—it has a nice little jeweler's heft in my palm. I try, leaning on my bare elbow, to remember through the haze of time if these are Marine issue, or just some trinket an old leatherneck had 'crafted' to memorialize a burnished valiance far from home.

Except I don't want to wonder over the origin of cuff links, or whose starchy cuffs they might link; or if they were left for my private perusal, or are here by accident. If I were married to Sally Caldwell, I would wonder about that. But I'm not. If 'my room' on Fridays and Saturdays becomes Colonel Rex 'Knuckles' Trueblood's on Tuesdays and Wednesdays, I only hope that we never cross paths. This is a matter to be filed under *'laissez-faire'* in our arrangement. Divorce, if it works, should rid you of these later, destination-less stresses, or at least that's the way I feel now that welcome sleep approaches.

I set the cuff links on the table and lie now more awake than asleep, listening to the children's voices and, farther away, nearer the continent's sandy crust, a woman's voice saying, 'I'm not hard to understand. Why are you so goddamn difficult?' Followed by a man's evener voice, as if embarrassed: 'I'm *not*,' he says. 'I'm not. I'm really, really not.' They talk more, though the sounds fade in the light airishness of Jersey seaside.

But then, gradually, I can hear the beach voices again, the slap of a book being closed, a feathery laugh, somebody's sandy sandals being slapped together, a palm being smacked on someone's tender, red back and the searing 'owwwweeeee,' while the tide fondly chides the ever-retreating shingle.

What I feel rising in me now is a strange curiosity as to what exactly in the hell I'm doing here; and its stern companion sensation that I really ought to be somewhere else. Though where? Where I'm wanted more than just expected? Where I fit in better? Where I'm more purely ecstatic and not just glad? At least someplace where meeting the terms, conditions and limitations set on life are not so front and center. Where the rules are not the game.

Time was when a moment like this one—stretched out in a cool, inviting house not my own, drifting toward a nap but also thrillingly awaiting the arrival of a sweet, wonderful and sympathetic visitor eager to provide what I need because she needs it too—time was when this state was the best damned feeling on God's earth, in fact was the very feeling the word 'life' was coined for, plus all the more intoxicating and delectable because I recognized it even as it was happening, and knew with certainty no one else did or could, so that I could have it all, all, all to myself, the way I had nothing else.

Here, now, all the props are in place, light and windage set; Sally is doubtless on her way at this instant, eager (or at least willing) to run up, jump in bed, find once more the key to my heart and give it a good cranking-up turn.

Only the old giddyap is vanished, and I'm not lying here a-buzz and a-thrill but listening haphazard to voices on the beach—the way I used to feel, would like to feel, gone. Left is only some ether of its presence and a hungrified wonder about where it might be and will it ever come back. Nullity, in other words.

Someplace far, far away I seem to hear footsteps, then the softened sound of a wine cork being squeezed, then popped, a spoon set down gently on a metal stovetop, a hushed radio playing the theme music of the news broadcast I regularly tune to, a phone ringing and being answered in a grateful voice, followed by condoning laughter—a sweet and precious domestic sonority I so rarely feel these days that I would lie here and listen till way past dark if I only, only could.

I lumber down the stairs, my teeth brushed, my face washed, though groggy and misaligned in time. My teeth in fact don't feel they're in the right occlusion, as if I'd gnashed them in some dream (no doubt a dismal 'night guard' is in my future).

It is twilight. I've slept for hours without believing I slept at all, and feel no longer fuguish but exhausted, as though I'd dreamed of running a race, my legs heavy and achy clear up to my groin.

When I come around the newel post I can see, out the open front-doorway, a few darkened figures on the beach and, farther out, the lights of a familiar oil platform that can't be seen in the hazy daytime, its tiny white lights cutting the dark eastern sky like diamonds. I wonder where the freighter is, the one I saw before—no doubt well into harbor.

A lone, dim candle burns in the kitchen, though the little security panel blinks a green all-clear from down the hall. Sally usually maintains lights-off till there's none left abroad, then sets scented candles through the house and goes barefoot. It is a habit I've almost learned to respect, along with her cagey sidelong looks that let you know she's got your number.

No one is in the kitchen, where the beige candle flickers on the counter for my sake. A shadowy spray of purple irises and white wisteria has been arranged in a ceramic vase to dress up the table. A green crockery bowl of cooling bow ties sits beside a loaf of French bread, my bottle of Round Hill in its little chilling sleeve. Two forks, two knives, two spoons, two plates, two napkins.

I pour a glass and head for the porch.

'I don't think I hear you with your bells on,' Sally says, while I'm still trooping down the hall. Outside, to my surprise it is almost full dark, the beach apparently empty, as if the last two minutes had occupied a full hour. 'I'm just taking in the glory of the day's end,' she continues, 'though I came up an hour ago and watched you sleep.' She smiles around at me from the porch shadows and extends her hand back, which I touch, though I stay by the door, overtaken for a moment by the waves breaking white-crested out of the night. Part of our 'understanding' is not to be falsely effusive, as though unmeant effusiveness was what got our whole generation in trouble somewhere back up the line.

She's seated in a big wood rocker, in a long white caftan slit up both sides to let her hike her long legs and bare feet up. Her yellow hair is pulled back and held with a silver barrette, her skin brown from beach life, her teeth luminous. A damp perfume of sweet bath oil floats away on the porch air.

'I hope I wasn't snoring,' I say.

'Nope. Nope. You're a wife's dream. You never snore.'

She gives me the look then. Her features are narrow, her nose is sharp, her chin angular and freckled—a sleek package. She is wearing thin silver earrings and heavy turquoise bracelets. 'You *did* say something about Ann—speaking of wives, or former wives.' This is the reason for the look.

'I only remember dreaming about somebody not getting his insurance premiums paid on time, and then about if it was better to be killed or tortured and then killed.'

'I know what I'd choose.' She takes a sip of wine, holding the round glass in both palms and focusing into the dark that has taken over the beach. New York's damp glow brightens the lusterless sky. Out on the main drag cars are racing; tires squeal, one siren goes 'woop'.

Whenever Sally turns ruminant, I assume she's brooding over Wally, her long-lost, now roaming the ozone, somewhere amongst these frigid stars, 'dead' to the world but (more than likely) not to her. Her situation is much like mine—divorced in a generic sense—with all of divorce's shaky unfinality, which, when all else fails, your mind chews on like a piece of sour meat you just won't swallow.

Somewhere on the water a boat neither of us can see suddenly becomes a launch pad for a bright, fusey, sparkly projectile that arcs into the inky air and explodes into luminous pink and green effusions that brighten the whole sky like creation's dawn, then pops and fizzles as other, minor detonations go off, before the whole gizmo weakens and dies out of view like an evanescing spirit of nighttime.

Invisible on the beach, people say *Ooooo* and *Aaahhh* in unison and applaud each pop. Their presence is a surprise. We wait for the next boomp, whoosh and burst, but none occurs. 'Oh,' I hear someone say in a falling voice. 'Shit.' 'But one was nice,' someone says. 'One ain't enough a-nuthin,' is the answer.

'That was my first official "firework" of the holiday,' Sally says cheerfully. 'That's always very exciting.' Where she's looking the sky is smoky and bluish against the black. We are, the two of us, suspended here as though waiting on some other ignition.

'Did you sell a house today?'

'I'm letting my clients simmer.'

'You're very skillful at your profession, aren't you? You sell houses when no one else sells them.' She rocks forward then back, using just her shoulders, the big rocker grinding the porch boards.

'It's not a very hard job. It's just driving around in the car with strangers, then later talking to them on the phone.'

'That's what my job's like,' Sally says happily, still rocking. Sally's job is more admirable but fuller of sorrows. I wouldn't get within a hundred miles of it. Though suddenly and badly now I want to kiss her, touch her shoulder or her waist or somewhere, have a good whiff of her sweet, oiled skin on this warm evening. I therefore make my way clump-a-clump across the noisy boards, lean awkwardly down like an oversized doctor seeking a heartbeat with his naked ear, and give her cheek and also her neck a smooch I'd be happy to have lead to almost anything.

'Hey, hey, stop that,' she says only half-jokingly as I breathe in the exotics of her neck, feel the dampness of her scapula. Along her cheek just below her ear is the faintest skim of blond down, a delicate, perhaps sensitive feature I've always found inflaming but have never been sure how I should attend to. My smooch, though, gives rise to little more than one well-meant, not overly tight wrist squeeze and a willing tilt of head in my general direction, following which I stand up with my empty glass, peer across the beach at nothing, then clump back to take my listening post holding up the doorframe, half aware of some infraction but uncertain what it is.

Possibly even more restrictions are in effect.

What I'd like is not to make rigorous, manly, night-ending love now or in two minutes, but to have *already* done so; to have it on my record as a deed performed and well, and to have a lank, friendly, guard-down love's afterease be ours; to be the goodly swain who somehow rescues an evening from the shallows of nullity—what I suffered before my nap and which it's been my magician's trick to save us from over these months, by arriving always brimming with good ideas, and setting in motion day trips to the *Intrepid* Sea-Air-Space Museum, a canoe ride on the Batsto, a weekend junket to the Gettysburg battlefield, capped off by a balloon trip Sally was game for but not me. Not to mention a three-day Vermont color tour last fall that didn't work out, since we spent most of two days stuck in a cavalcade of slow-moving leaf-peepers in tour buses and Winnebagos, plus the prices were jacked up, the beds too small, and the food was terrible. (We ended up driving back one night early, feeling old and tired—Sally slept most of the way—and in no mood even to suffer a drink together when I let her off at the foot of Asbury Street.)

'I made bow ties,' Sally says very assuredly, after the long silence occasioned by my unwanted kiss, during which we both realized we are not about to head upstairs for any fun. 'That's your favorite, correct? *Farfaline*?'

'It's sure the food I most like to *see*,' I say.

She smiles around again, stretches her long legs out until her ankles make smart little pops. 'I'm coming apart at my seams, so it seems,' she says. In fact, she's an aggressive tennis player who hates to lose and, in spite of her one leg being docked, can scissor the daylights out of a grown man.

'Are you over there thinking about Wally?' I say for no good reason except I thought it.

'Wally Caldwell?' She says this as if the name were new to her.

'It was just something I thought. From my distance here.'

'The name alone survives,' she says. 'Too long ago.' I don't believe her, but it doesn't matter. 'I had to give up on that name. He left *me*, *and* his children. So.' She shakes her thick, blonde hair as if the specter of Weasel Wally were right out in the dark seeking admission to our conversation, and she'd rejected him.

'What I *was* thinking about—because when I drove all the way to New York today to pick up some tickets, I was also thinking it then—was you, and about you being here when I came home, and what we'd do, and just what a sweet man you always are.'

This is not a good harbinger, mark my words.

'I *want* to be a sweet man,' I say, hoping this will have the effect of stopping whatever she is about to say next. Only in rock-solid marriages can you hope to hear that you're a sweet man without a 'but' following along afterward like a displeasing goat. In many ways a rock-solid marriage has a lot to say for itself. 'But what?'

'But nothing. That's all.' Sally hugs her knees, her long bare feet side by side on the front edge of her rocker seat, her long body swaying forward and back. 'Does there have to be a *"but"*?'

'Maybe that's what *I* am.' I should make a goat noise.

'A butt? Well. I was just driving along thinking I liked you. That's all. I can try to be harder to get along with.'

'I'm pretty happy with you,' I say. An odd little smirky smile etches along my silly mouth and hardens back up into my cheeks without my willing it.

Sally turns all the way sideways and peers up at me in the gloom of the porch. A straight address. 'Well, good.'

I say nothing, just smirk.

'Why are you smiling like that?' she says. 'You look strange.'

'I don't really know,' I say, and poke my finger in my cheek and push, which makes the sturdy little smile retreat back into my regular citizen's mien.

Sally squints at me as if she's able to visualize something hidden in my face, something she'd never seen but wants to verify because she's always suspected it was there.

'I always think about the Fourth of July as if I needed to have something accomplished by now, or decided,' she says. 'Maybe that comes from going to school in the summers for so long. The fall just seems too late. I don't even know late for what.'

I, though, am thinking about a more successful color tour. Michigan: Petoskey, Harbor Springs, Charlevoix. A weekend on Mackinaw Island, riding a tandem.

Sally raises both her arms above her head, joins hands and

does a slinky yoga stretch, getting the kinks out of everything and causing her bracelets to slide up her arm in a jangly little cascade. This pace of things, this occasional lapse into silence, this unurgency or ruminance, is near the heart of some matter with us now. I wish it would vamoose. 'I'm boring you,' she says, arms aloft, luminous. She's nobody's pushover and a wonderful sight to see. A smart man should find a way to love her.

'You're not boring me,' I say, feeling for some reason elated. (Possibly the leading edge of a cool front has passed, and everybody on the seaboard just felt better all at once.) 'I don't mind it that you like me. I think it's great.' Possibly I should kiss her again. A real one.

'You see other women, don't you?' she says and begins to shuffle her feet into a pair of flat gold sandals.

'Not really.'

'What's "not really"?' She picks her wine glass up off the floor. A mosquito is buzzing my ear. I'm more than ready to head inside and forget this topic.

'I don't. That's all. I guess if somebody came along who I wanted to see'—See. A word I hate. I'm happier with 'boff' or 'boink,' 'roger' or 'diddle'—'then I feel like that'd be OK. With me, I mean.'

'Right,' Sally says curtly.

Whatever spirit has moved her to put her sandals on has passed now. I hear her take a deep breath, wait then let it slowly out. She is holding her glass by its smooth, round base.

'I think you see other men,' I say hopefully. Cuff links come to mind.

'Of course.' She nods, staring over the porch banister toward small yellow dots embedded in darkness at an incomprehensible distance. I think again of us Divorced Men, huddled for safety's sake on our bestilled vessel, staring longingly at the mysterious land (possibly at this very house), imagining lives, parties, cool restaurants, late-night carryings-on we ached to be in on. Any one of us would've swum ashore against the flood to do what I'm doing. 'I have this odd feeling about seeing other men,' Sally says meticulously. 'That I *do* it but I'm not planning anything.' To my huge surprise, though I'm not certain, she scoops a tear from the corner of her eye and massages it dry between her fingers. This is why we are staying on the porch. I of course didn't know she was *actually* 'seeing' other men.

'What would you like to be waiting on?' I say, too earnestly.

'Oh, I don't know.' She sniffs to signify I needn't worry about further tears. 'Waiting's just a bad habit. I've done it before. Nothing, I guess.' She runs her fingers back through her thick hair, gives her head a tiny clearing shake. I'd like to ask about the anchor, ball and chain, but this is not the moment, since all I'd do is find out. 'Do you think *you're* waiting for something to happen?' She looks up at me again, skeptically. Whatever my answer, she's expecting it to be annoying or deceitful or possibly stupid.

'No,' I say, an attempt at frankness—something I probably can't bring off right now. 'I don't know what it'd be for either.'

'So,' Sally says. 'Where's the good part in anything if you don't think something good's coming, or you're going to get a prize at the end? What's the good mystery?'

'The good mystery's how long anything can go on the way it is. That's enough for me.' My life at this period *par excellence*. Sally and Ann are united in their distaste for this view.

'My oh my oh *my!*' She leans her head back and stares up at the starless ceiling and laughs an odd high-pitched girlish *ha-ha-ha*. 'I underestimated you. That's good. I . . . never mind. You're right. You're completely right.'

'I'd be happy to be wrong,' I say, and look, I'm sure, goofy.

'Fine,' Sally says, looking at me as if I were the rarest of rare species. 'Waiting to be proved wrong, though—that's not exactly taking the bull by the horns, is it, Franky?'

'I never really understood why anybody'd take a bull by its horns in the first place,' I say. 'That's the dangerous end.' I don't much like being called 'Franky,' as though I were six and of indeterminate gender.

'Well, look.' She is now sarcastic. 'This is just an experiment. It's not personal.' Her eyes flash, even in the dark, catching light from somewhere, maybe the house next door, where lamps have been switched on, making it look cozy and inviting indoors. I wouldn't mind being over there. 'What does it mean to you to tell somebody you love them? Or her?'

'I don't really have anybody to say that to.' This is not a comforting question.

'But if you did? Someday you might.' This inquiry suggests I have become an engaging but totally out-of-the-question visitor from another ethical system.

'I'd be careful about it.'

'You're always careful,' Sally knows plenty about my life—that I am sometimes finicky but in fact often not careful. More irony.

'I'd be *more* careful.'

'What would you mean if you said it, though?' She may in fact believe my answer will someday mean something important to her, explain why certain paths were taken, others abandoned: 'It was a time in my life I was lucky enough to survive,' or 'This'll explain why I got out of New Jersey and went to work with the natives in Pago Pago.'

'Well,' I say, since she deserves an honest answer, 'it's provisional. I guess I'd mean I see enough in someone I liked that I'd want to make up a whole person out of that part, and want to keep that person around.'

'What does that have to do with being in love?' She is intent, almost prayerful, staring at me in what I believe may be a hopeful manner.'

'Well, we'd have to agree that that was what love was, or is. Maybe that's too severe.' (Though I don't really think so.)

'It *is* severe,' she says. A fishing boat sounds a horn out in the ocean dark.

'I didn't want to exaggerate,' I say. 'When I got divorced I promised I'd never complain about how things turned out. And not exaggerating is a way of making sure I don't have anything to complain about.'

'You can probably be talked out of your severe view of love, though, can't you? Maybe that's what you meant by being happy to be wrong.' Sally stands as she says this, once again raises her arms, wineglass in hand, and twists herself side to side. The fact that one leg is shorter than the other is not apparent. She is five feet ten. Almost my height.

'I haven't thought so.'

'It really wouldn't be easy, I guess, would it? It'd take something unusual.' She is watching the beach where someone has just started an illegal campfire, which makes the night at this moment seem sweet and cheerful. But from sudden sheer discomfort and also affection and admiration for her scrupulousness, I'm compelled to grab my arms around her from behind and give her a hug and a smoochy schnuzzle that works out better than the last one. She is no longer humid underneath her caftan, where she seems to my notice to be wearing no clothes, and is sweeter than sweet. Though her arms stay limp at her side. No reciprocation. 'At least you don't need to worry how to trust all over again? All that awful shit, the stuff my dying people never talk about. They don't have time.'

'Trust's for the birds,' I say, my arms still around her. I live for just these moments, the froth of a moment's pseudo-intimacy and pleasure just when you don't expect it. It is wonderful. Though I don't believe we have accomplished much, and I'm sorry.

'Well,' Sally says, regaining her footing and pushing my cloying arms off in a testy way without turning around, making for the door, her limp now detectable. 'Trust's for the birds. Isn't it just. That's the way it has to be, though.'

'I'm pretty hungry,' I say.

She walks off the porch, lets the screen slap shut. 'Come in then, and eat your bow ties. You have miles to go before you sleep.'

Though as the sound of her bare feet recedes down the hall, I am alone in the warm sea smells mixed with driftwood smoke, a barbecue smell that's perfect for the holiday. Someone next door turns on a radio, loud at first, then softer. *E-Z Listn'n* from New Brunswick. Liza is singing, and I myself drift like smoke for a minute in the music: 'Isn't it romantic? Music in the night . . . Moving shadows write the oldest magic . . . I hear the breezes playing . . . You were meant for love . . . Isn't it romantic?'

At dinner, eaten at the round oak table, under bright, ceiling light, seated either side of the vase sprouting purple irises and white wisteria and a wicker cornucopia spilling summery legumes, our talk is eclectic, upbeat, a little dizzying. It is, I understand, a prelude to departure, with all memory of languor and serious discussion of love's particulars off-limits now, vanished like smoke in the sea breeze. (The police have since arrived, and the firemakers hauled off to jail the instant they complained about the beach's being owned by God.)

In the candlelight Sally is spirited, her blue eyes moist and shining, her splendid angular face tanned and softened. We fork up bow ties and yak about movies we haven't seen but would like to; we talk about possible panic in the soybean market now that rain has ended the drought in the parched Middle West; we discuss 'drouth' and 'drought'; I tell her about my real estate problems there, which leads somehow to a discussion of a Negro columnist who shot a trespasser in his yard, which prompts Sally to admit she sometimes carries a handgun in her purse, right in South Mantoloking, though she probably believes it will be the instrument that kills her. For a brief time I talk about my son Paul, noting that he is not much attracted to fire, doesn't torture animals, isn't a bed-wetter that I know of, and that my hopes are he will live with me in the fall.

Then (from some strange compulsion) I charge into realty. I report that there were 2,036 shopping centers built in the US two years ago, but now the numbers are 'way off,' with many big projects stalled. I affirm that I don't see the election mattering a hill of beans to the realty market, which provokes Sally to remember what rates were back in the bicentennial year (8.75 per cent). While she mixes Jersey blueberries in kirsch for spooning over sponge cake, I try to steer us clear of the too-recent past, talk on about my grandfather losing the family farm in Iowa over a gambling debt and coming in late at night, eating a bowl of berries of some kind in the kitchen, then stepping out onto the front porch and shooting himself.

I have noticed, however, throughout dinner that Sally and I have continued to make long and often unyielding eye contact. Once, while making coffee using the filter-and-plunger system, she's stolen a glimpse at me as if to acknowledge we've gotten to know each other a lot better now, have ventured closer, but that I've been acting strange or crazy and might just leap up and start reciting Shakespeare in pig Latin or whistling 'Yankee Doodle' through my butt.

Toward ten, though, we have kicked back in our captain's chairs, a new candle lit, having finished coffee and gone back to the Round Hill Fumé Blanc. Sally has bunched her dense hair back, and we are launched into a discussion of our individual self-perceptions: mine basically as a comic character; Sally's a 'facilitator,' though from time to time, she says, 'as a dark and pretty ruthless obstructor'—which I've never noticed. She sees me, she says, in an odd priestly mode, which is in fact the worst thing I can imagine, since priests are the least self-aware, most unenlightened, irresolute, isolated and frustrated people on the earth (politicians are second). I decide to ignore this, or at least to treat it as disguised goodwill and to mean I, too, am a kind of facilitator, which I would be if I could. I tell her I see her as a great beauty with a sound head on her shoulders, who I find compelling, which is true (I'm still shaken by being perceived as a priest). We venture on toward the issue of strong feelings, how they're maybe more important than love. I explain (why, I'm not sure, when it's not particularly true) that I'm having a helluva good time these days, but I fully admit that this part of my life may someday be—except for her—hard to remember with precision, and that sometimes I feel beyond affection's grasp but that's just being human and no cause for worry. I also tell her I could acceptably end my life as the 'dean' of New Jersey realtors, a crusty old bird who's forgotten more than the younger men could ever know. She says quite confidently, all the while smiling at me, that she hopes I can get around to doing something memorable, and for a moment I think again about bringing up the Marine cuff links and their general relation to things memorable, and possibly dropping in my wife's name—not wanting to seem unable to or as if her very existence were a reproach to Sally, which it isn't. I decide not to do either of these.

Gradually, then, there comes into Sally's voice some tone of greater gravity, some chin-down throatiness I've heard before and on just such well-wrought evenings as this, yellow light twiny and flickering, the summer heat gone off, an occasional bug bouncing off the front screen; a tone that all by itself says, 'Let's us give a thought to something a little more direct to make us both feel good, seal the evening with an act of simple charity and desire.'

My own voice, I'm sure, has the same oaken burr.

Only there's the old nerviness in my lower belly (and in hers too, it's my guess), an agitation connected to a thought that won't go away and that each of us is waiting for the other to admit—something important that leaves sweetly sighing desire back in the dust. Which is: that we've both by our own private means decided not to see each other anymore. (Though 'decided' is not the word. Accepted, conceded, demurred—these are more in the ballpark.) There's plenty of everything between us, enough for a lifetime's consolation, with extras. But that's somehow not sufficient, and once that is understood, nothing much is left to say (is there?). In both the long run and the short, nothing between us seems to matter enough. These facts we both acknowledge with the aforementioned throaty tones and with these words that Sally actually speaks: 'It's time for you to hit the road, Bub.' She beams at me through the candle flicker as though she were somehow proud of us, or for us. (For what?) She's long since taken off her turquoise bracelets and stacked them on the table, moving them here and there as we've talked, like a player at a Ouija board. When I stand up she begins putting them on again.

The hall clock chimes ten-thirty. I look around as though a closer timepiece might be handy, but I've known almost the exact minute for an hour.

She's standing now beside the table, fingers just touching the grain, smiling still, like my most steadfast admirer. 'Do you want me to make more coffee?'

'I drive better asleep,' I say, and produce a witless grin.

Then off I go, rumbling right down the hall past the winking green security panel—which might as well have changed to red.

Sally follows at a distance of ten feet and not fast, her limp pronounced for her being barefooted. She's allowing me to let myself out.

'So, OK.' I turn around. She's still smiling, no less than eight feet back. But I am not smiling. In the time taken to walk to the screen door I've become willing to be asked to stay, to get up early, have some coffee and beat it to Connecticut after a night of adieus and possible reconsiderations. I close my eyes and fake a little weaving stagger meant to indicate *Boy, I'm sleepier than I thought and conceivably even a danger to myself and others.* But I've waited too long expecting something to happen to me; and if *I* were to ask, I'm confident she'd simply phone up the Cabot Lodge in Neptune and check me in. I can't even have my old room back. My visit has become like a house-showing in which I leave nothing but my card in the foyer.

'I'm real glad you came,' Sally says. I'm afraid she might even 'put 'er there' and with it push me out the door I came through months ago in all innocence.

But she doesn't. She walks up, grasps my short shirtsleeves above my elbows—we are at eye level—and plants one on me hard but not mean, and says, in a little breath that wouldn't extinguish a candle, 'Bye-bye.'

'Bye-bye,' I say, trying to mimic her seductive whisper and translate it possibly into hello. My heart races.

But I'm history. Out the door and down the steps. Along the sandy concrete beach walk in the fading barbecue aroma, down sandy steps to Asbury Street, at the lighted other end of which Ocean Avenue streams with cruising lovers on parade. I crawl into my Crown Vic, though as I start up I crane around and survey the shadowy cars behind me on both sides, hoping to spy the other guy, whoever he is, if he is, someone on the lurk in summer khakis, waiting for me to clear out so he can march back along my tracks and into my vested place in Sally's house and heart.

But there's no one spying that I can see. A cat runs from one line of parked cars to the one I'm in. A porch light blinks down Asbury Street. Lights are on in most all the houses, TVs warmly humming. There're nothing, nothing to be suspicious of, nothing to think about, nothing to hold me here another second. I turn the wheel, back out, look up briefly at my empty window, then motor on.

The literary break of the year!

As Swansea hosts the UK Year of Literature & Writing 1995, why not take the opportunity to hear some of the greatest writers and enjoy a short break in Swansea, with the outstanding Gower Peninsula on the doorstep.

Criminal Pursuits 19-21 May
Folk Writes 26-29 May
Dylan Thomas Month 1-30 June
The Importance of Being Elsewhere (Irish Writing) 13-18 June
The First Literature Proms 11 August-9 September
Chiness Moon September
Under the Veld 27-30 September
Star Crossed Lovers 7-21 October
Readers of Today, Writers of Tomorrow 7-14 October
Welcome to the Nightmare 27-31 October
Speaking in Tongues 2-5 November
Press, Peace and Politics 7-12 November

The Ghost Story 17-19 November
Caledonian Companions 25 November -2 December
Out of This World 7-11 December

Visiting Writers Include:
Kenzaburo Oe
Seamus Heaney
Bono
PD James
Maxine Hong Kingston
Jonathan Coe
Sarah Dunant
Czeslaw Milosz
Terry Pratchett
James Kelman
and many more

For more information on the Festival Programme and to book tickets and accommodation telephone: **01792 652211**
For more information on Swansea Bay, Mumbles and Gower, telephone: **01792 468321**

Beautiful bays, beaches & books

GRANTA

ROMESH GUNESEKERA
THE HOLE

M y mother was the one who told me he was dead. I ran into the bathroom and bolted the door. There was a small window in there with two round jail-house bars. I held on to them hard. I was only ten. I let the tears roll down to the sides of my mouth, and licked them to harden my insides. I wanted to cry gushingly, but I couldn't. He had gone too fast from our world of make-believe. It has taken me all of thirty years to learn to mourn properly.

Alone, I turned on the hot water. The geyser ignited with a small explosion, and a trickle of warm water formed a thin column merging silver with rust, quivering into a pale green pool. I wanted the comfort of running water, nothing more. Water was his element. He loved everything about it: the algae, the microbes, the aquatic ferns, the gouramis, guppies and angel fish he kept in a dozen tanks around the house. He loved swimming, growing up half-submerged, long, tall, fish-lipped, almost a *mer*man. And the water had felt for him. It entered him. It thinned his blood, it settled in his knee, swelling it until it was too painful for him even to cycle. The doctors syringed it out one afternoon, while I shot down the hill on my red bike. I could coast without hands and, where the slope was steepest by the Muslim cemetery, with my feet up on the handlebars. He wanted to try it when I told him about it, but his leg kept going bad. The knee kept filling up with water, like a boat with a hole in it, every couple of weeks he would list, and the doctors would have to bail him out.

O ne day, he said we had to build a bunker. 'We are going to hole up. No one will be able to come close.' He grinned. He was losing weight, and his face appeared bonier every day. His teeth were enormous. His big lips seemed undone, bubbling with ill wind.

'OK. Yes, OK.' I would do anything for him. He was fifteen.

We got hold of a couple of spades and started to dig a hole in his father's back garden. He marked off a rectangle—six-by-four—and we dug deep into the buffalo-blade lawn. 'It's got to be deep enough to stand in,' he said. I had to cart away the spare earth and pile it up next to the chicken sheds. By the end of the day, we had a hole as big as a grave.

His father came home that evening and saw the grim hole in the middle of his lawn. He stood by the fish tanks and looked at us, but he said nothing. His face was a mask. He must have seen the knee swelling up again, his son dropping into the ground as if into the sea.

That night, I stayed over. I slept in a small camp-bed on the upstairs veranda. He had to sleep with a splint fastened to his leg. He'd grit his teeth every time he shifted. From my bed, I could see the garden. The plastic sheet we used to cover the pit gave a glow, and I whispered to him reports of ghosts and gangsters and trapped stars. He would call back from some darker world commands for our escape and then instructions for building a new shelter above the pit. 'We are going to have to dismantle the tree house, move it down.'

'But why?' We had taken ages over the tree house. Hauling planks and boards on pulleys up a huge breadfruit tree in the wasteland next door. There was my blood on the tree where I had cut my hand hacking a branch to make the platform. From it we could survey the whole neighbourhood: a sea of unkempt gardens and wild fruit trees. We could see into the German ambassador's bedroom, where the curtains were kept open and the afternoons unrestrained. 'I like the tree house,' I whispered.

'It's time to go underground, now,' he whispered back. 'I can't climb any more.'

The next day, we took down the tree house. He stood on the ground and handled the rope, letting down the chair we had hauled up before, then the doors we had used for walls, the tin roof and, finally, the platform itself. I stayed up on the Y-shaped branch that supported it, watching it all disappear below me. Finally, I undid our pulley system and let everything slide down.

Out on the lawn, he laid out all the pieces of the new edifice, like the components of an Airfix model, around the pit: two planks on one side, a board, a pole, two sheets of corrugated tin, two old panelled doors we had scavenged from a disused building, wire mesh, wooden posts. Even a bead curtain.

He climbed down into the pit and lined it with plastic sheets.

207

Then he lay down in the hole and grinned at me, 'OK, this will stay dry, for sure.'

By midday, we had a new shack built over the pit. There was a small door through which you could crawl in and then drop down into the pit. You could use the viewing-gap to keep watch. I hankered after the old tree house, high up and far away, but he kept patting the ground around him saying, 'This is it. This is our place. We are in the earth.'

We spent the rest of the day in our hole in the garden, pretending the chicken squawks from the backyard were the transmissions of enemy patrols combing the Colombo jungle.

A few days later, his leg completely gave way, and he was rushed to a cancer hospital abroad. That night, I went over to collect my things from his veranda. A storm broke, and I stayed up there alone, watching the lightning, the pulse of a petrified, brilliant sky. A flash hit the tin roof of our shack in the middle of the garden. For one searing, beautiful moment it was incandescent; then the whole world turned dark again. Water poured out of the sky and flattened everything.

He never saw the little shack in the middle of the garden again. And I never saw him again.

NORMAN LEWIS
HEMINGWAY IN CUBA

I met Ian Fleming at Cape's annual party. Jonathan Cape made no secret of disliking Fleming, had read only the first chapter of *Casino Royale* and nothing whatever of his subsequent books, but reluctantly accepted that he was likely to become the firm's best-selling author since T. E. Lawrence.

When I arrived at the party, I was shunted off into a side room of which Ian was the only occupant. He was prone to fits of paranoia, and at that moment was in a foul mood, having taken it into his head, quite wrongly, that the party was for Cape's less prestigious authors. He soon recovered, and asked me if I wrote poetry. When I replied that I did not, he seemed disappointed. He admitted to being bored with thrillers of the kind he wrote, and enjoyed the company of those who had dedicated their lives to higher literary ideals.

He then began to quiz me on the Caribbean. It was generally known that during the war he had been assistant to the Director of Naval Intelligence, and from the way his questioning went, it seemed clear that although he was now foreign editor of the *Sunday Times*, his link with intelligence had not been severed, and that his field of operation was Latin America.

He wanted to talk to me about Cuba, and I told him that I had visited the island twice, had travelled from one end of it to the other and still had friends there with whom I exchanged occasional letters.

During the war, I had also been engaged in intelligence duties at a fairly low level, and it was clear that Fleming was aware of this. He asked me if I would consider visiting Cuba on behalf of the *Sunday Times*. This sounded to me like an interesting temporary escape, and I said that I would. He explained that an uprising had taken place on the island, and he was convinced that the reports passed to him through official sources tended to play down the importance of what was happening. He believed I might be able to get nearer the truth.

At this point, a strange convergence of interests became evident. Fleming believed that Ernest Hemingway was in contact

Opposite: Ernest Hemingway at his farmhouse Finca Vegia in Cuba.

with the revolutionaries, and that he was the man I should see. The trouble was that Hemingway had taken himself off to live in isolation on a farm somewhere outside Havana, and Jonathan Cape, his publisher, was the only man in England in touch with him. Jonathan was anxious to hear news of what was expected to be Hemingway's final masterpiece, and Fleming was convinced that if Cape could be induced to write a letter to him on my behalf, he would see me. This Jonathan Cape agreed to do, and the arrangements for the journey went ahead.

It was a Sunday in late December 1957 when I arrived in Havana. I was carrying a letter of introduction to a New Zealander named Edward Scott who edited the *Havana Post* and lived in the Sevilla Biltmore Hotel—rather splendidly, Ian told me, in the penthouse flat. At Ian's request, Scott had reserved a room there for me, but had since been called away to Pinar Del Rio, leaving me a note saying that he might be held up there for two or three days. I unpacked, took a quick bath and decided to take a short tour of the neighbourhood.

The Sevilla Biltmore was on the Prado, Havana's principal street, which even now, at half-past eight in the morning, was full of strolling, loudly chattering crowds, the men smoking tremendous cigars. There were many American tourists, some of them behaving rather erratically, and I was told by the man at the kiosk from whom I bought the morning edition of Scott's newspaper that most of them were drunk and would probably remain so over the whole of their weekend in Havana. His words were confirmed by the number of bars advertising, in English, HANGOVER BREAKFASTS.

I carried on down to the port, where at this hour the Galician shark fishermen were bringing in their blood-lacquered boats, and then went on to the Malecón, the greatest sea promenade in the world. Nothing had changed in the nineteen years since my last visit. Once again, I was overwhelmed by the flowering, scented spaces, the grey, time-scoured walls with their granite facets glistening, the thrusting femininity of the women, the playful arrogance of the men, the soft growl of negro voices through the spray spattering over the sea wall, the rust-choked barrels of cannons that had last been fired at the English pirates, the millionaires' seaside houses like wedding cakes turned to stone and painted red, blue or yellow according to the owner's political allegiance.

Despite these outward appearances, profound changes had taken place. Batista—formerly known as 'the handsome mulatto' —had taken on and defeated the ferocious colonels of the old regime, but now Batista too was old, and had himself been defeated by success and time. Instead of laughing at his opponents, he shot them, and the city was filled with unmarked graves.

One of the old reactionary officers, Enrique Loynaz, had actually survived and, not only that, had risen to the rank of general. By the greatest of good luck, I had a letter of introduction to him, and the next day I paid him a call. He took me to see General García Velez, the other surviving hero of Cuba's war of independence against Spain.

Velez was an anglophile and for twelve years had been ambassador to Great Britain. Since his return to Cuba, he had done his best, against considerable odds, to create for himself a West End of London environment, filling his flat with heavy Victorian furniture imported from England. The room in which he received us was overflowing with fringed lampshades, antimacassars and aspidistras. He was ninety-four and believed the fairly sedate surroundings in which he lived might help him to last out to a hundred.

The horrors of war had left Velez a pacifist, whereas Loynaz, despite a variety of wounds, was as bellicose as ever. The story of his most dramatic escape from death was held ready for such occasions, and as soon as the pretty mulatta in lace cap, apron and gloves had brought the Earl Grey tea, he launched into it.

It happened at Babinay in 1898, as the war was drawing to a close. The Cubans could already taste victory, and the Spanish were preparing to sell their lives dearly behind a seven-foot stockade. Loynaz, a poor horseman at the best of times, as he readily admitted, was now compelled by custom to mount a white horse and lead the final charge.

'I was never a good jumper,' he said. 'I fell, landing on the horse's neck, and one of the Spaniards brought down his machete on the top of my head.'

Both Velez and I were ordered to examine the result. There was a trough about six inches long on his skull, and its edges could still be felt through the skin.

'Three American presidents have felt that wound,' Loynaz said, 'Harding, Teddy Roosevelt and—I forget the third. Anyway, I managed to scramble back into the saddle, holding my brain in with my fingers. They got me to the nearest house. There was a couple staying there on their honeymoon, and we commandeered their bed. It was a month before I was on my feet again, and I noticed a remarkable thing. Up until then, I had suffered from headaches all my life. Now they were gone. My doctor said that opening up the skull had made more space for the brains.'

It was now García Velez's turn. 'Do you think he'd like to see the album, Enrique?' he asked.

'I'm quite sure he would,' Loynaz replied.

Velez found a bunch of keys on a shelf and took them into the next room. He returned with his album and, displacing an aspidistra, made room for it on a low table.

He opened it carefully, explaining that he had inherited it from an ancestor named Francisco Miranda. Loynaz released a preliminary cackle as I found myself looking down at a wisp of hair as dry as hay stuck to the centre of a yellowed page over an illegible scrawl of faded ink.

'What you see there is pubic hair, one of fifty-one examples donated by the great ladies of Miranda's acquaintance,' said Loynaz.

'What on earth made them agree?' I asked.

'It was a passing craze,' Velez said. 'It did a woman's reputation no harm to have had an association with a man of the standing of Francisco Miranda. All the women were after him.' He stroked the filaments of hair with a fingertip. 'This is La Perechola La Segunda,' he said. 'She was the greatest actress ever to appear on the South American stage. Pay no attention to the message. It's a fake. She couldn't write. Nine out of ten of them couldn't.'

'May we see the greatest of the conquests?' Loynaz asked.

'You may,' Velez said. He leafed cautiously through the pages, then stopped.

'This one should be in a museum,' Loynaz said.

'It should. Where it could be properly looked after, before it's lost altogether. I've offered it to the National Museum, but they seem to be toffee-nosed these days.'

This time, the writing was legible under the ragged little tuft: a splendid, arrogant K, half-smothered in entwining curlicues. 'Catherine,' Loynaz murmured reverently.

Velez nodded. 'The Great Queen.'

'Apart from the remains in the Kremlin vault, this is all that has survived of the body of Catherine the Great of all Russias.'

I expressed all the wonder expected of me, yet a lurking doubt remained. Later, after Loynaz and I had left, I asked him whether he thought the Catherine part were true.

Loynaz patted at the cavity in his skull as if to confirm that the brains were still in position. It was a gesture that suggested he might not be sure of the facts.

'No reason why it shouldn't be,' he said. 'Miranda was forty-odd at the time, an absolute ram. Catherine put up money for his adventures and invited him to stay in Moscow. She was very lustful. And besides, she was fifty-eight.'

On my next visit to Velez, I asked him about the political situation. People, I said, were talking of the Castro revolt and its chances of success. What was it all about? My question gave Velez the chance to ride his favourite hobby-horse: the scandalous treatment Cuba, and he himself, had received at American hands after the War of Independence. This, he believed, had sown the seeds of almost all the nation's subsequent troubles.

'The war was over before they arrived,' Velez said. 'They dropped like vultures out of the sky to pick up the spoils. For six years, the Yankees ran the country and snapped up everything worth having. Hence Castro.'

'What do you mean?' I asked.

'A lot of middle-class boys see Castro as their only chance of getting anywhere. Don't ever believe Karl Marx has anything to do with it. We're talking about high-school boys who can't find nice white-collar jobs. Fidel started out as a lawyer. He went in for revolutions because he only had ten clients, and they were too poor to pay. Do you know how the present bother started? It was over an incґease in bus fares. That's the cause of the trouble: university drop-outs who refuse to walk.'

The next morning, Scott returned, and we met in the hotel coffee shop. His appearance came as such a surprise that for a moment I thought that I had picked out the wrong man. Ian had told me that James Bond was an amalgam of four actual persons, one of whom was Scott. But the man before me was short and somewhat plump, with rosy cheeks, small blue eyes and the expression of a confiding child. He had once been a champion boxer, but had put on weight since then.

As this one-quarter of James Bond read my letter of introduction very slowly, folded it with great care and put it into the breast pocket of his shirt, I took in further details of his appearance: the small feet encased in brilliantly polished shoes, the gold fountain-pen and the small, dimpled hands. In moments of concentration, as while reading the letter, his expression became wary and stern.

'Let's go and talk things over,' he suggested. He guided me to the lift, and we went up to his flat which was at the end of a long passage scented with wax polish and fine cigars. We passed first of all into a small anteroom, in which stood, elegantly posed, a quite naked negress. At first, I took her to be a statue, but in passing I could not help noticing the goose-pimples produced by the chill of the air-conditioning. Scott glanced at her as we passed into his office.

I later learned that Scott believed frequent intercourse to increase mental creativity, and I wondered if he had simply forgotten that the girl was there. He kept a register in which he entered the details of several thousand encounters over the years. It was a compulsion he shared with John F. Kennedy, who occasionally popped over to Havana for random excitements of this kind, and Scott had had the pleasure of showing him round.

'Why do you want to see Hemingway?' he asked.

Photo: Burt Glinn (Magnum)

'Because Ian thinks that he and Castro may be working together.'

Scott gave a bellowing laugh. 'Hemingway, of all people!'.

'There's some story that he met Castro when he was hunting in the mountains.'

'The only mountain Hemingway hunts in is the Montana Bar. He's a burnt-out case. Any time you want, you can see him in there. His friends bring him king-sized prawns. He chews them up and swallows the lot, shells and all.'

Scott's dislike of the great man stemmed from an incident that happened at a party to celebrate the Queen's birthday given by the British Ambassador, at which Ava Gardner had appeared on Hemingway's arm. In a moment of high spirits, the actress had taken off her pants and waved them at the crowd. Scott, who considered himself an ultra-patriot, objected to this insult to the Crown. In the wrangle that followed, Hemingway, known for his aggression, threatened to thrash Scott to 'within an inch of his life'.

'Next day,' Scott said, 'I sent him a formal challenge to a duel. Don't laugh. This is a serious matter.'

'Do people still fight duels in Cuba?' I asked.

'They do. Frequently. Right now, they have a couple of victims in the city morgue, mixed up with the student revolutionaries.'

'Do you think he'll accept?'

'No, I think he'll back down. Anyway, in case he doesn't, how about being my second?'

'Sorry,' I said. 'It would make a good story, but nobody would ever believe it.'

Scott seemed to want to impress on me that his talk of duels was not to be taken lightly, and took me off to a private shooting gallery in the offices of the *Havana Post*. The far end of the room had been fixed up with an arrangement of the kind that might have been used in a fairground; playing cards were clipped to moving wires in a way that allowed them to move laterally at varying speeds, jerking up and down simultaneously.

He then produced two sinister-looking pistols. He set the cards in motion, bobbing and ducking on their wires, and we took aim. I failed to hit anything, and so did he.

'Pst . . . missed it again. Pst . . . this isn't my day. Pst . . . not again! I don't believe it. Pst . . . I'm not altogether happy with the way these fit into the hand. May have something to do with it. Hang on while I slow the thing down.'

I expected no better of myself, but for someone who was a quarter of James Bond, it was not good enough, and it occurred to me that it might be as well for him if Hemingway did turn his challenge down.

B ack at my hotel, a call came through from Ian Fleming. 'How's it all going?' he asked.
'Fairly well,' I said.
'Have you talked to the writing man?'
'Not so far,' I said.
'Do your best to see him.'
I assured him that I would. Fleming had just re-read *The*

Above: Hemingway and Fidel Castro, 1961.

Old Man and the Sea, and was more convinced than ever that it was a masterpiece. He had the book open by the telephone and read me a favourite passage. I agreed with him that it was superb but could not see that this literary skill had any bearing upon the author's judgement of a political situation. 'People say he keeps out of politics these days,' I said, 'but I'll go on trying to have a word with him.'

Some days later, a letter arrived from the great man saying that he had heard from Jonathan and would be pleased to see me. It was written in a small, neat hand, with a certain formality of tone. He would be sending a car to pick me up the next day.

The car duly arrived, and I was driven to Hemingway's converted farmhouse in the hilly outer suburbs of the city. The retreat was protected by a high fence over which hardly more than the roof was to be seen. There was a gate on the approach road, secured by a heavy padlock and chain. When we stopped, the driver got out, thrust a huge key into the padlock and let us through. I wandered a short way up a drive to the house, little realizing that each step was taking me closer to an experience which would change my outlook on life, not instantly, but in a most fundamental way.

I was about to enter the presence of a being of a heroic, almost legendary kind, who had reconstructed the literary architecture of the twentieth century and had now, with his recent book, been awarded its highest prize. In addition to these achievements, Hemingway had had the courage and the vision to speak out on the side of the Spanish Republican government when it was under attack not only from Spanish rebels but from the troops sent to Spain by Mussolini and from Hitler's Luftwaffe, which first practised on Spanish territory its techniques of mass destruction. He had pleaded with the English, the inventors of non-intervention, to realize that they would be next, and even then he was a big enough man for his warnings to be listened to, even if they were subsequently ignored.

The driver pushed open the door and shoved me through it into a narrow passage with another door at the end. I tapped on this, and a growl came from the other side which I took to be an invitation to enter. I did so, and found myself in some kind of bedroom lined with bookshelves. Bottles were stacked within reach of the bed on which Hemingway was sitting. He hauled himself to his feet and turned to face me. He was in his pyjamas, and I was shocked and bewildered by what I saw. He had remained forever young in my imagination, boisterous and vigorous in the never-ending fiesta of life. But here was an old man, slow-moving, burdened with flesh.

He mumbled a welcome and, moving slowly under the great weight of his body to find the drinks, poured himself, to my astonishment, a tumbler of Dubonnet, half of which he immediately gulped down. Above all, it was his expression that shocked me, for there was an exhaustion and emptiness in his face: the corners of his mouth were dragged down by what might have been despair, and his eyes gave the impression that he was trying to weep.

Two objectives of this visit were to be kept in mind, the first being Jonathan Cape's hope for the imminent delivery of the book Hemingway had been reported as working on for several years. A cautious reference to this subject provoked something close to an outburst of fury. Wasted and watery eyes swivelled around to focus on me with suspicion. What did I want? What had I come for? 'Is this an interview?' he asked coldly.

There was something about him which reminded me of Massart in *For Whom the Bell Tolls*—'one of France's great modern revolutionary figures,' Chief Commissar of the International Brigade, a 'symbol man' who cannot be touched. With infallible discernment, Hemingway had described this great old man's descent into pettiness, and now I was amazed that a writer who had understood how greatness could be pulled down by the wolves of weakness and old age should—as it appeared to me—have been unable to prevent himself from falling into the same trap. How grotesque, but how sad, must have been his appearance at the embassy party with Ava Gardner on his arm.

I hastily assured him that I was no more than a messenger from a very old and devoted friend, his enthusiastic publisher, who had hoped that I would be able to convey his heartfelt congratulations on the success of *The Old Man and the Sea*.

Humble pie produced the reverse of the desired effect.

Hemingway embarked on a tirade over what he saw as Cape's parsimonious handling of the publication. 'They didn't want to spend money on it,' he said. To make sure the American edition had a good dust-jacket, he had hired a first-class artist himself, but the English version had been done on the cheap, and sales had suffered. At this point, someone rattled at the back door, and Hemingway lurched towards it with a cry of irritation to suppress the female twitterings that came through.

The subject of Scott's challenge now came up. 'Do you know this guy? I hear you've been seen around with him. Is he a friend of yours?'

'I had an introduction from London. I've seen him a few times.'

'He's been built up as some sort of dead-eye Dick. You think that's true?'

'I've no way of knowing,' I said, 'but I doubt it.'

'Take a look at his,' he said. He handed me a copy of a letter he had written to the *Havana Post*. I read it. He had taken note, he said, of a challenge to a duel made by Edward Scott, the newspaper's editor. This he had decided not to take up in the belief that he owed it to his readers not to jeopardize his life by its acceptance.

'Dignified?' he asked.

'Very,' I said.

'Give me your frank opinion. What do you feel about this business yourself?'

'I wholly agree with you. The thing's absurd. Even if this is Cuba, it is the twentieth century.'

'Right,' he said. He nodded vigorously, smiling for the first time in the course of our meeting. 'That's the way it is.'

I was astonished, in view of the macho posturing for which he had become famous, that he was prepared to give this publicity to what many of the paper's readers would see as a loss of nerve and of face.

As there was nothing more to be done for Jonathan Cape, only Ian Fleming's interest remained to be served. I took the plunge.

'How do you see all this ending?' I asked. 'Can Castro pull it off?'

Comrade Massart's cautious, watery, doubting eye was on me again. 'My answer to such questions is bound to be that I live here,' Hemingway said.

In my letter to Fleming, in which I reported on my meeting with Hemingway, I wrote:

> There was something biblical about it, like having the
> old sermon about the vanities shoved down your throat
> in the middle of whatever you happen to be doing with
> your life in the workaday world. They give funny names

to the buses in this town, and there's one that runs past the hotel that says WE JUST RAN SHORT OF GREATNESS, which just about sums him up, although perhaps understating the case. This man has had about everything any man can ever have wanted, and to meet him was a shattering experience of the kind likely to sabotage ambition—which may or may not be a good thing. You wanted to know his opinion on the possible outcome of what is happening here. The answer unfortunately is that he no longer cares to hold opinions, because his life has lost its taste. He told me nothing, but he taught me more than I wanted to know.

GERMAINE GREER
SHANGHAI EXPRESS

When I sent off my cheque for two berths on 'A Railway Cruise along the Silk Route . . . aboard Mao's State Train richly endowed with walnut panelling and brass fittings', I hadn't actually grasped the fact that if you travel from Samarkand to Shanghai, you spend most of your time in China. Nor had I any idea what a package tour was like. To judge from the list of things Ann and I were advised to bring with us—a pillow, a torch, comfortable rubber-soled shoes, medications, toiletries, razor-blades, reading matter, booze, raincoat, folding umbrella, bath towel and toilet paper—packages have great difficulty in adapting to changed circumstances. Most of the packages on the tour were seasoned members of the Hundred Countries Club and spent a good deal of their time in the bar discussing the countries they had 'done' rather than observing the one they were actually in. The unstated premise of such discourse is that foreigners behave incomprehensibly, and only the British are sane, clean and honest. Successful travel-writing in English projects the same subliminal message. Packages are interested in sight-seeing, getting a tan, souvenir-buying, being photographed against exotic backgrounds and, in this case, train-spotting.

After a night on Uzbekistan Airways, during which one of our elderly number fainted, presumed dead, we had to wait an hour or two at Tashkent airport for our connecting flight to Samarkand. I spent the time watching the hurrying, early-morning people, the women crudely made-up, their black hair bleached orange, lime green and cadmium yellow; their clothes cheap, ill-fitting and encrusted with glitter; their shoes plastic and stiletto-heeled; the men spivvy and unshaven in crumpled suits and collarless shirts. The only sign that we were in central Asia rather than Times Square was that many of the men wore traditional Uzbek caps, the same ones that you may see in the photographs of kulaks being exported to Siberia in the 1920s. With a dollar bill I bought a Coke and a handful of aluminium coins from a street stall. My parched fellow packages watched in horror as I swigged from the dirty bottle. The courtyard of the domestic terminal building boasted a *haaz*; I remembered Gustav Krist's thrillingly ghastly description of extracting a filaria worm in *Through the Forbidden Land* and peered in looking for snails.

Photo: Bradshaw (Katz)

227

No snails. Beside the tank someone had planted a peppery-smelling basil with a green leaf and purple flowers. Nobody objected when I gathered its seed.

We dropped down into Samarkand over irrigated fruit gardens and trodden-earth floors where small things, black and bronze, red and gold, had been laid out in neat squares to dry in the sun. Did I see coffee? Were they prunes or figs or what? 'Cotton, I should think,' said a package, consulting the wrong page of her guidebook. Ann and I fell in line and shuffled out of the airport on to a bus that bucked and bounded down the pot-holed boulevard in clouds of pinky-grey dust and threw us into the Hotel Samarkand for lunch. We shuffled out again to clamber over open trenches to gaze obediently at Gur Emir, its outside and its in, and to goggle at the jade cenotaph of Tamberlaine. Here we heard for the second time that the disturbance of Tamberlaine's remains coincided with the Nazi invasion of the Soviet Union, and his re-interment with the victory at Stalingrad. I was more interested in living women than dead tyrants. Through the doorways of the mud-brick houses, I could see courtyards where women wearing trousers of Uzbek silk under vividly patterned nylon velvet smocks squatted to their daily tasks. Every courtyard had a divan where the men could sit, smoke, play chess and converse on a higher plane.

Sleep-deprived and dyspeptic as we by now felt, the blue and gold splendours of the Registan, 'the noblest public square in the world', with its wonky minarets built to hold up the sky as if it were Ulug Bek's tent, all but overwhelmed us. Where the transfixed heads of executed miscreants once dripped blood into the sand, a hundred pennants fluttered, red, apricot, green and blue. Under the arch of the vast portico of the Sher Dor *madrase*, boys in plum-coloured track suits waited in formation; on the lower level, girls in white, with frothing pompoms on their heads wriggled nervously. Gangs of shouting youths endeavoured to spread padded felt mats and rugs, apparently for a wrestling match. On an upper tier, something disturbingly like morris dancing was going on. The over-amplified voice of a man in a suit, interrupted by bursts of patriotic music, bounced off the kingfisher-blue glaze and gold leaf. The Registan was alive and well and functioning as the town square of Samarkand, regardless of us and our buses, growling and gushing clouds of stinking black smoke as they waited to take us to meet our train.

The train boasted four dining-cars: an Oriental one, a Gothicky one, a red-plush one and one Fascist-chic. There were also a cavernous lounge bar, with very little in the way of drinks, and an entire carriage of shower-rooms. In all of these, Ann and I spent as little time as possible, choosing instead to loll on the cut velvet of our tall, mahogany-panelled compartment and stare out of the window. We were to be looked after and given water boiled in her samovar by a motherly young person called, naturally, Olga. We clattered out of Samarkand back towards Tashkent, through outcrops of dirty heavy industry and small fields of cotton. The cotton was one of the low-growing strains that produce more bolls and less stalk so that the crop can be harvested by tractors, but in these tiny fields men and women were plucking it by hand, bent double. Many miles to the west, the fishing industry of the Aral Sea has collapsed because the lake has shrunk to half its extent and a third of its volume as a result of vast irrigation schemes for cotton-growing. Every year, more and more land is lost to production through salination. As the workers toted their bales and piled them on donkey carts, Ann and I sat silent, appalled at this glimpse of what lay behind Soviet self-sufficiency in cotton.

Because every time Olga could get into our compartment, she pulled the curtains, we unhooked the curtain rod and hid it. She asked us to pull the window blinds down in case rocks should be thrown at the train. We chose to unscrew the light-bulbs and watch the dusk creep over the countryside. Two small boys ran up the steep side of the embankment; each flung a stone with all his small might. By night, bigger people used catapults to do more serious damage. The thick outer pane of our window was broken when we boarded the train; by morning, the corridor window too was a star burst of cracks. At first, we thought it was our foreignness that provoked these attacks, but the workers' trains that passed us on the way down from Irkutsk had been given the same treatment. Ann and I smiled and waved as an ad hoc way of finding out how the other travellers felt about us. Each time their big chapped faces lit up with hilarious astonishment.

The element of drama in our expedition was provided not by the spectacular scenery or the savage hordes that inhabited it, or by the giant spiders and man-killing scorpions of legend, or even by the stone-throwers, but by the lavatories. The train-fanciers among us probably knew the unpalatable truth about human waste flushed from trains travelling at speed. If I had known it then I would have been even more constipated than I was. When British engineers recently spent three days flushing hundreds of gallons of whitewash down train lavatories while technicians ran alongside the train catching the droplets on black card, they discovered that the whitewash was distributed not only all over the people standing by the line but funnelled back on to and into the train itself. When droplets of the real thing were examined they were found to be ten times more concentrated than household sewage. Within hours of departure from Samarkand, the gleaming coachwork of our train was stuck all over with shards of loo paper. If we wanted to get down from the train, we had to wait while white-gloved attendants wiped the goo off the handrails. Despite washing its face and cleaning its teeth in boiled water, within two or three days most of our party was racked by gripes, squits and scours. Touchingly, the packages all believed that the train was a haven from the insalubriousness of Asia. When I bought a netful of Hami melons, famed since antiquity as the sweetest-scented in the world, I was informed by a package that, because they take up so much water, melons carry cholera.

We were shaken to sleep long before we rolled over the Sir Darya. None of us noticed when we switched from the Transcaspian Railway to the dreaded Turk–Sib on which so many nomad herdsmen had travelled to exile and death. When the next day broke we were in Kazakhstan, running between treeless tablelands that looked as if they were covered in brown suede. 'Oh look,' quacked one of our number, 'they've cut down all the trees for firewood.' She seemed not to see the evidence of fifty years of Soviet tree-planting schemes, or to have noticed that the mud-brick houses had no chimneys on their corrugated fibro-cement roofs. There has never been any timber in this part of Kazakhstan, or on any part of the great steppe, just as there never was in Dakota. The nomads dealt with the continental extremes of heat and cold by insulating themselves in all weathers with sheepskin; they lived in yurts, cocoons made of layers and layers of sheep's wool beaten into felt. In exceptionally severe winters, many froze to death. What was amazing me was that even the meanest houses we saw had electricity. The reaction of the packages to the Electrification of the Soviet Union was to complain that the overhead power lines ruined their photographs.

The packages complained a lot—about the bunks, about the food, about the hot-water situation (which was going to get a lot worse). More annoying than their querulousness, though, was their unconscious superiority. 'Oh look,' someone would say in a tone of deeply compassionate condescension, when she looked up from her Joanna Trollope long enough to glimpse a little of Central Asia, 'They're *trying* to build a retaining wall!' Remote from any earthly comfort, in one of the most inhospitable regions of the world, gangs of workers had built hundreds of miles of impressive wall which she could have seen if she would, but the packages, bar a train-spotter or two, were not given to giving credit where credit was due. The sight of exhausted workers asleep in the heat of noon called forth volleys of satirical remarks. A man proudly wheeling a new bicycle was judged to have stolen it. While I was wondering how travel writers could tell Tartars from Kirghiz and Sarts and Hui and Kazakh and Tajik and Uzbek, my fellow packages had it all sussed. 'Well, at Samarkand you could see that there's been a lot of intermarriage with the Chinese,' one remarked as she picked over her lunch, to murmurs of general agreement. Travel, I decided, narrows the mind.

At every station in Kazakhstan, dozens of cheery, red-faced peasant women and children waited with piles of melons, apples and nans and bottles of koumiss to sell. At night, they rolled themselves in quilts and slept where they were. There were too many of them, far too many melons, too few trains, and the passengers had too little cash, but still the women smiled broadly at us and positively fell about when I gave a whole dollar for a bottle of fiery local brandy. At Chu, our train stopped to take on water. When the local train pulled in on the far side of ours, the vendors wailed in disappointment and bundled up their wares, half-carrying and half-dragging them towards the edge of the platform, swung them down, dropped to their knees and began crawling under our train. The guard raised his flag. The whistle blew. Believing that the Russian train might roll over the Kazakh people, I began shouting. A package patted my arm, 'Don't worry. They won't come into the train. They're crawling under it,' he said soothingly.

All that day and the next night, we kept moving fast through Kazakhstan. On the embankments, long straggling stems of wild hollyhock, with green-throated flowers of fragile silvery white, alternated with pincushions of blue miniature asters. Kazakhstan is the size of Western Europe and the fourth nuclear power in the world, but most westerners have never heard of the place. To the north-west, south of Semi-Palatinsk where Dostoevsky was exiled in 1854, eighteen thousand square kilometres were used as a nuclear test site from 1949 to 1990. Nowadays the Polygon, as the area is called, is a tourist attraction. Nowhere in the Soviet Union was collectivization more confused and inefficient in its organization, or more catastrophic in its effects, than here. The number of Kazakh households was halved; four-fifths of the Kazakh herds perished, first because they were slaughtered to prevent nationalization, then because the people had nothing else to eat. Despite poor planning and inadequate financing, the collectivization drive succeeded in its main aim of virtually obliterating the Kazakhs' pastoral way of life. We saw some yurts near the branch line that went off towards Bishkek; a few transhumant pastoralists still drive their herds across the Chinese border to summer pasture in the Heavenly Mountains.

The irrigated fields were far behind us; instead a fenceless, ditchless, treeless plain rolled to the horizon on every side. It should have been grassland; instead, it was thin stubble. In the 1950s, thirty million hectares of the steppe were ploughed up in Krushchev's Virgin Lands Programme; we were looking at the result. Along the railway line and wherever the fine light soil was on the move, triple rows of trees had been planted in a last-ditch attempt to prevent the dust-bowl effect. Wrapped in its scarf of

vaporized excrement, our train tore through a thousand-mile avenue of salix and alder, past hundreds of abandoned projects, feed-lots with no cattle, batteries with no chickens, machine houses with no tractors, only solitary horsemen trotting across the endless sloping plain, some with strings of horses; some with cows, donkeys and sheep. Since the 1920s, when more than a million Kazakhs died of hunger, the population of Kazakhstan has more than doubled. I began to wonder if, on the dappled face of the great steppe where most of the topsoil seemed to have blown away, I was seeing the lineaments of approaching famine.

For hours, low scarps rolled by like breakers in a brown ocean, patterned with shifting purple shadow. There was never a time when there was not to be seen glowing against the deep blue sky a cenotaph, sometimes domed, sometimes painted in white and blue, always in a railed enclosure. Throughout Kazakhstan, the houses were flimsy, drab and uniform, but the graves, no matter how isolated, were solid, individual and fantastic.

We arrived in Alma-Ata ahead of schedule in a clear, zingy morning. On the bus, our Kazakh guide explained that

Kazakhs love to give their daughters names connected with the heavens and in particular the moon. She placed her thumb on her snub nose and moved her hand clockwise to explain that to be moon-faced, as she certainly was, was to be a Kazakh beauty. Screwing up her eyes in a grim attempt at a smile, she described the great changes that had overtaken her country. 'One day everybody Communist; next day everybody democrat. One day nobody believe in God; next day everybody believe in God. Now we have millionaires,' she went on incredulously, 'yes, millionaires! They buy Chinese junk, sell it and get rich *over*night!' Her pale face darkened with rage.

The name Alma-Ata means, she told us, father of apples. Our buses roared through the tree-lined streets of a grandiose provincial capital, with public buildings and parks on a gargantuan scale. We lumbered up towards the fir-clad Heavenly Mountains on our way to marvel at the Medeo winter sports centre, though there was no ice in the famous rink, and the speed skaters were training on roller-skates in the parking-lot. Moonface led us off up five hundred or so granite steps to the top of what seemed to be an enormous dam. Idiotically, all those of us with hips and knees in working order made the lung-burning climb after her, only to find that in the valley beyond the rampart there was no water, nor had any torrent crashed into it in the past ten years or so. Somebody's projections about melting snow-water were clearly badly wrong. Our one morning on the ground in Kazakhstan had been deliberately squandered on an exhausting and fatuous exercise.

On the rubber-kneed way down, I questioned Moonface about the Russians and Ukranians who form the majority of the present-day population of Kazakhstan. 'They can learn Kazakh or go,' she said. 'For them Kazakhstan was a punishment. We don't throw them out because we know they have nowhere to go.' What of the Russian teachers? 'They lost their jobs. It will not be like Serbia, because the Russians and Ukranians do not have their own territory.' In fact, the Kazakhs, though settled, have chosen to remain in the rural areas, while the cities are predominantly European; the present situation in Kazakhstan has more in common with the agony of Serbia than Moonface realized. 'All subjects in secondary and tertiary schools will be taught in Kazakh, perhaps not right away because the language is not yet sufficiently developed,' she went on. Moonface had scant regard either for truth or for our intelligence, telling us not only that Kazakhstan produced sixty per cent of the wheat grown in the Soviet Union, but that the ragged herds we had seen were cross-bred Merino sheep. Before we left the bus, she had begun trying to sell Communist memorabilia, unused Young Pioneer badges and crackling new red flags. Unmoved by her pallid desperation, none of us bought anything.

After years of hosting Soviet delegations, the Hotel Otrar knew exactly what to do with us. On each table in the famous yurt-shaped restaurant stood bottles of beer, sparkling wine and American vodka. At the end of our repast, we were

235

invited to take the remaining hooch with us. It was the last time alcohol of any drinkability was to be so easily available. In an attempt to confer some cutesy-tootsy local colour, a waitress presented the oldest member of our troop with a boiled sheep's head. Many of the party were already manifesting a marked disinclination to eat anything, which the appearance of the sheep's head did nothing to dispel.

By now, Ann and I knew that we were sealed inside a hermetic capsule, a suppository for insertion in the rectum of China, totally isolated from contact with the Land of Seven Rivers. We tried to find a street market in Alma-Ata, to see who was selling, and who was buying, and what they were paying. It was already clear that in Kazakhstan there are serious food and other shortages (cement for example) and considerable inflation. We had got as far as ad hoc fabric shops set up in the foyers of public buildings when it was time to run back to the hotel for lunch, or we would miss our buses and the train and cause an international incident. As our train slid off along the Turk–Sib Railway, we realized that Kazakhstan was slipping through our fingers as Uzbekistan had. All we knew of Alma-Ata was that its inhabitants had no idea whatever of how to grow the apples for which they had been famous for thousands of years. The apple trees we saw were full of dead wood and disease. Transhumant pastoralists don't grow apples. Historically, Alma-Ata is less a Kazakh capital than a cosmopolitan city with significant minority populations, including a large number of Jews. Moonface told me that the Jews had all left, but I saw Stars of David painted on the balcony walls of a dingy high-rise, whether in pride or derision I could not tell. The Kazakhs have long and bitter scores to settle; the peaceful creation of a Kazakh nation out of the present population is less likely than conflict, if only because the economic future is of the bleakest.

North of Alma-Ata, the treeless steppe gave way to desert. We saw cairns of irregular black stones marking the graves of the many men who died of thirst and disease during the building of the Turk–Sib Railway. Today, workers on remote sections of the track brave the harsh climate in miserable collections of mud-brick huts and tents. Even so, when we went into our smiling-waving routine, their grimy faces were split by smiles, and they invariably waved back, dwarfed by sliding hills of dark shale and heaved-up torrents of jagged stones. At the eastern end of Lake Balkash, our train switched tracks to travel south-east along the northern edge of the Dzungarian spur of the Heavenly Mountains, across the choppy bed of a long-dead inland sea. On either side lay lakes opaque as oyster shells crusted with carbon salts. A bird coasted briefly on the train's bow wave. 'A seagull!' Ann and I cried in astonishment.

Once we crossed the platform at the frontier post of Druzhba to board the new train, we were entirely in the hands of China Rail. Every step we took, everything we saw, was under their benign control, personified by the chef de train, a broad-shouldered woman with pigtails bound with tinsel, and a face like a boiled ham with a mouth lipsticked on it. She made a rat-tat-tat speech of welcome in a little-girl voice, and we all applauded in the accepted Chinese fashion. The new train was an almost - exact copy of the Russian one, but without the showers and hot water. The plush bunks and seat-backs had frilly white covers, and had been embellished with embroidered antimacassars; the windows were impenetrably draped in machine-made nylon lace.

After the loneliness and dilapidation of northern Kazakhstan, we were unprepared for the tall buildings with glittering blue mirror windows, the many brick walls, hangars and huts of the Chinese rail terminus at Alataw-Shankou. We saw the first of the stockpiles of coal that we were to see everywhere in China, where eight hundred million tonnes are mined every year and distributed to every production unit in the country. Most of the freight trains that passed us were carrying coal; most of the sidings and yards we saw were black with it; coal left its dirty trail in every rural hamlet. Instead of using friable sun-dried brick for construction, as we had seen everywhere in Kazakhstan, the Chinese erected small coal-fired kilns and fired their bricks on the spot. As the train slid silently along the seamless modern track past the terminal building, a young woman in a uniform with shiny red and gold tabs stepped on to a railed dais, raised a handful of crimson-lacquered fingernails to the peak of her cap and saluted gravely.

Behind us and ahead of us lay the hundreds of miles of

crystalline salt-bush plain that rippled in the afternoon heat. We seemed to be flying over a swirling sea of dirty cream with blown crests of copper-green foam. Though there was, for many miles, no sign of animal life, patterns in the shifting sand showed that someone, many people perhaps, had been at work, cutting, binding and planting numberless bundles of reeds, or plaiting long ropes of grass to make a net to keep the sand from flowing over the rails, or laying flints in patterns to stop the embankment blowing away. Occasionally, half-buried matting stretched between the dunes and fences of bound reeds betokened a dwelling tucked into the sand. Once in a while, we glimpsed vivid-faced women leading strings of horses between pink-flowered clumps of tamarisk.

Although Xinjiang has been Chinese for little more than a hundred years, the weird landscape of lime-green sky, silver-grey dunes and orange shadows already seemed to me Chinese. Perhaps because the Chinese have been recording the shapes of their landscape in every imaginable medium for upwards of five thousand years, it was inevitable that I should see Chinese-ness in the worn tussocks and saw-edged mountains and dumpling-shaped clouds. The great blankness of the steppe under its fathomless over-arching sky had given way, even in this desert, to something deeply inscribed by a human presence. In answer to my wave, the Dzungar herdsmen blew kisses. Astonished to find anyone living in such a desolate place, let alone people as happy and healthy as these seemed to be, I stayed with my nose pressed to the denuded window until all I could see was an occasional swaying light amid the glinting salt-pans.

The next dawn broke over an immense stony plain where billions of blue, pink and white plastic bags bobbed like so many tethered pearly balloons. If my fellow packages had been awake to see it, they would have complained most shrilly, but the Great Plastic Bag Plain was an odd, rather than unsightly, emblem of the failure of Maoist Communism to instil any responsibility for public spaces in the heart of the average Chinese. When trains from Urumqi and points further east began to pass us, we could see that they were absolutely filthy, not with vomit, as I thought at first, but with food remains unceremoniously dumped at high speed. In traditional Asian thinking, only private space is pure, and all public space polluted. The body is purified, the kitchen and compound are cleaned, and the excrement and kitchen and animal refuse dumped in the street. No one would dream of transferring snot to a handkerchief and stuffing it in a pocket; instead they blow their noses using their fingers and fling the snot to the ground where it belongs, with the dust and droppings. The Chinese all hawk revoltingly and loudly as a warning to avoid the flob which will certainly follow. In the Provincial Museum at Xi'an, I heard one of the museum's ponderous, uniformed guards heartily hawking and turned to see him spit a great gob on to the museum's polished floor. Some of the most beautiful pots ever made by human hand are Chinese spittoons.

A t night, our train seemed to travel extraordinarily fast. We passed Urumqi in the dead of night and tore on down into the Durfan depression, the second deepest dent on the globe, 154 metres below sea level and the hottest place in China. The oasis became visible through the heat as a cliff of bright green that turned out to be double rows of tall poplars, closely planted wherever they could drink up the run-off from the irrigated fields, to provide shade, reduce evaporation and salination, and protect the crops from the sand storms that bear down on Durfan thirty times a year. Remains found in excavated ruins prove that poplars have been grown in the oasis towns in exactly this way for thousands of years. Durfan is famous for raisins that have kept their green colour because they have been dried in the shade, and almost every dwelling has a drying-house built with a flat roof of openwork brick. As our buses squeezed themselves through the narrow, shaded streets, we could see through gateways beds of bright flowers, and women sitting under shady loggias overgrown with melons and ornamental gourds, de-stalking raisins, while their children ran out to see the foreigners. The water comes from the famous *kareez*, kissing cousin of the Iranian *qanat* but, unlike the *qanat*, still fully functional. The melting snow-water from the Heavenly Mountains is collected in underground wells on the lower slopes and brought down along underground channels lined with round flints to the edge of the city, where it surfaces as fast-running milky-green streams. One of the obligatory sights in Durfan is the underground working of the *kareez*; as we peered obediently into its depths, one of our number, a retired Belgian railwayman who was never seen without his pork pie hat and his video camera, overbalanced and fell in. His wife made a grab at him, missed and fell in herself. Such are the perils of being tall and paunchy in a country of more neatly built people.

After lunch, our Chinese guardians allowed us an unsupervised hour among the Kazakhs, Uighur and Hui in the Durfan bazaar. The women of one ethnic group—we didn't know which—wore dresses of all-over sequinned material in shades of luminous yellow, turquoise, magenta and red. Others wore crêpe-de-Chine gowns loaded with beading. A group of particularly burly women affected bursting pink camiknickers and short jackets. All completed their ensembles with dirty brown stockings and crunched-up high-heeled shoes. Best dressed were the babies, of whom there was no lack. In one donkey cart, we saw three small sisters dressed identically in magenta sequins, and a smaller brother in a sparkling beaded cap. We bought a pair of shoes for nine yuan and four pairs of glittery drop-earrings for ninety. Where other people had been pestered by money-changers, we saw none; where others had been forced to pay in dollars, we were asked to pay the yuan price displayed and were given the right change. In a region where most people are said to be still illiterate, the vendors had marked their prices in pencil on torn pieces of cardboard. We sniffed at spices, tasted the extraordinary array of dried fruits, many of which we had never seen before: sand dates and Chinese dates, tiny brown apricots and large, flat, brick-red pears, bronze prunes and purple dates. The famous green raisins I found to be as hard as the hobs of hell. We peered into cooking pots where slabs of sheep's fat shuddered amid shawls of tripe, and sheep's heads gazed skyward with popping eyes. The traders were most diverted to find that I had donkey-bells hanging from my waist and jingled as I moved, like a cart. Though the ubiquitous presence of coal meant that the place and the people presented a rather grimy appearance, there were few flies and only two beggars. We were looking for some indication of control of commercial activities, but there was none. Even the staple crop of raisins we found piled by the hundredweight waiting for a buyer. We had seen the cotton cooperatives and the government coal yards, but the produce market seemed completely unregulated.

That night, we gathered speed once more and arrived at Liujiang station long before, instead of after, breakfast. No use of toilets could be permitted. The dismay of the packages was heart-rending. Eventually, word came that on terra firma the soft-class waiting-room had been unlocked so that the arse-shotten could have access to the toilets. Clad in shorts and sun-hats and carrying banners of loo paper, we trooped down the platform and began queueing outside toilets that had no water and were soon in a noisome condition. Organizing bucket drill so that we could sluice away the worst of it proved quite impossible because the single standpipe and both the buckets were in the men's loo. No ruse, no ranting could persuade the men on one side to assist the women on the other. The very idea seemed an indecent suggestion. Yet it is the Europeans who think that the Chinese are mad.

Then we toddled off to the buses that would carry us to Dunhuang, one hundred and twenty kilometres away across the Gobi, there to see the Mogao grottoes with their thousands of Buddhas. On the way, we encountered a herd of Bactrian camels chomping majestically on the camel thorn. The bus stopped, we all got out to take photographs and got back in again. At the grottoes, a willowy old woman with minute bound feet was walking among the tourists with her hand out. Our group and our guides took a dim view of begging. I slipped her ten yuan, bowing to take the sting out of it if I could, and was horrified to see tears come into her eyes. She swayed away with the flickering movement that was the point of foot-binding, slightly averting her head, as if she would have preferred not to have been given anything. Could this be the impenetrable indifference of the Chinese?

I am ashamed to say that after five days and nights on the train, on terra firma I was seasick; straining my eyes upward through the dancing lights of the torches and the crush of people inside the grottoes made my head reel. Beautiful as Serindian painting may be, it is hardly pleasant to have it beetling over one as one measures one's length on a catarrh-speckled floor. While our packages were herded with hundreds of others through a one-way circuit of the caves, I sat outside, giddily watching people paying to dress up in Mandarin costume and be photographed. As the packages emerged, one of them, who wore the same pair of corduroy trousers for the whole two weeks and farted loudly and often, asked me why genitalia, so important in all primitive painting, were invisible in these images. Had some censorious authority obliterated them? At the entrance to a cave, I had seen a beautiful young monk in a saffron robe, seated in the lotus position on a low wooden stool, his hands laid upwards on his knees, tips of index fingers against thumbs, his eyes fixed on a point on the floor six feet before him, sedulously avoiding the too-muchness of the world. It was hard to believe that my questioner was of the same species.

At the next great sight wheeled on for us, namely the southern end of the Great Wall in Jiayuguang, after the formalities were over and we could move in and ask about things that we were really interested in, we found out that our young guide was delighted to be six months pregnant with twins. How did she know? She had had an X-ray. After a moment's consternation, we managed to establish that she meant an ultrasound scan. No, she did not know the sex. And no, there would be no penalty for bringing forth twins. She would not be sterilized after the birth, because sterilization is not offered to women of her age after a single pregnancy. Jiayuguang is a frontier outpost, and the rules may be more easily relaxed there, even for the urban population, but still it was strange. We had been told that in China, 115 boys are born for every hundred girls, and that they already have fifty million surplus males, but how did anyone know? Who was counting? It occurred to me that a government that did not want its population skewed would tell its people that it was skewed already.

Our suspicions that we were seldom going to achieve contact with living China were confirmed in startling fashion when we got to Xi'an. As we trudged out of the station, four tall, slender, very fair-skinned young women in ruby-red velvet cheongsams split almost to the waist swayed towards us and presented us, nonplussed, smelly and dishevelled in our shorts and sun-hats, with a red carnation each. As soon as we were all embussed, a police car slid out in front of us, lights flashing, siren wailing, and took off with the buses thundering along behind, nose-to-tail, at fifty miles an hour. The Russian Consul whose forty mounted Cossacks used to slash at the faces of Chinese who failed to leap out of the way of his carriage could hardly have behaved worse than we were now forced to. Our screaming buscade bore down time after time on hundreds of massed cyclists at traffic lights to sail through on the red, while lorries swerved and braked, cyclists fell off, carts were overturned and wives and babies tumbled in the dust.

That night, Ann and I skipped our hotel meal and went out to eat in the street; at the first stall we were given a small helping of fried pancakes. A skinny man who came in after us wolfed a huge bowl of them while his toddler son looked on, then paid his eleven yuan and left. Our bill was also eleven yuan. I shook my head and said one of my three words of Mandarin, making a disparaging gesture towards the bowl. The cook tossed his head and flung his hands down, fingers splayed, meaning that if we thought his pancakes were rubbish, we needn't pay for them. In another stall we had dumplings with a hot and acrid soup-sauce. Brilliant. We were in China, and China was in us and China was delicious. That night, I kept waking up, thinking the train was in a siding because my bed wasn't shaking. In one of my waking moments, I realized that all the stall-holders in the alley charged eleven yuan for whatever it was the customer wanted to eat. In the wrong again. Damn.

The next day, the police car was in attendance again to shriek us out to the Huaqing Hot Springs and the Terracotta Warriors. It was perhaps a reaction to our unintentionally despotic behaviour that brought on my attack of disgust at the magnificent sight of the Terracotta Warriors, 'eighth wonder of the world'. What can the potters have felt, making those witty, sensuous, optimistic figures just so that they could be buried for ever with a megalomaniacal stiff? I was supposed to be aghast that peasants are stealing funerary figures and selling them on the black market, but I was actually glad. As a tourist I was useless. At the Longmen caves, I was less interested in the endless replications of smirking stone Buddhas which seemed to me to have more to do with obsessive-compulsive disorder than religion or art, than in the gangs of Young Pioneers who ran riot all up and down the stairs, capturing the crabs out of the ditches to put down each other's necks and swiping at each other with their red flags. Among these brats were the first obese people I saw in China.

In 1949, the Chinese were a sick people, visited periodically by starvation, plague, smallpox and cholera, with thirty million cases of filariasis, eleven million cases of schistosomiasis and half a million lepers. Eighty-two million suffered from Keshan disease. Endemic goitre afflicted a quarter of the population. Four per cent were infected with tuberculosis, which caused two hundred deaths per hundred thousand annually. Life expectancy was thirty-five years. To transform this situation in less than fifty years into the China I saw is an achievement of unimaginable magnitude. The Chinese now have to pay the price of their success, but the evidence is that they are paying it. What is certain is that the rich world paid none of it. The Chinese people did it themselves. Yet this too we seem to hold against them. Famine is so recent in the Chinese memory that the commonest greeting is not 'How do you do?' but 'Have you eaten?', but now no Chinese is malnourished. Our favoured trading partner, Brazil, troubles itself not at all that millions of its people go hungry to bed every night, and yet we like Brazilians much, much better than we like the Chinese.

The Chinese are the healthiest population I have ever seen. My fellow packages would say that that must be because they kill the sick and disabled. Not in Shanghai they don't, because in Shanghai the only people licensed to drive single-seater motor-scooter-cabs are the disabled, who clip their crutches on to the side of the cab and whizz round the city earning an independent living. None of the Shanghai travel writers have bothered to record this obvious little fact. Why is that, I wonder? If crippled drivers tried to buzz around London as they do around Shanghai, they would be run into the ground and mashed by aggressive motorists and oppressed motor cycle couriers. Yet it is the Chinese who are cruel and careless, so I'm told.

Morning after morning, I watched from the train as the peasants pulled their carts from the manure heap to the fields, tipped the manure out in neat piles, spread it and hoed it in. I would pull down the window to sniff the morning air. Nothing. European agriculture stinks of propellant and diesel and silage, but Chinese farming smells of nothing. What I expected, having seen the privies that clung to the back walls of the compounds, and the dark heaps that accumulated below, was the bouquet of composted human dung as I have savoured it in Brazil and India and a dozen other places. Sniff though I might, I smelt—nothing. I don't know why. All Chinese drink copious amounts of tea; their water intake is probably close to the ideal and they clearly place great store on bodily purity. The Han Chinese smell not of scent or sweat or breath, but of nothing. (The same could not be said of the Diarrhoea Express.) As I watched the people walking home through the fields for their lunch, I thought: 'If we must have an eighth wonder of the world, let it not be ten thousand Buddhas or six thousand terracotta warriors. Let it be the 1.2 billion Chinese who have doubled their life expectancy in less than fifty years.' A glossy-skinned, flat-bellied and straight-backed people. A people who at any age can sit on their heels and get up again without putting a hand to the ground. A nation of cyclists and walkers, not sitters. A people with appetite and food that deserves it. Everywhere else, the peasant farmer is under sentence of death, losing his land, his livelihood and his way of life. The Chinese farmer has all three.

Ann and I decided to watch for sick animals, so common in the rest of Asia. We saw a pig being skinned, but it was both very fat and quite dead. The English think the Chinese are wicked and mad because they eat dogs and horses. It must be madder to breed untold numbers of animals, fatten them up and refuse to eat them because they are concubines for emotionally inadequate humans. Ann and I, both cat-women, hadn't seen a single cat. China seemed a land without cats. When we met our first grimy little long-hair, tethered to the wall in a street stall in Xi'an, we didn't know if she was there to eat or be eaten. We thought probably both.

We never got the chance to eat cat; though we had been served kid and rabbit and tripe, on the train or off it we were served meals of such unbelievable blandness that we had to buy a bag of green chillies to serve as a condiment. The crowning insult was a banquet at Xi'an, at which twenty different kinds of equally tasteless dumplings were served without any sauces or seasonings whatsoever. These we were expected to wash down with flat beer and thimblefuls of something hot and revoltingly sweet which they said was rice wine. As usual, the packages, for whom I was actually beginning to feel sorry, ate next to nothing. On the last day, a package raised her voice to announce that she was going to complain to the tour operator because her travel agent had promised international cuisine. In that moment all became clear: the tasteless brown stew was the Chinese version of *boeuf bourguignonne*; the white one was chicken *à la* king. As both were rigid with monosodium glutamate and we had to eat them with rice, we had never tumbled.

From Xi'an to Shanghai we travelled through a yellow fog of industrial pollution thickened with Third World dust. My eyes and nostrils hurt, and the inside of my mouth turned red raw. Perhaps Shanghai would show us the faceless Chinese horde. For two days, we blundered through the narrow alleys, intruding on every kind of domestic scene. Sensibly, the people defended themselves by pretending we weren't there. When two workers in basket helmets wedged a cycle cart loaded with thirty-foot bamboo scaffolding across an intersection, the shoal of cyclists came quietly to a halt. I caught the eye of a woman cyclist and shrugged, as if to signify that it was quite a funny situation. She grinned, pulling down the corners of her mouth in a droll grimace to match my own. Then the blockage was cleared, and she flowed past with the rest, leaving a tiny gleam of comprehension hanging in the dirty air.

'Why do travel writers notice that Chinese bicycles have no

brakes and not that they have no locks?' asked Ann.

On the Bund, an old woman in neat jacket and trousers was collecting cans and plastic bags. Scavenging and recycling are big, big business now. I offered her a yuan for a photograph. She shook her head and put the money back in my hand. She wanted only my beer can. She was a businesswoman, not a beggar or a scrap of local colour.

In a backstreet market, we found live carp swimming lazily about in a cycle cart lined with polythene to make a mobile pond. Other carts had been pedalled in from the countryside, laden with cabbages, lettuces and herbs, pearl-coloured fungi, sprouted alfalfa and soy, lotus seed and lotus root, chillies and aubergines, all carefully picked over and cleaned. The shoppers sniffed and poked among the carts with an absorption approaching reverence. Joking, the vendors asked what we would like. A huge blue cabbage? A pair of live ducks? A bouquet of chicken's feet? A wobbling slab of tofu? I used my three words, 'Hello! No, [but] beautiful,' and they, remarkably, understood.

When I looked up at the dirty-grey apartment blocks and saw pots of chives in the windows and strings of red peppers hanging from the balconies, I knew that, despite the nuclear tests in the Taklimakan desert, it will not be the Chinese who destroy the earth. It will not be a nation of resourceful cooks and diligent gardeners, of herbalists and husbandmen, that cancels human history. If you have picked your way through Brazilian *faveladas* and Indian slums and Ethiopian famine shelters and think that what the planet needs most desperately is good housekeeping, China will ease your pain.

Politically Incorrect

Get a different perspective on the week's events with The Spectator.

Lively, informed comment on politics and current affairs; reviews of books, film, TV, music and art; some of the best columnists currently writing; plus Michael Heath's selection of the very best of the week's cartoons.

TIMOTHY GARTON ASH
GOLDEN KIDS COMEBACK

Hips. Some never have them. Most have them but lose them. A few have them and keep them. That woman in the dress circle: she still has them. And they're moving to *'Hey Jude, don't make it bad . . . '* Her husband sits uncomfortably beside her. He's lost them. *'Remember to let her under your skin . . . '* Remember?

It's November 1994, and we're at the Lucerna Palace in Prague, built by a millionaire architect–developer in the early years of this century, expropriated by the Communists, but now returned to his sons, Ivan and Václav Havel. Tonight's guest stars are the Golden Kids, a sixties pop group who haven't performed together for nearly twenty-five years, since they were banned by the Communist authorities after the Soviet invasion. They are Marta Kubišová, now aged fifty-three, Václav Neckář, fifty-two, and Helena Vondráčková, forty-seven. They wear black. They jive. They sing 'Hey Jude' and 'Massachusetts' and 'The times they are a'changin'' and 'The Mighty Quinn' and even, God save us, 'Congratulations'.

The audience, like the Golden Kids, is middle-aged: men in sheeny suits, white shirts and ties, women in blouses, as if for the opera. They sweat amid the faded Jugendstil gilding and candelabra. Sometimes they clap along. But when the Golden Kids sing 'Suzanne', there's just total silence.

> *Suzanne takes you down*
> *To the place by the river*
> *And she shows you where to touch her*

Tense and heavy with regret: the silence of the middle-aged remembering sex.

There's another story being played out on stage this evening: the story of Marta and Helena. Marta Kubišová was a Czech heroine of '68. A song called 'Hymn for Marta' became a rallying song of that time. So after Husák took over from Dubček, following the Soviet invasion, she was banned. For twenty long years, until 1989, she did odd jobs, worked as a clerk, had close friends among the dissidents. In the middle of the Velvet

Revolution she made her first comeback. A moment at once rapturous and terribly sad. Barely able to sing for the engulfing emotion, she whispered into the microphone: *Časy se mění*, The times they are a'changin'. Helena Vondráčková took a quite different path after 1969. She went on performing, was seen often on television. She collaborated.

Now their paths have met again. Will virtue have its reward? Or does none of that matter any more? Helena, tall, blonde and still very much in practice, seems to have it at first. She's younger, more professional, and the audience knows her from television. Perhaps they even feel a little easier with her. For most of them collaborated too, or at least, made their little compromises to keep their jobs. Marta, black-haired, older, shorter, is a shade slower, and you feel the nervousness in her voice. Oh, time that is intolerant of the brave and innocent . . .

But somewhere in the middle of the evening, the emotion begins flowing towards her. People bring bouquets of flowers up on stage after every number (opera habits, again), and the flower count is going Marta's way. Then the whole concert stops, and the stage is suddenly full of embarrassed men in suits. They represent Supraphon, Fiat, Interbanka, Seagram—the commercial sponsors of the evening. Awkwardly they hand out platinum discs and bottles of champagne. You try to imagine Citicorp and Chrysler distributing prizes at the Woodstock revival, wiping the mud from their pin-striped lapels. And there's a raffle: first prize, a Fiat Punto. The prize-winners come up on stage, say a few words into the mike and kiss the stars.

One, a comfortable-looking man in jeans, shambles up and says he'd like to thank all the performers, every one, 'but above all, above all, Mrs Kubišová.' And we all applaud loud and long, and we all know what he's thanking her for, and it's not for her singing that evening, it's for her twenty years of silence. And now everyone is sweating, and everything is mixed up together, the Marta of then and the 'Mrs Kubišová' of now, the pop heroes of the sixties and the business heroes of the nineties, the memories of sex and the memories of national protest, and today's hope of a Fiat Punto.

Yet there's an even bigger circle closing here: a European circle. For these are also our songs; this is our past. Sixty-eight was one of those very rare moments when the experience of people in Western and Eastern Europe really did meet. For all the differences between Prague and Paris, Liverpool and Leipzig, people under thirty here and there moved to the same rhythm, sang the same lyrics, shared something of the same protest, the same emancipation. Then the Russian tanks rolled in, and the paths of experience diverged, like those of Marta and Helena; and the years slipped away.

Now, a quarter-century on, East and West have come together again, like Marta and Helena, here in the Havels' Lucerna Palace, in this post-modern stew of middle-aged longing and regret, under the sign of Seagram, and the shared meaning of history is:

Yeh yeh yeh yeh yeh yeh yeh da da da da, da da da da
Hey Jude da da da da da da da.

Nominees for the

R E E F
Romesh Gunesekera

**A love story set in the spoilt paradise of Sri Lanka;
the story of a boy becoming a man in a world
stumbling to the brink of chaos.**

'A delectable first novel about growing up.' *Guardian*

'A book of the deepest human interest and moral poise.'
Independent on Sunday

'A sensuous feast of delight, incessantly pleasurable
to read.' *The Times*

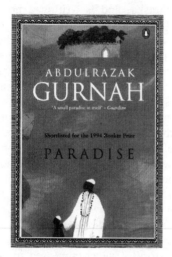

Notes on Contributors

Philip Gourevitch is a journalist and lives in New York City. He is a contributing editor to the *Forward*. **Tran Vu** fled Vietnam by boat in 1979 at the age of sixteen. After a year in a refugee camp in the Philippines, he was taken by the Red Cross to France, where he now lives. **Paul Eggers** worked for the UNHCR in Malaysia in 1980. He lives in Lincoln, Nebraska, and is writing a novel. **Bao Ninh** was born in 1952 in Hanoi, where he still lives. During Vietnam's 'American War', he was one of five hundred soldiers to serve in the Glorious 27th Youth Brigade, only ten of whom survived. His first novel, *The Sorrow of War*, was published in 1993. **Ed Grazda**, whose work appeared in *Granta* 21, is currently completing *Asia Calling*, a book of photographs from the past ten years. He is also working on a project documenting the mosques of New York City. **Redmond O'Hanlon** is the author of *Into the Heart of Borneo* and *In Trouble Again*. An account of his search for the Congo dinosaur appeared in *Granta* 39. **Julian Barnes** is working on a collection of short stories occasioned by historical meetings between the English and the French. His last contribution to *Granta*, 'Trap. Dominate. Fuck', appeared in *Granta* 47. **William Boyd**'s novels include *The Blue Afternoon*, *Brazzaville Beach*, *The New Confessions*, *A Good Man in Africa* and *An Ice Cream War*. A new collection of short fiction, *The Destiny of Nathalie X* (the title story of which appeared in *Granta* 48), will be published in Britain this summer. **Richard Ford** is the author of *A Piece of My Heart*, *Rock Springs* and *The Sportswriter*. His new novel, *Independence Day*, will be published on the Fourth of July. **Romesh Gunesekera** grew up in Sri Lanka and the Philippines and now lives in London. He is the author of *Monkfish Moon*, a collection of stories, and *Reef*, a novel, which was shortlisted for the 1994 Booker Prize. Both are published by Granta Books. Described by Graham Greene as 'one of the best writers of our century,' **Norman Lewis** is the author of thirteen novels and nine works of non-fiction. He is currently working on a further volume of autobiography, to be published in Britain by Cape next year. **Germaine Greer** is a *Guardian* columnist, a Fellow of Newnham College, Cambridge, and a director of Stump Cross Books. Her next book, *Slipshod Sybils*, a collection of essays on women poets, will be published by Penguin later this year. **Timothy Garton Ash**'s account of visiting Erich Honecker in prison, 'The Visit', appeared in *Granta* 45. His books include *The Polish Revolution*, *The Uses of Adversity* and *We the People*, all published by Granta Books. He lives in Oxford, where he is a Fellow of St Antony's College.